TITLES IN THE SOFTWARE QUALITY INSTITUTE SERIES

Practitioner's Handbook For
USER
INTERFACE
DESIGN And
DEVELOPMENT

R.J. Torres

PRENTICE HALL PTR
UPPER SADDLE RIVER, NJ 07458
WWW.PHPTR.COM

Editorial/production supervision: *Mary Sudul*
Acqusition Editor: *Paul Petralia*
Editorial Assistant: *Justin Somma*
Marketing Manager: *Debby vanDijk*
Manufacturing Manager: *Alexis R. Heydt*
Cover Photo: *Tony Stone Images*
Cover Design Director: *Jerry Votta*
Series Design: *Gail Cocker-Bogusz*

© 2002 Prentice Hall PTR
Prentice-Hall, Inc.
Upper Saddle River, NJ 07458

The publisher offers discounts on this book when ordered in bulk quantities.
For more information, contact
Corporate Sales Department,
Prentice Hall PTR
One Lake Street
Upper Saddle River, NJ 07458
Phone: 800-382-3419; FAX: 201-236-714
E-mail (Internet): corpsales@prenhall.com

Printed in the United States of America

10 9 8 7 6 5 4 3 2 1

ISBN 0-13-091296-4

Pearson Education LTD.
Pearson Education Australia PTY, Limited
Pearson Education Singapore, Pte. Ltd
Pearson Education North Asia Ltd
Pearson Education Canada, Ltd.
Pearson Educación de Mexico, S.A. de C.V.
Pearson Education — Japan
Pearson Education Malaysia, Pte. Ltd
Pearson Education, Upper Saddle River, New Jersey

Contents

CHAPTER 12
Principles, Guidelines, and Style Guides

CHAPTER 13
Mockups, Simulations, and Prototypes

CHAPTER 14
Usability Evaluation

CHAPTER 15
Iteration

PART 3
Getting Serious

CHAPTER 16
High Level Design

Chapter 17
Specification Techniques   *295*

Chapter 18
Low-Level Design   *313*

Preface

Although there are a large number of software products in the world today, the number of software user interfaces with high usability is painfully small. Furthermore, the number of software products with overall high usability is even smaller. These days, as in the past, it takes more than just a pretty interface to achieve high and competitive overall user satisfaction. An aesthetic interface with in-depth character is what users, customers, and business sponsors are seeking.

This is a daunting task for software designers and developers who are under constant pressure to reduce product cost, reduce development time, deliver increasing features, and improve quality relative to competition in a rapidly changing world wide environment. People in the software development business today (and in particular, those focusing on user interface and usability) must approach the job with caution and humility – there are lots of things to learn and do very quickly and effectively. No one person has all the answers to deal with so many simultaneous and competing challenges.

The primary goals for this book are to

1. Make essential distinctions between the overall usability of a software product and its user interface. Overall usability is a function of many parameters that must be accounted for and user interface is only one factor.

2. Provide very practical, specific, effective, and "best practice" guidance and techniques to achieve software products and user interfaces on schedule, with high overall usability, and with high user satisfaction. The guidance and techniques are provided in a way that is immediately applicable to current software user interface projects.

The focus of the text is on application software user interfaces, which is where the majority of user interface work exists. However, the techniques are applicable to development of software user interfaces for operating systems. In a more general sense, the general concepts are applicable to user interfaces of systems of different types.

Let's begin by discussing the task, the audience, and criteria that this text addresses.

The Task

Of course, the task that is explored in depth is that of planning, designing, constructing, validating, and deploying user interface software that meets requirements and helps achieve product goals for the user interface and usability in general. Each key subtask is described, rules of thumb (heuristics) provided, and examples explored. The intent is to provide effective guidance to achieve effective results. The guidance provided is typically not described in any other publication. Guidance in the text is experience-based and derived from a large number of projects, i.e., the school of hard knocks.

The Audience

There are several intended users of this information.

- Product personnel responsible for user interface planning, requirements analysis, design, online help, performance support, tutorials, and training
- Product personnel responsible for implementing all aspects of a product user interface, including implementation design, construction, and test
- Product personnel responsible for evaluating the usability of software user interfaces, help, performance support, tutorials, and the overall usability of product software
- Development Managers responsible for planning and tracking software development and the effectiveness of results

Measurable Criteria

A major objective is to guide a software developer who understands the basics of user interface development to design and implement better user interfaces more effectively.

- Designing a better user interface means achieving higher usability and user satisfaction than was achieved prior to using this text or any other text or source of guidance.
- Achieving the result more effectively means producing a better user interface faster, on or ahead of schedule, with fewer user interface and usability defects, on larger product feature sets, and with fewer resources than before.

In addition, this book is intended to be a more complete reference for user interface design and development than others available.

Acknowledgments

Jim Stone—a friend, supporter, and co-conspirator.

Jim Kubie—a friend, supporter, and tireless usability advocate.

Esther— for always being there.

There are others who have influenced and supported my journey in software usability engineering. Here are but a few: Ted Kerr, Roy Klastin, Jim Willette, John Kent, Steve Jacobs, Murray Turoff, and Dick Osterman.

R.J. (Bob) Torres
Colleyville, TX
June 2001

Part

Preliminaries

Some introductory material is provided in the first set of chapters. Basics on the project, User Centered Design, people, teamwork, user interfaces, and tools are intended as prerequisite knowledge for UI and usability work. The material is basic but should provide a "jump start" to get into the more serious work of design and development.

The following topics are discussed:

1

Introduction

The design of a user interface (UI) appears to be relatively simple at a high level—everyone has an opinion about what is right and wrong in any given UI. Just about anyone is able to design parts of any UI, though few are able to handle the entire job and various aspects of design through deployment. Even fewer people are able to prototype or implement a software UI, much less deploy it to users on schedule and within constraints.

> **Rule of Thumb:** Anybody can design a UI, anybody can design a client/server application, anybody can design a web-based application, and anybody can design a database—just look at the evidence in the sea of software in the world today. It's when a design must meet challenging constraints for competitiveness, UI, usability, consistency, cost, resources, skills, and schedule that the need for special expertise becomes evident.

Numerous opinions about a UI don't work when:

- The design of software must meet stringent criteria for the UI, usability, consistency, and integration

- Implementation must occur within resource and schedule constraints placed on a design and implementation team with a certain set of skills
- Strict accountability for results is tracked

The process of designing a UI is highly complex, nonlinear, nondeterministic, and nonorthogonal. Complexity is normal in software and even more so in the UI because of the large number of factors and unknowns. Design is nonlinear because there is not necessarily a fixed, orderly, and straight-line path from start to finish. The process of design is nondeterministic because there is no equation to produce the same results given the same inputs, and it would be almost impossible to produce the same results even under duress. UIs are nonorthogonal in the sense that a decision in any one facet of a design can influence other facets in not always pleasantly surprising ways.

Statistical independence is not joy that is available in creating UIs and systems—it's more of a puzzle.

> **Rule of Thumb**: UI design and development is surprisingly complex and easy to underestimate relative to planning, requirements, and deployment.

In order to simplify a discussion of such a broad topic and be effective at the same time, a "best practices" approach for UIs and usability is provided for people involved in software planning, design, implementation, testing, and deployment. The focus is on identifying the right things that must be done correctly in order to achieve success. These right things are the basics that are independent of the current industry buzzwords used to name them.

This chapter covers:

- A project—keeping things real
- A challenge
- Major causes of project failure (or success)
- An approach to processes
- An approach to solutions
- Best practices

The basic layout of the text is to present chapters in a somewhat linear and design task oriented flow. However, each chapter is somewhat independent of preceding ones for those with a need to reference information in a different order.

A project introduced in this chapter is used throughout the text. It is the basis for exercises designed so a reader can experience a comprehensive set of real-world design and implementation situations and tasks.

The opinions of the author, readers, UI and usability engineering experts, or others are important to a product's success, but users and/or usability testing ultimately determine whether a solution meets requirements or whether one solution is better than another. In fact, a large number of alternative solutions may satisfy the likely requirements for the project, but what determines the best design possible?

A Project—Keeping Things Real

The market research department has convinced senior management of the viability of a potential new product. As a result, and in spite of very tight budget and headcount constraints, management has approved the immediate assignment of a small team to pursue initial validation of project concepts and likely development costs.

The Application. The project is to deliver a software application supporting scheduling and attendance of events at major conferences like Guide, Share, and Computer Human Interaction (CHI). Conference events include tutorials, workshops, presentations, and after-hours sessions. Likely users of the software are conference attendees, as well as conference personnel who define and maintain events for the system.

The Platforms. The conference scheduling application is intended to operate on three hardware and operating system platforms:

- Laptop computers running Microsoft Windows
- Network computers running Windows/NT or UNIX
- Interconnected personal digital assistants (PDAs)

Web-based and kiosk support may be important for a later release of the software, though this is not known with certainty at the time of project kick-off. Market Research has an action item to return with an answer to this question and others within three months.

Tools. The implementation languages are not known. No development languages or tools are standardized for project development at this facility. However, Java, C++, Visual Basic (VB), and HTML are leading candidates for all or part of the software. Several other languages and tools are in use within the development organization, but no other development tools have been discussed or finalized for use on the project.

The Team.   The project startup team consists of an experienced and aggressive software development manager and two software developers. One of the developers is very experienced in client-server software infrastructure, and the other developer is experienced in GUI-based client software applications. Both are experienced leading software teams.

The members of the team are relatively new to the parent development organization and have not worked together before. None of the team members have developed software for PDAs, Java, object-oriented software, Web-based technology, or UNIX.

The initial market research personnel have been reassigned to other locations and jobs, but their management is finding personnel to complete remaining work items. The Senior Management Team of the project startup team has agreed to provide marketing and other support if the project proves promising. No other staffing is available for more than minor consultation.

The Schedule.   Market research predicted potential first year sales of over 10 million units of the software worldwide if delivered within 15 months at a certain price. Competition is anticipated and is expected to erode the sales prediction significantly with any delay beyond 18 months. Potential units are well over 50 million if extensions to support scheduling of educational, sporting, and other events are considered.

Senior management has requested a weekly 15-minute status meeting with the leader of the project team. Senior management has requested a preliminary assessment, project schedule, and likely resource estimates within 30 days from today. The project leader has agreed to the requests made by senior management.

Any questions?

A Challenge

The project is not too unreal as a description of how development of shrink-wrapped applications begins. For software developers working on internal applications, the scenario is not too far off the mark with minor modifications. For example, what if the development project is intended to provide a solution for scheduling internal education first, and then the solution is to be extended, packaged, and marketed externally at a later time?

There are many challenges in today's software development environment. There is severe pressure to reduce costs, shorten schedules, achieve more predictable plans, deliver higher quality, provide easier to learn and use software, learn and use new technologies and tools, and to achieve better results relative to competition and other factors.

A Very Broad Topic.   A very large portion of user satisfaction with a product or its usability is typically attributed to its UI. This is a very large and unsupported burden. A broader view of usability is required. In addition, a broader view of user interface and how it is designed and implemented is required.

Before addressing ease of use as a topic, a broader and common understanding of factors that drive user satisfaction is required. Several studies have demonstrated that user satisfaction is a function of a small number of factors. An equation to represent user satisfaction as a function of these factors is:

User Satisfaction =
Function of (FEATURES, USER INTERFACE, RESPONSE TIME, RELIABILITY, Installability, Information, Maintainability, and Other Factors)

The capitalized factors are the most significant in the equation. Certainly, it is easy to find examples where a product is not usable if:

- Key functional features are missing

- The user interface is missing key features, has poor appearance and behavior, and places high knowledge and interaction demands on users

- Response time and throughput are slow

- The system does not stay up and/or causes work or data to be lost

The factors in the equation can be refined further—for example, UI has components related to appearance, behavior, user knowledge demands, and user interaction demands. Other factors can certainly be added to the equation.

The bulk of a user's focus is getting a job done quickly, easily, and reliably with tools that automate, augment, and facilitate the task. Ease of install/ deinstall is important because it sets the initial and final tone of a user's experience with a product. Ease of software upgrade is as important as other interactive features of a product. Information (training, tutorials, help, and performance support) is important during initial or later learning but is not necessarily task relevant unless used during an infrequent or complex task.

There are many other factors, such as consistency, integration, and cost, that affect user satisfaction depending upon role, environment, task, and situation.

> **Rule of Thumb**: All factors in the user satisfaction equation and their relative importance must be kept in mind during product planning, requirements analysis, design, implementation, test, and deployment.

The focus of the book is on usability in general and the UI in particular. Only high-level guidance and considerations are made for performance and reliability; the importance of these factors cannot be minimized.

Risky Business.   Software development is a high-risk endeavor in even the best of cases. There are many examples of software development horror stories—where projects fail due to cancellation, significant schedule slips, rejection by users, or significant cost overrun. There are many examples in the media of the horrors visited upon users and purchasers of software that is deficient in the major areas that contribute to user satisfaction.

One of the major goals of the book is to address the risk areas relative to usability and UI, that is, where things can go wrong. Pragmatic approaches and specific guidance that are immediately applicable to design and usability efforts are provided.

Timely.   Although there is much that is not known, many things are known about users and UI technology. There are also many things known about how to achieve good development plans, designs, software, tools, evaluation, and iteration. In particular, accepting an effective and rapid iterative process within constraints is a best practice approach to achieving desired results.

The guidance provided applies to achieving results quickly by requirements personnel, designers, trainers, writers, developers, testers, usability engineering personnel, team and project leaders, and managers—everyone involved in software development must do a broader and more effective job.

Effective.   Just as developers are under pressure to reduce cycle time, UI and usability engineering personnel are under pressure to produce better results in a more effective manner. This pressure means that

- Product personnel do the right things right
- Usability engineering cycles are reduced without compromising results

It is possible for results and UI quality to improve dramatically and quickly—perhaps with fewer resources. This gives potential promise to a fantastic future for end users.

Causes of Software Project Failure or Success

An exploration of sources such as Brooks, McConnell, and Keil reveals common themes as to why projects fail or succeed. Failure takes the form of major cost overruns, schedule delays, project cancellation, and user rejection. Success takes the form of a product that meets requirements, is delivered roughly on schedule and within constraints, and has a long and positive relationship with its users. These themes are explored briefly here. The root causes of failure and success are explored throughout the book.

User Involvement.   Understanding users, their environment, tasks, constraints, pressures, and goals is essential to delivery of a product that meets needs. Methods are available for effectively involving users in requirements, design, construction, evaluation, and throughout deployment and usage.

> **Rule of Thumb**: A user or business representative may not be able to define needs in a way that can be translated easily into requirements or a usable design. However, a user can certainly be adamant about what is liked or disliked about your product when it is made available for testing or use.

Requirements.   Business and functional needs are the most common and easiest requirements to gather. However, requirements for UI features, usability, consistency, and integration are overlooked very often. Many times, UI features are defined implicitly if not unconsciously in expectations.

With up to 50 percent of software code bulk related to the UI, more effort is required to understand the requirements for product features that are visible to users. In addition, requirements for usability, consistency, and integration must be defined explicitly and measurably. Compliance is then measurable and testable in product plans and evaluation efforts.

> **Rule of Thumb**: Once defined, requirements must be controlled and managed. Project teams must beware of requirements and feature creep by users and the project team. Feature creep kills!

Planning.   Developers are thought to be schedule optimistic, but a more likely cause of schedule optimism is being work unaware. This is basically a skills and experience issue relative to current UI technology. There is a large volume of detail, expected behavior, and redundancy associated with many UI styles and features.

Developers responsible for a UI may not be aware of the volume of very fine detail until after the second or third time around. Unfortunately, by that time the more experienced developers have moved on to other tasks, and a new set of developers is working on UI software and encountering the same old UI speed bumps—a costly and vicious cycle.

Planning must provide sufficient time for skill building, use of UI and usability quality methods, and tracking and reporting results. In addition, plans for UI and usability tasks may need to be provided at a lower level of detail than is provided for other areas of a project.

Skills.   There is a large amount of learning required for new software development efforts. There are relatively new operating systems, new languages, new application architecture styles, new user interface styles, and lots of new technologies and tools. Each new thing requires time to learn just the basics, more time to internalize and make the basics operational, and then even more time to learn how to exploit. Exploitation means being able to use tools and techniques quickly and to best effect for users. The more things that must be learned concurrently, the higher the risk to a project.

Old Rule of Thumb: There are three major causes of project failure:

- A team that has not worked together before
- An operating system that the team has not used before
- New hardware that the team has not used before

The presence of any two of the three causes leads to a major project failure.

New Rule of Thumb: There are six major causes of project failure:

- A team that has not worked together before
- An operating system that the team has not used before
- New hardware that the team has not used before
- A new UI style that the team has not used before (e.g., nongraphical user interface for a PDA)
- A new design paradigm that the team has not used before (e.g., OO)

- Other new technologies that the team has not used before (e.g., multimedia)

The presence of any two of these causes leads to a major project failure.

Project failure is defined as project cancellation, major project delays, significant cost overruns, inability to deliver major project features, inability to achieve major product criteria, or product rejection by the user community. Major project failures are not fun.

Design Practice.

It is always better to design prior to implementing and even better to formulate architecture as input to design. Just as there are good practices in software development, there are good practices in UI and usability. Involving users, multidisciplinary teams, design reviews, prototyping, evaluating, iterating, and evolving rapidly are all good development practices if requirements are to be met. If these techniques were used more often by experienced and inexperienced software development teams, many more products would succeed.

Rule of Thumb: Follow good design practice earlier rather than later.

Risk Management.

Forewarned is forearmed. Knowing that software and UIs are high-risk areas, a product team can be proactive in managing the course of events. More anticipation of problems and solutions is required. Given the vast experience of most software development groups, there must be more learning about awareness of typical problems and solutions.

Plan templates help encode and reuse organizational knowledge. Project teams can proactively address the things that typically go wrong—and badly. A template for a risk list of common UI and usability problems is potentially a common and reusable component for project planning; e.g., "too many steps" and "desktop unfriendly screen size."

The same things seem to go wrong repeatedly. The software "deja vu all over again" phenomenon is explored further as the project is experienced. A major task of software UI and usability is avoiding the tar pits and pitfalls of UI and usability problems.

Rule of Thumb: Projects have a better than random chance of succeeding with the right planning, execution, and tracking.

An Approach to Processes

Just having a great process documented does not guarantee a great product. Painting by the numbers does not create great art. Many great artists developed drafts (models or prototypes) of their great works and iterated on their methods and approach until a great work of art was delivered. Understanding needs and success criteria, having a design vision, delivery of the vision, measuring delivery against criteria, iterating until the right design is instantiated—these are very important.

A necessary and sufficient process is described in this book. Since this is not a cookbook, techniques to allow variations and deviations from a basic theme are provided as well. Techniques to judge sufficiency of execution are described.

An Approach to Solutions

Just as there are lots of ways to skin a cat, there are lots of ways to skin a UI. Better solutions are achieved when options are considered. However, the search for alternatives is likely to be constrained by time, cost, skills, movement of technology, availability of resources, competition, or all of the above—and more. At some point, a single solution must be chosen for delivery to users.

> **Rule of Thumb**: Beware of the search for the best design possible. Invariably, any design can be improved upon, but a design that meets all project requirements is what customers really want.

Techniques to generate alternatives, including generation of alternatives to problems discovered during development are described. Techniques to judge sufficiency of alternatives and selection criteria are also described.

Best Practices

An experience-based approach is employed for selection of described techniques. The techniques have been proven to work on multiple projects that include shrink wrapped and internal application software. Use of the techniques does not automatically guarantee success—the wrong things can be done with the right practices. Not using the techniques does not automatically guarantee failure. There are a small number of projects that are lucky or that are right for the wrong reasons.

Rule of Thumb: Using the right techniques the right way improves the likelihood of success in a significant manner.

The Remainder of the Journey

The journey undertaken in the remainder of this book is one based upon the project and the School of Hard Knocks. The reader is to experience

- Planning
- Requirements
- Analysis of users and tasks
- Design of UI, help, training, and graphics
- Instantiating a design in a specification, prototype, style guide, and product
- Evaluating a proposed product
- Iterating to fix what's broken and not break what's right
- Deployment

Rule of Thumb: A software developer should be a sadomasochist and really enjoy this type of work.

Back to the Project

The project lead has come into your office unexpectedly. He gives you a brief project overview. He also tells you about his commitment to senior management. He tells you how he is organizing the project and whom he has selected as the lead for the non-UI work.

He says that he has spoken with your manager and tells you that he would like to appoint you as the technical lead for the UI work, and expresses his confidence in your skills and abilities. You are currently finalizing some documentation on your previous project and are unassigned to any other project. In spite of the many concerns that you have about schedule and scope, you realize that your choices are somewhat limited in the current environment in the development orgainzation.

The project lead asks you to put together your thoughts about the approach, schedule, and resource needs for the project's UI. He would like to meet with you in 30 minutes. The team lead for the non-UI work will be there as well.

Any questions?

References

Brooks, F., *The Mythical Man Month*, Addison-Wesley: New York, 1995.

Clements, P., et al., *Constructing Superior Software*, Macmillan Technical Publishing: New York, 2000.

McConnell, S., *Rapid Development*, Microsoft Press: Redmond, WA, 1996.

Keil, M., et al., "A Framework for Identifying Software Project Risks," *Communications of the ACM*, Nov. 1998.

Torres, R., "User Centered Practices in a Customer's World", IBM Interact 98 Conference Proceedings, Yorktown Heights, NY, 1998.

Torres, R., "Graphical User Interfaces: Design and Development Overview," Share 81 Conference Proceedings, Aug. 1993.

User-Centered Design Through Delivery

2

Software UIs are receiving increased attention and importance as a feature of competitive advantage. As product feature lists grow longer and more complex, users responsible for product purchases look to the UI as a solution to complexity. If a product's UI catches a user's attention and is simple to learn and use, and has the right price and features, then the product may gain competitive advantage. A competitive edge may be obtained if claims of reduced training costs and productivity gains are real.

Achieving a product with a competitive advantage and edge doesn't happen by fiat, art, or magic. Although there are many techniques that improve the probability of achieving tough goals and successful products, there are no silver bullets in methods or tools. Concerted, systematic, hard work is required on the part of management and technical personnel. A process for design and development of a product includes several steps Plan, Requirements, Design, Implement, Evaluate, Iterate, and Deploy when requirements are satisfied.

These steps are similar to what a gourmet chef does to generate great meals. The basic steps lead to many recipes as variations in ingredients and implementation details are made. Not all recipes are great. However, a skilled gourmet chef knows which recipes to keep and offer to customers, and which recipes to throw away.

This chapter provides an overview of a UI planning, design, and development process that, when applied with integrity, diligence, and perseverance, can yield great UI recipes. The topic is necessarily broad, but an overview of key elements is provided together with references for further exploration. Each process step is explored in more detail in subsequent chapters.

The following topics are discussed:

- Key principles
- A user's view
- A developer's view
- A system's view
- An overview of a process
- Back to the project

Key Principles for Being User Centered

There are a few conditions under which you may know if a project is being conducted in a user-centered manner. The following are essential to being user centered:

1. Understand users and their tasks. Involve users in all aspects of a product life cycle.

2. Set measurable goals. User- and business-based success criteria are established.

3. Design a total user experience. The total experience of a user with a product includes packaging, marketing, training, hardcopy documentation, setup, install, screens, graphics, help, other performance support, upgrade, and uninstall.

4. Evaluate. Test with real users to determine whether goals are met or problems exist.

5. Iterate. If goals are not met or problems exist, then repair and revalidate. It is important to realize that you can never get it perfect the first time.

Rule of Thumb: Anticipate the need to extend and evolve a product's design and implementation.

There are many design and development practices and techniques that, when used in conjunction with principles of user-centered design, help ensure success in developing software products that achieve user and business goals.

A User's View

A typical end user is overwhelmed easily by the many features of GUI-based operating systems and applications. Although basic UI features are learnable within 30 minutes, learning and exploitation of the full features of a UI style and a using application can be somewhat lengthy. Web UIs (WUIs) and handheld UIs (HUIs) can be similarly intimidating for initial learning, though there is less to learn because of constraints imposed by a system.

Users perceive computing systems as tools that should support and facilitate completion of work in a real-world environment. End users are task-oriented and conceptualize tasks in terms of real-world domain objects (see Figure 2.1). An end user then determines how a computing system is used to accomplish a task.

Rule of Thumb: A difficult to use or perplexing system gets in the way of doing real work.

Merely providing the basic elements of any UI style does not guarantee an easy-to-learn and use software application. For example, use of a GUI style does not guarantee usability of a GUI-based application. By the same token,

FIGURE 2.1
A user's task-based view of a computing environment.

use of a Web UI style or a handheld UI style does not guarantee usability of a software implementation.

An end user's problem is further complicated when multiple heterogeneous applications and systems are required in the natural course of work. UI styles of legacy and more modern software are quite different. Aside from the natural hardware, operating system (OS), and application differences, there are differences in even a single UI style, as demonstrated by several common GUI styles, e.g., Apple OS/7, Windows, and Open Software Foundation (OSF) Motif. In these cases, the goal of a UI is to make unneeded features transparent and as consistent as necessary across computing systems.

A Developer's View

The features and mass of today's hardware, OSs, UI styles and technologies, and development tools can overwhelm a typical software application development team. The complexity of a programming task is easily measured in terms of "foot-pounds" of documentation, CDs, and diskettes as well as a large specification and innumerable programming instructions.

A software development task is complex and requires focused attention to a multitude of very fine details at many levels of abstraction and translations (see Figure 2.2). Developing a UI for an application only makes the task more nonlinear, nonorthogonal, and nondeterministic. The problem of a

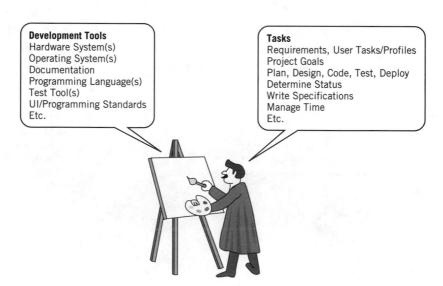

Development Tools
Hardware System(s)
Operating System(s)
Documentation
Programming Language(s)
Test Tool(s)
UI/Programming Standards
Etc.

Tasks
Requirements, User Tasks/Profiles
Project Goals
Plan, Design, Code, Test, Deploy
Determine Status
Write Specifications
Manage Time
Etc.

FIGURE 2.2
A developer's task-based view of a development environment.

software development team is made more complicated when multiple systems are required to perform tasks.

A UI development task is complicated further when porting an application across environments and platforms. There are long lists of systems differences to account for when trying to implement the application-layer of software, e.g., system services, display controls and widgets, font and graphics support, and so forth. For GUI-based software, a developer quickly learns that even with portable languages and porting tools not all windows, icons, menus, and pointers are created equal.

An additional complication for software development teams is the rapid pace of change in hardware, OSs, programming languages, application domains, relevant technology, and UI styles and techniques. As an example, just as GUIs are dominating the desktop, Web- and PDA-based software and UI styles are becoming very popular and must be accommodated.

A Systems View

A system and its software communicate with a user in a presentation language of visual and auditory information, as well as nonverbals like response time, reliability, behavior, and other human factors (see Figure 2.3).

A user communicates with a system and its software in an action language of keyboard, mouse, audible, or touch information. Sometimes a system or its software imposes constraints on a user associated with inputs within a certain time period (response time), error-free communication (reliability), and a well-behaved approach to usage (behavior).

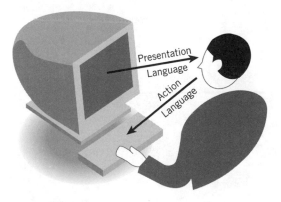

FIGURE 2.3
A systems view of human computer interaction.

For communication of information in presentation and action, the language is composed of semantics (meaning), syntax (structure), and physical mappings. A high degree of multiple skills are required for design and understanding on the part of the computer and user.

An Overview of a Process

Conventional design processes are varied in approach (see Figure 2.4). Major variables associated with a development process include the degree to which it is outside-in or inside-out, 1-shot (no iteration) or N-shot (many iterations), and big bang (a.k.a., all or nothing) or evolutionary.

An inside-out approach focuses on the system internals first, while outside-in focuses on the UI and end user visible product features. Depending upon the complexity of the project and the technologies employed, it may be appropriate to work on the internals and externals simultaneously using an integrated approach.

Iteration refers to the amount of engineering planned for the product, especially the UI. An iterative design and development approach focused on building a UI and its major usability factors is considered a software development best practice. Selection of such an approach does not prohibit or preclude a development team from using a similar approach to contain the risk of non-UI work or use of other technologies on the product.

Evolutionary design and development focuses on building the project using an approach of incremental growth and refinement of a product. Layers of

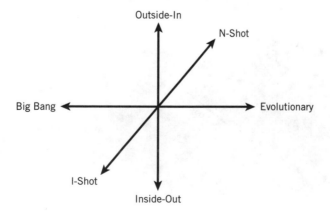

FIGURE 2.4
Major process variables affecting usability and UI.

features are designed and implemented in a staged fashion. A big bang approach is an all-or-nothing, go-for-broke development effort—all software designed and developed concurrently.

> **Rule of Thumb**: The best approach to employ is iterative, evolutionary, and outside-in.

Typical Steps.   Modern design and development processes are portrayed as iterative in nature and utilizing rapid prototyping techniques. Essential to the success of such projects is user involvement. However, depending on the experience of a development team, technical approach used, and tools selected, the number of iterations can be very small and the prototyping not rapid.

The design process depicted in Figure 2.5 does not assume any particular UI style and can support GUI, non-GUI, Web, PDA, OO, or procedural styles of interaction. Some notions explored in follow-up chapters include:

- The process looks like a waterfall model of development. However, development is really an upstream (uphill) process—it doesn't get easier as time elapses. It is more like swimming upstream than swimming downstream.

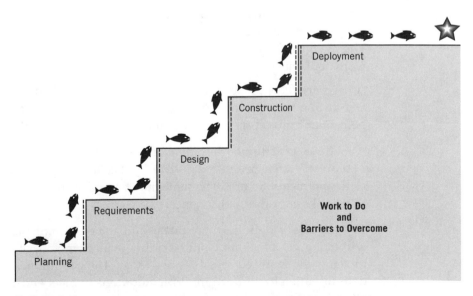

FIGURE 2.5

A conventional design and development process—the big steps.

- The volume and complexity of work increases as time goes on.
  - A small body of requirements is translated into a larger body of UI screens, help, and training.
  - The UI screens and help are translated into implementation design that must interact with system infrastructures, networks, and data bases.
  - The implementation design easily translates into tens—or hundreds—of thousands of lines of programming instructions (code) written in obtuse and picky programming, database, and communications languages and data structures.
  - The code is tested to demonstrate reliability, performance, quality, as well as compliance to functional, UI, and usability requirements.
  - The number of people involved in development increases over time. Unfortunately, the amount of work required of each individual does not decrease as more people become involved.

In practice, there are no tidy or discrete ending points to many aspects of the process; e.g., design typically continues during construction as requirements, design, or construction defects are corrected. Multiple project phases typically overlap; e.g., planning (risk management) and requirements (control) continue throughout a project's lifetime.

Iteration is not depicted but may be required to successfully exit any process phase because it may take a few tries to jump over the next waterfall. Iterative and evolutionary processes are variations of the basic waterfall model. The major difference is the number of iterations experienced prior to software deployment.

A key part of the process is the construction phase. Product implementation and testing are performed during this stage of development and can take 50 percent of a project schedule even if planned and managed properly.

> **Rule of Thumb**: Iteration and successive refinement are likely required to ensure that software application UI, usability, and other requirements are met. The same may be true for other key product factors like critical response times.

The process is definitely nonlinear and nondeterministic. Even subtasks within a given block may not be orthogonal. Remember that commitment to achieving required results is necessary. The commitment may require a determination to perform multiple iterations to meet end-user needs. Iteration is not to be performed solely for the sake of iteration but to achieve user goals.

A Better Way.   A better and more strategic process alternative to most development is user-centered design (UCD). Product development is still swimming against an upstream process. However, facilitation methods and techniques are provided to help smooth out some of the edges of the process. Use of a skills-based approach that is iterative, evolutionary, and staged for development of functional, UI, information, and other features helps to ensure that all requirements are met.

> **Rule of Thumb:** Painting by the (process) numbers does not guarantee success. Hard work committed to achieving requirements is needed.

A Broader View of Being User-Centered.   The concept of UCD has been successful in varying degrees across a number of projects for a number of years. If numerous companies practice UCD and if it is so great, why are there so many poor products?

Part of the answer is that UCD on the surface is too design oriented. The implications of UCD go beyond predesign and early design and apply to the more difficult phases of detailed design, implementation design, and preservation of design integrity during implementation and follow-on activities. That UCD must be carried forward during the not-so-much-fun phases of software development must be made explicit and facilitated.

> **User-Centered Product Development**—a software development process that is multidisciplinary, iterative, and focused on achieving product goals for UI, usability, and other measurable product factors throughout the product life cycle.

The intent of a user-centered product process is illustrated in Figure 2.6. Key notions of user centeredness are embedded in the graphic—planned iteration embedded in the development process, multidisciplinary product team, meaningful user participation, and ongoing evaluation and evolution until requirements are met.

The process is UCD with extensions. UCD is focused on what a product team must do in order to achieve software, UI, usability, and other goals. Although the figure depicts one iteration per development milestone, there can be multiple iterations within each development phase. The point is to iterate until requirements are satisfied.

Plan.   Given a very difficult task, formulating a plan together seems a reasonable first step.

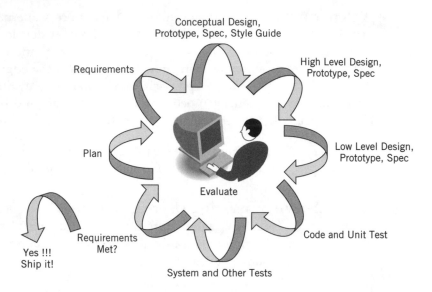

Conceptual Design,
Prototype, Spec, Style Guide

High Level Design,
Prototype, Spec

Requirements

Low Level Design,
Prototype, Spec

Plan

Evaluate

Code and Unit Test

Requirements
Met?

Yes !!!
Ship it!

System and Other Tests

FIGURE 2.6
A user-centered process.

A product plan focused on UI and usability process elements in a measurable way helps take some of the magic out of the process, and contains some of the risk. In order to achieve success:

- A product plan specifically accounts for schedule milestones of each process step and its UI and usability deliverables, including dependencies, assumptions, and technical approach
- A plan identifies and addresses the major risk factors
- A plan incorporates as many facilitating techniques as possible; i.e., approaches that reduce risk and ensure requirements are met
- A plan's execution specifically accounts for and tracks the quality of UI and usability deliverables with respect to plan
- A management approach is defined for proactive involvement. Along with other management tasks, setting up the right team with the right skills is extremely important. The concept of a multidisciplinary team is made explicit with the formation of a team of individuals with the required skills.
- Responsibility and accountability are assigned
- Goals to ensure product UI and usability objectives and criteria are established

Planning is discussed further in Chapter 8.

Requirements.   Requirements for end-user interfaces, usability, consistency, and integration are typically high level and lacking in specificity. In comparison to functional features, requirements for UIs and usability leave quite a lot to the imagination. Because of the lack of clarity and expectations, some very imaginative UI and usability results are obtained. Tasks that are typically performed during a requirements phase include:

- User descriptions, discussed in Chapters 3 and 10.
- User tasks, discussed in Chapter 10.
- Current usability, discussed further in Chapter 14.
- UI features, discussed in Chapter 5.
- Trends, discussed in Chapter 20.

Requirements for UI, usability, and consistency are discussed in Chapter 9.

Conceptual Design.   Usually not discussed explicitly in processes or plans, a conceptual design can be thought of as the architecture for a UI. A conceptual design is a collection of high-level descriptions, abstractions, and overview information that gives developers and end users a big picture about a product, its structure, and its UI:

- Concepts are abstract ideas generated from instances, while a design is a deliberate organization of elements that make up a system.
- A conceptual design is like an outline or a blueprint that describes a product's main features, the arrangement of its parts, and its intended use.
- A development deliverable associated with a product's conceptual design is a user-oriented overview presentation and document describing a product's features and user interface.

Providing a vision and an intended user's model are discussed in Chapter 11, while design principles and guidelines are discussed in Chapter 12.

Design.   Design is an underlying scheme or arrangement of elements that makes up an entity. A UI design is a collection of end-user perceptible features of a software program that includes user input and interactions and system response to user input and interactions. There are many approaches to design of a UI-based application. A key consideration is to break the design down into more granular and comprehensible deliverables—building a pearl. Design iterations and layers are conducted because of the mass of detail to comprehend, integrate, and manage. Concurrent UI and non-UI work is performed to ensure that user visible and infrastructure components integrate and support each other properly.

Extensive design discussions are provided in Chapters 16, 17, and 18.

Prototyping.   Prototypes and simulations are effective tools for the early evaluation of a design. A simulation, or model, is an instantiation of a design, but one not necessarily built using the intended implementation platform. Depending on the timeframe, design questions, skills, and tools available, a story board or paper mockup may be an appropriate design representation method. A prototype is an instantiation of a design built using its intended implementation platform, including hardware, OS, implementation languages and tools.

Different types of simulations and prototypes address questions of depth and breadth of UI or system feature representation, fidelity of UI representation, and construction medium. Because of the many dimensions involved, different names are assigned to the notion of a prototype: UI, functional, low-fidelity, high-fidelity, light-weight, and so forth. It is always better to define the tool and its constraints carefully.

More extensive discussion of prototyping is provided in Chapter 13.

Specification.   A UI specification is an instantiation of a product design in documented form. It describes and depicts user actions and software appearance and behavior in specific situations. Typical specifications are potentially quite large, even for simple applications.

More extensive discussion of specification is provided in Chapter 17.

Construction (Code and Unit Test).   UI software is the ultimate instantiation of a design and evolves through several stages; for example, simulation, prototype, construct, and document. Similarly, non-UI software evolves through stages to construction and documentation. Conventional wisdom dictates that software is written three times before it's right, and prototyping helps achieve this prior to entering deployment environments.

More extensive discussion of construction is provided in Chapter 19.

Evaluation.   All evaluation techniques involve potential users of the product. Techniques are applied early and as often as necessary to ensure that requirements are met. A best practice approach is one that has actual user involvement in all aspects of planning, design, construction, evaluation, and deployment. Such methods are called participatory.

Evaluation techniques are available to span the entire lifecycle of a product. However, these occur at discrete points during the development cycle versus ongoing involvement at a more granular level.

More extensive discussion of usability evaluation methods is provided in Chapter 14.

Iteration. Overall criteria for achieving UI goals must be clearly specified, understood, and accepted by management and developers. Agreements must go beyond superficial acceptance to true personal commitment by an entire product team. Once a design for a UI is developed, it may need iteration many times in order to meet goals. An entire design may need to be discarded if goals cannot be met.

A more extensive discussion of iteration is provided in Chapter 15.

Deployment. Of course, once a product meets requirements and user needs, it is deployed for end use. At this point, there are follow-up activities like evaluating with users not involved in the development and conducting

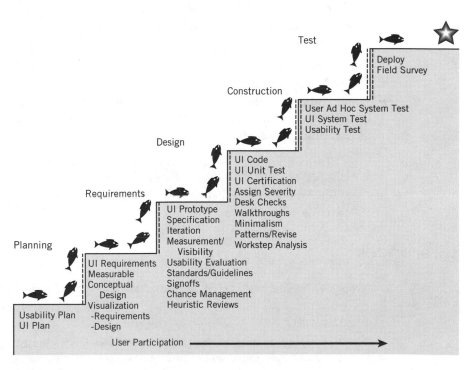

FIGURE 2.7
The UCD process with key facilitation techniques.

pilot tests. There are also user tasks performed on the product that have not been evaluated or anticipated during design and development. There are likely to be new product requirements due to changing business needs. It is good to evaluate a product on an ongoing basis after deployed to end users.

A more extensive discussion of deployment is provided in Chapter 19.

Back to the Project

You've just returned from the initial meeting with the project lead and your peer team leader for the non-UI software. During the meeting, you were given an assignment to meet with the project lead to discuss project development processes, methods, and techniques. You've had a chance to read this chapter but nothing else. Update your initial thoughts about an approach for planning, requirements analysis, design, development, and testing. Update your first pass on schedule, activities, and resource needs for the project's UI and usability in general.

The project lead would like to meet tomorrow and you have two hours to identify major process considerations for the project.

At this point, it is probably a good idea to begin researching information. For example, locate references to supplement information about UCD, usability engineering, GUI, WUI, and handheld UI. Other information to inquire about is related to evolutionary and iterative software development processes of a rapid nature. (There is certainly no need to search for slow development processes).

> **Rule of Thumb:** Establish a habit of searching the Web using keywords related to the project. Although a very large amount of information is indicated in search results, it is easy to sort through for relevance.

References

Brooks, F., *The Mythical Man Month*, Addison-Wesley: New York, 1995.

Clements, P., et al., *Constructing Superior Software*, Macmillan Technical Publishing: New York, 2000.

Gould, J., et al., "Making Usable, Useful, and Productivity Enhancing Computer Applications," *Communications of the ACM*, Jan. 1991.

Karat, C., "Cost-Benefit Analysis of Iterative Usability Testing," ACM/SIGCHI Tutorial, May 1991.

Mayhew, D., "Managing the Design of the User Interface," ACM/SIGCHI Tutorial, May 1991.

McConnell, S., *Rapid Development*, Microsoft Press: Redmond, WA, 1996.

Nielsen, J., *Usability Engineering*, Academic Press: New York, 1993.

Nielsen, J., "The Usability Engineering Life Cycle," *Computer*, Mar. 1992.

Randall, N., "A Look at Usability Testing," *Windows Magazine*, Sep. 1992.

Rettig, M., "Interface Design When You Don't Know How," *Communications of the ACM*, Jan. 1992.

Shneiderman, B., *Designing the User Interface*, Addison-Wesley: Reading, MA, 1987.

Torres, R., "Graphical User Interfaces: Design and Development Overview," Share 81 Conference Proceedings, Aug. 1993.

Torres, R., "Graphical User Interfaces: An Introduction," Share 81 Conference Proceedings, Aug. 1993.

Understanding Peopl

Designing and implementing a UI for OSs and application software is a challenging process.

Two sets of people are described in the previous paragraph—users of software development tools and users of OS and application software. In many cases, a user of software development tools uses application software as well. However, given the challenges of both types of people, there are opportunities to improve UIs for both developers and users. Developers can employ better processes and techniques to deliver software, and users can take advantage of the resulting software.

Although there is wide variation of computer input, processing, and output device characteristics, there is an even greater distribution in the input, processing, and output characteristics of people. A developer must understand that users have strengths, limitations, and weaknesses. Designing around user weaknesses can result in efficient and satisfying software for internal and shrink- wrapped software.

Rule of Thumb: For those working on mission-critical or life-critical software, secure the services of a skilled usability engineer. Otherwise, ensure that necessary and sufficient psychological and ergonomic skills are available for team support and consultation.

The goal of this chapter is to provide insight and sensitivity to physical, physiological, psychological, and sociological aspects of how a user is affected by learning and using software. More complete human factors, ergonomics, and organizational expertise is desirable to complement and supplement skills of software development, computer science, UI, graphics, and information science.

This chapter discusses:

- Ergonomics and human factors

- The ergonomics of software

- Sociological ergonomics

- Implications to software design and development

- Back to the project

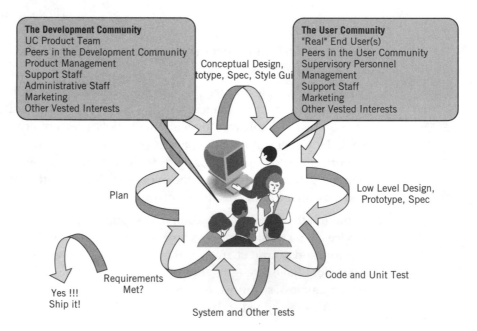

FIGURE 3.1

People, people, people.

Ergonomics and Human Factors_____

That there are many human-related factors around which hardware should be designed is well known and characterized, as in the "Ergonomics Handbook" produced by IBM. Within the context of hardware design, the goal of applying ergonomic principles is to improve effectiveness and job satisfaction.

In addition, there are several nonphysical, human-centered considerations around which software should be designed. While hardware factors are focused on physical attributes of people, software factors consider psychological (nonphysical) attributes, which are not as well known or understood as physical factors. Thus, a focus on user involvement and testing with users is needed. In addition, there are factors related to environmental and sociological considerations.

> **Rule of Thumb**: Walk around and notice the differences in people. Appreciate the differences and note how other users are not like you.

A software UI must be designed correctly, independent of hardware factors, and it must utilize computer hardware and OS features to a user's advantage. As with hardware, the goal of applying ergonomic principles to software is to improve effectiveness and job satisfaction.

Definition.   Ergonomics is the understanding of the relationship between people and their work. The term is used synonymously with human factors, which discovers and applies information about people to the design of tools, tasks, and environments in order to achieve productive and comfortable work.

Productive work provides business value in a tangible way. Productivity is measurable in metrics, such as time to complete a task in an error-free manner. On the other hand, comfortable work provides business value in a less tangible way. Comfort is measurable in terms of user satisfaction or attitudes about a product's ease of use.

Software ergonomics and software human factors have been used to describe the study and application of user-centered information to design. Application software used on a computer system certainly qualifies as a tool applied to achieve work.

Ergonomics of Hardware.   Classical   hardware   considerations involve anthropometrics (the study of physical dimensions of male and female human beings). Other design factors include posture, the back, arm and hand strength, and conditions in the physical work environment. Within an intended user population, there is great diversity of human physical characteristics that must be accounted for in a well-designed tool.

Ergonomics Principles.   There are two major principles of ergonomics:

- Fit the person to the job
- Fit the job to the person

Fitting a person to a job equates with training and practice, while fitting a job to a person means designing tools and tasks to match the capabilities of people. Although the most common use is related to hardware, there is broad applicability of ergonomics to software. There are also several useful extensions.

As with hardware, there is great diversity in human psychological and organizational characteristics and behavior. In addition, there is significant diversity in tasks, task variations, education, experiences, skills, and styles for performing these tasks.

Ergonomics and Human Factors of Software _____

A better understanding of people relative to the task of using computer software to accomplish work is needed, regardless of whether a user is a software developer or a user of application software. Figure 3.2 depicts a very simple model of human information processing.

In the field of cognitive psychology (the study of human learning and thinking), there are many variations on what the elements are. However, a simple model describes general functions that are important aspects of human cognition. A full understanding of the human information processing system may well be a final frontier.

Salient features for a designer to be aware of and sensitive to include human

- Sensation and perception
- Learning and memory
- Attention and performance

A user gathers information from computer software via sight and sound. In the future, a user will use touch as well as sight and sound to gather information.

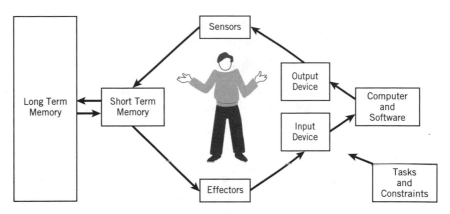

FIGURE 3.2
Human information processing.

A major physical requirement is for the human factors of computer hardware and software to be perceived by a user and sensitive to user input. Application software visual and auditory input to a user must be within sensory ranges. From the sensory buffers, information flows to short-term memory, where pattern recognition processes are invoked to deal with ambiguity, context, identification, and interpretation.

> **Rule of Thumb**: Lack of sensitivity to human features leads to unproductive, hard-to-learn, hard-to-use, and disliked software.

Short-Term Sensory Store.

Sensory buffers in the human information processing system temporarily store fixed images long enough for analysis by a user.

Although a high level of detail is stored, the information is held for a very short period of time. There are believed to be multiple sensory storage areas—one for each sense. Iconic storage is used to store visual information, while echoic storage saves sound information. The icon is a visual record that preserves spatial relationships while the echo preserves temporal relationships. Information in each buffer decays rapidly.

Short-Term Memory.

The part of human memory that retains a limited amount of information about current time is called short-term memory. Information is

- Stored automatically
- Retrieved with very little effort
- Relatively small (7 +/- 2 items)

- Retained by rehearsal
- Relatively slow (compared to input rates)
- Easily lost by distractions or lack of attention

Conscious thought (calculation, interpretation, and reasoning) occurs in short-term memory. The size of short-term memory is small and characterized as having a size of seven plus or minus two. This number is misused in various contexts.

Long-Term Memory.   Information about past experiences is contained in long-term memory. Information is

- Stored and retrieved with effort
- Dependent upon personal interpretation
- Very large (billions of items)
- Organized hierarchically with effort
- Relatively permanent in duration
- Recognized more quickly than recalled

Long-term memory holds knowledge of past events as well as all acquired information and skills. Components are episodic, semantic, analogue, conceptual, and word.

Intermediate-Term Memory.   The part of human memory that keeps track of the current problem-solving approach, stores interim results, and modifies future plans is intermediate-term memory. In contrast, long-term memory stores rules and experiences relative to the current task, and short-term memory formulates the best plan of action for the moment.

Information Processing.   There are methods of processing that deal with learning, attention and decision making. Learning is a complex process that takes many forms, such as memorization, understanding of concepts and rules, and motor skills for repetitive and seemingly automatic procedures (see Figure 3.3). People learn by building upon pre-existing knowledge.

True knowledge and skills are ultimately stored in long-term memory. Highly learned skills are compiled in human memory, meaning that they can be carried out automatically. As one might expect, attention connotes conscious awareness and processing of information. Attention is selective, focused, or divided.

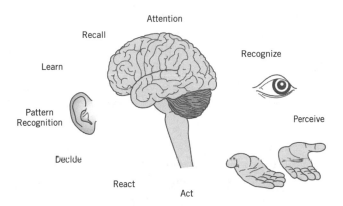

FIGURE 3.3
Components of information processing.

Seeking information, evaluating alternatives and outcomes, and selecting a course of action is decision making. Analyzing and solving problems is subject to counterintuitive behavior or biases typified by

- More information improving confidence but not necessarily accuracy
- Rules of thumb (heuristics) being used more often than precise algorithms
- Optimal problem-solving approaches not always being used

Physical Challenges. People responsible for design of a software product must be very sensitive to the physical challenges that a general user population encounters. Up to 5 percent of a general user population experiences some form of physical challenge. Over 70 percent of challenged users access the Internet.

Although these sound like small numbers, the actual number of individuals affected by supportive software is quite large when one considers the entire working population of a large business or an entire country. The term used for support of users with special physical needs is accessibility. The concept is extensible to users with special cognitive needs, but this is beyond the scope of what is discussed here.

> **Rule of Thumb**: Consider the accessibility factor as an opportunity to better support a user population by being aware of and sensitive to needs on a very broad scale.

A critical challenge for perception is its major dependency upon vision. There are limitations to the use of some color combinations. There are also restrictions for users who have forms of uncorrectable vision or blindness. A more common impact results from the needs of vision correction on the design of display screens. Up to half of a general user population requires some form of vision correction and half of that group requires use of bifocal vision correction. There are other restrictions for users with macular degeneration (tunnel vision), cataracts in aging populations, and other severe but less common conditions.

The use of sound in a UI for gaining user attention or the use of speech for obtaining user input may be ineffective because not everyone can hear. There are other physical challenges that designers must be sensitive to.

A starting point to gain additional insight and awareness are web sites such as

- http://www.textmatters.com/guides/visually_impaired.html
- http://www.w3.org/WAI/GL/

There is also useful accessibility information on web sites of major computer vendors.

Other Challenges.   Other factors come into play for users of computers and software. For example, there are effects of age on learning and perception, distinct learning styles (visual or auditory), and distinct styles of thought (right brain and left brain). There is quite a bit left to learn about human perception and cognition, as well as learning how to apply the knowledge correctly.

Sociological Ergonomics

Up to this point, consideration has been given to only a single individual in interaction with a computer system and independent of other people. However, in an increasingly connected and interdependent world, no individual (or software application) is an island. The vast majority of users and developers do not interact in a vacuum. A user is more likely to be interacting with a computer, customers, developers, supervisors, peers, and peer groups (see Figure 3.4).

As a result, there are several sociological factors to consider in design and software. Along with fitting an individual to a job, one must fit groups and organizations to jobs and available technologies, and vice versa. Group dynamics and organizational behavior are very real and cannot be ignored.

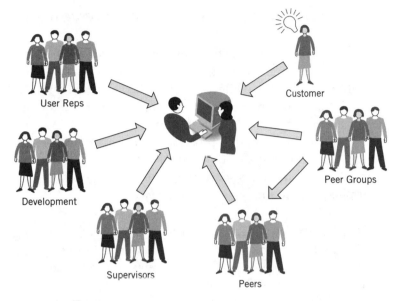

FIGURE 3.4
Social view of design.

The most obvious social factors are pressures that arise from a user's customers, supervisors, managers, work groups, and peers. There are also related work pressures associated with

- Visibility of how time is used
- What errors or mistakes happen and their implications
- How software supports a user's and group's tasks and informs of errors
- Motivation, competition, cost, and other business factors

There are also the ergonomics associated with common forms of communication, culture, and language. Individuals and work groups have norms and mores about the availability of certain types of information to others. Some aspects of this factor are related to privacy or value of information. There are also factors about how some individuals and work groups like to manage or control their time and resources. This is noticeable in use of electronic calendars and who can view and/or schedule use of an individual's or group's time.

The notion of social ergonomic factors should not be ignored or minimized during the rush to deliver products. Issues of turf, ownership, communication, cooperation, interests, and goals are always present. To be sure, it requires further study.

Implications of Software Design and Development _____

There is more than meets the eye and ear, touch, scent, sound, taste, and mind. A design must work around the strengths and limitations of a user or collection of users while exploiting the strengths and limitations of computer hardware and software. As with hardware, ergonomics in software is not a one-time activity but an ongoing and evolving process to optimize software in the tasks and processes of a work environment. Based upon the ergonomic principle of fitting the job to the person (and vice versa) in the context of human and social factors, there are general guidelines that can be applied to user and organizational benefit.

Use Ergonomic Hardware and UI Styles.   Having the right hardware and operating system UI style and tools is a required starting point. In many cases, it is possible for application user interface software to overcome deficiencies in basic hardware and operating system UI styles and tools. Overcoming basic problems in the system platform typically translates into extra work for an application developer or imposes limitations on an application UI. When fundamental problems cannot be overcome, a user typically experiences the consequences.

Remember the User(s).   Regardless of the software and the tasks being performed, know the users. Be cognizant of the distribution of ages, genders, characteristics, skills, knowledge, and limitations. Consider a user population's physical, psychological, and sociological factors. Be aware that there are acceptable ranges for human perception and processing. Keep it simple to learn and simple to use. Make it look good. Where possible, user tasks can be made simpler via software-supported automation, support, and augmentations.

> **Rule of Thumb**: Create a poster and look at it often as a reminder of the eventual users of the software to be delivered.

Don't Demand too Much (or too Little).   There are user performance limits that even the best software design cannot overcome, such as the content and speed of short-term memory. By the same token, software developers can employ a model of an intelligent user who learns and uses a computer system, application software, and task related job aids and information to get everyday work done better and faster.

> **Rule of Thumb**: Avoid the stupid user syndrome.

Exploit Existing Knowledge. Use familiar terms and concepts. Maintain cognitive fidelity with a user's and work group's task, objects, and work aids, as opposed to absolute mimicry of an end user's environment and objects. Exploit learning techniques related to peer, group, or technological means.

Facilitate Learning. Explicitly and consciously provide analogies and conceptual models. Allow a user to learn the system in stages by supporting exploration without penalty. Good organization and layering of features helps a user organize the structure of an application. Be consistent in semantics, syntax, and low-level physical device usage. Analogies and associative devices of any type are extremely important in the learning process.

Don't Overload Short-Term Memory. Information and options should be clearly visible and accessible. Provide defaults where possible to assist recognition. Use reminders and chunking of information where appropriate.

Exploit Long-Term Memory. Icons, visualization, terms, and models play a big role in supporting long-term memory. Use of recognition instead of forcing recall of features and data helps end users. Use of different forms of input, output, and views are important to accommodate different learning styles.

Design for Error. Think in terms of managing trouble. Application software should be tolerant of user error and minimize its effect. Feedback on system status and reversibility for destructive actions is important. Be cognizant of opportunities for error and consequences, and how to avoid errors. For errors where recovery is painful, actions should be difficult to perform and be confirmed prior to being performed.

Facilitate Developing Automatic Procedures. For high use tasks and actions, design interactions that are easy to internalize as reactive procedures. With a little practice, tasks that take few, or easy to perform, steps lead to user work habits that require minimal effort. Use of shortcut keys and some direct manipulation actions are examples of such automatic procedures.

Assist Decision-Making and Task Flow. Provide decision aids as an essential feature of applications. Support individual and group oriented task flows in various forms, such as decision trees, matrices, visualization of work steps and information via trees or maps, and cooperative workgroup environments. Provide ways for users to organize information meaningfully through chunking, ordering, searching, and partitions.

Use System Defaults and Customization Features.   Use system defaults and customization features. Observe what characteristics are employed by key platform software for such features as font, control size, sounds, and colors. Developers should vary from platform defaults and styles with care. In addition, the UI must stay within the sensory bounds of users.

> **Rule of Thumb**: A UI is in the receptors of a perceiver.

Utilize System Provided Accessibility Features.   Many OSs provide or support features and technologies that allow accessibility by users challenged in many ways. Application software avoids doing anything that prevents use of accessibility features. If anything, application software should support existing technologies instead of utilizing a roll your own approach.

Keep Learning.   Find two or three references and sources of information about software and social human factors. With as much information as exists on the Internet, find two or three web sites from technical experts. References and experts must talk to you and make sense relative to your needs and the needs of your users. Apply what is learned.

Back to the Project

The project manager has asked for a preliminary description of the likely users for the product's software. The project manager is not asking for a specific audience description or specific characteristics of each user—just general characteristics of users and work groups and the likely influence this has on the design direction of the product.

In addition, the project manager would like a contrast of end user characteristics to those of developers (he is trying to explain to upper management how end users differ from developers, management, and customers). In terms of developers, the project manager would like an assessment of what characteristics and kinds of processes and tools would facilitate product development.

Be sure to continue your research for the project.

As usual, the project manager needs an answer quickly. You have 30 minutes.

After the meeting with the project manager, continue your research.

Any questions?

References _____

Brown, J., and Newman, S., "Issues in Cognitive and Social Ergonomics," *Human Computer Interaction*, vol. 1, 1985.

Ergonomics Handbook, IBM Corp., Purchase, NY.

Ergonomic Design for People at Work, Eastman Kodak Co., New York, 1983.

Lachman, R., et al., *Cognitive Psychology and Information Processing*, Lawrence Erlbaum Associates, Hillsdale, NJ, 1979.

Mayhew, D., *Software User Interface Design*, Prentice Hall: Englewood Cliffs, NJ, 1992.

Norman, D.A., *The Design of Everyday Things*, Doubleday: Currency, NY, 1990.

Sanders, M.S., and E.J. McCormick, *Human Factors in Engineering and Design*, McGraw-Hill: New York, 1987.

Shneiderman, B., *Designing the User Interface*, Addison-Wesley: Reading, MA, 1987.

Torres, R., "Ergonomics of Software," Westlake Reflections, 1992.

Vecchio, R., *Organizational Behavior*, The Dryden Press: Chicago, IL, 1991.

A User-Centered Product Team   4

Even for relatively small projects, the design of a software UI is a daunting task. If a complex suite of software applications is being developed, new technologies are being utilized, severe competitive factors are involved, and severe project constraints are imposed, well, that's another story.

The number of critical skills involved in today's UI styles and applications is somewhat large. Skills involved in any software project are UI, software development, software and performance testing, graphics and visualization, training, help, performance support, human factors, business planning, workflow, business transformation, project management, and change management.

Many projects do not have people with these skills, and many project teams are unaware of the skills required. This is an area of high risk and a major cause of project failure. Critical skills for user-centered product teams are identified in this chapter.

A reason for lack of skills in this area is that this set of skills is not generally taught with any detail in most educational or company programs for software developers/engineers. This requires the developers to learn it on their own.

Traditional organizations may cause severe people-oriented problems due to organizational behavior and consequent group dynamics. There is at least one better way for success using user-centered product teams operating under different organizational models.

This chapter presents the critical team based information in the following areas:

- The ergonomics of software development
- Implications to software development
- A different perspective on a team model
- Required development skills
- An approach to skill building
- Skills for managers
- An analogy
- The project and a user-centered product team

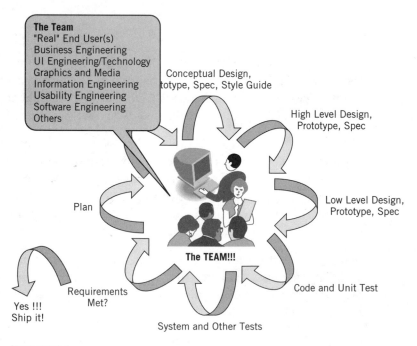

FIGURE 4.1
A user-centered product team.

The Ergonomics of Software Development

If software development were easy, there would be more software available today. If developing easy to learn, easy to use, and productive software were easy to achieve, there would be more of it as well. As it is, the bulk of software products and UIs tend to be very average and do not meet user and business needs. Some of this software is actually very bad by any number of metrics.

Why? It is very difficult to develop software products based upon current methods and skills of software engineering. However, even with the best of processes, painting by the process numbers is not sufficient to achieve desired results. A critical ingredient is having the right people with the right skills to:

- Work with many different people in development and business organizations
- Understand current business users, processes, and future needs and goals
- Translate ambiguous requirements to increasingly precise and voluminous detail
- Use tools and techniques that are not necessarily suited to software development
- Evaluate and repair design and implementation quickly and effectively

Recall that ergonomics is about fitting the person to the job and fitting the job to the person. Not all people necessarily fit the job or its tools. Similarly, the job and its tools are not necessarily suited to most people.

There are myriad precise details to consider in all aspects of a UI. There are potentially hundreds of issues and differences in users, groups, and organizations to resolve. There are transitions from customers to business leaders to users to product requirements to UI designs to UI tools to infrastructure design to implementation (code) to information to test cases to user manuals to deployment.

A better process (like UCD) certainly helps. Better tools to support the transition from requirements through implementation and testing would certainly help. The next best supporting factors are the right people with the right skills and a relatively detailed and pragmatic approach to managing the volume of details and issues.

Implications of Software Development

Getting the right people with the right skills on a user-centered product team organized the right way is a good thing to do—a best practice.

Rule of Thumb: The organizational, group, and individual challenges of product development are orders of magnitude more difficult than any technical challenges. The challenges appear to be 80 percent people and 20 percent technology.

I don't get no respect!　All the members of a conventional software development effort say this in one form or another. Because of the nature of a user-centered product team, there may be only a few reasons for anyone to say or hear comments about lack of respect:

- Lack of individual skill that is not being remedied
- Poor interpersonal skills
- Poor group dynamics

The members of a user-centered product team are drawn from the key skill areas involved in software development. Also included on the team are other major contributors and stakeholders, such as a representative from the user community. Depending upon the product under development, other skill areas or stakeholders may be required.

Critical Goals.　A user-centered product team has the major goal of effective delivery of a product that meets requirements for usability, UI, and consistency. In addition, the team requires clear project management, management support, tools, facilities, and the right attitude to tackle a tough job.

Critical Engineering Skills.　The term engineering is applied to various skill areas because no one person or group has all the right answers, even for their respective skill area. As a result, an iterative and evolutionary approach is used to achieve a solution. UI design and development for current UI styles and a majority of business software is a high skill and high teamwork effort. Depending upon the product under development, the required skill set can include people to perform engineering tasks for other skill areas. Table 4.1 depicts a set of primary skills required for today's software.

TABLE 4.1
Potential skill areas

Primary skills	Potential skill areas
Operating system UI style	Advertising
Application UI style	Packaging
Business knowledge	Product planning
Human factors	Product support
Graphic and visual design	Management
Information design	Leadership
Prototyping design/develop	Communication
Product architecture/design/develop	Group dynamics
UI styles and standards	Organizational behavior

Rule of Thumb: The importance of the various skills and the appropriate number of people with each skill type requires careful planning to secure.

Skills are mapped to specific roles within a user-centered product team as depicted in Table 4.2. In some cases, there is overlap in skills and responsibilities. However, well-defined assignments, deliverables, and teamwork resolve any ambiguity. One person can perform one or more roles. For example, a team leader may perform roles of UI design, standards formulation, and prototyping. A team member with graphic design skills may perform roles of graphic design and information design. Close working relationships among the members of a team are needed to ensure success.

Rule of Thumb: Each person must have sufficient skills and be ready, willing, and able to perform more than one role. People must be multifaceted and multitalented.

TABLE 4.2
Major roles on a user-centered product team

Role	Skills required	Typical sources of skill
UC team lead	Leadership, team building, planning, tracking, communication, risk assessment, reporting	UI engineering
UI	Interaction techniques, UI structure and flow, widget behavior and selection, standards, tools, technology, specification	UI engineering

TABLE 4.2 *(continued)*
Major roles on a user-centered product team

Role	Skills required	Typical sources of skill
Graphics and media	Layout, visualization, color, fonts, audio, animation, and graphic tools	Graphic, visual, and media engineering
Information	Technical writing, performance support, layout, training, information tools	Information engineering
Storyboard and mockup	Storyboarding and low-fidelity representation techniques for UI, information, graphics, and others	All
Simulation and prototype	Programming language, development tools, and high-fidelity representation techniques for UI, information, graphics, media, and others	UI software engineering
Product evaluation	Design, conduct, analyze, report user feedback and evaluations; knowledge of people and interaction with hardware and software	Usability engineering
User/business representation	Business knowledge, user profile, user environment	Business engineering
Management sponsor	People management, strategy, planning, tracking, risk management	Software and UI Engineering

User Interface Engineering.   Personnel skilled in UI technology, UI standards, implementation tools, and exploiting the UI for an application are essential to product success. UI design personnel are responsible for formulating approaches for conceptual models, object and action definitions, the structure and flow of screens, appearance and behavior, and all the fine details associated with user interaction and the response of the system. The UI designer may be responsible for documentation of guidelines and specifications for the product.

UI Software Engineering.   Personnel skilled in design and implementation of UI software are required for developing interactive prototypes and/or product level software. The task involves use and exploitation of widgets available, design and use of algorithms and data structures to support UI appearance and behavior, software installation, performance tuning for response times, and so forth.

Rule of Thumb: Team members involved in UI prototyping must understand the differences in what must be designed and implemented for prototype and product software.

Graphics and Media Engineering.   Personnel skilled in design and implementation of visual and graphic constructs for the UI are required. In GUI and WUI, specific visual themes may be designed and graphic elements designed, such as icons, bitmaps, JPEGs, and GIFs. A graphics engineer may be involved in audio-visual tasks to produce multimedia and animation deliverables.

Information Engineering.   Personnel skilled in design and implementation of training, tutorials, help, and electronic performance support are required on the team. The task involves design and implementation of information useful and usable to support initial learning, performing infrequent tasks, or solving problems.

Usability Engineering.   Personnel skilled in human behavior, perception, learning, ergonomics, and cognition are extremely important. Human factors and engineering psychology skill is required to design and conduct user surveys and evaluations of system usability.

Business Engineering.   Personnel skilled in doing the real world work of a business are essential to the team. A business engineer is a real user—one actively doing the work of the business instead of a person who used to do that work. Knowledge of the application domain, business rules, business data and values, and user success criteria is required. Knowledge of success criteria for the business and factors important to design tradeoffs cannot be underestimated. The business engineer must be familiar with usage of current systems relative to the proposed product.

User-Centered Product Team Sponsor/Manager.   Along with a technical team lead, a responsible manager must be appointed to oversee the user-centered product team. Along with the technical team lead, the team sponsor/manager is accountable to product management for delivery of a product that meets requirements within constraints.

Other Critical Skills.   Other skills may be needed for a project. Someone on the team must be responsible for exploring other potential skill areas and the possible implications to the product and the team. Some skill areas with potential importance to a UC product team include business planning, business transformation, change management, performance evaluation, project management, and workflow.

Rule of Thumb: Talk with technology awareness personnel, explore new concepts and potential applicability to the project, and get help as soon as possible.

A Different Perspective on the Team Model

A lot has been said about how small team efforts tend to be very successful, especially when new technologies are being implemented. However, development in the large or huge has a tendency to water down results achieved. Small teams work best when the right technical people, motivations, rewards, management, and support are in place.

A major challenge for large or huge project development efforts is to establish a concept of teams of high performing small teams working together and generating high performance results.

Rule of Thumb: A challenge for leaders and team members is to preserve the atmosphere and characteristics of a small team regardless of the number of people involved on a project.

FIGURE 4.2
Building blocks for effective small teams.

Good People.   Much of the focus is necessarily on having the right technical skills, but there must also be an abundance of soft skills. These include perseverance, dedication, flexibility, inquisitiveness, ego-less, friendliness, and just being nice. Building a good team depends on getting good people with the right skills.

> **Rule of Thumb**: It is better to wait for good people to become available than to wait for available people to become good and behave well.

Entrepreneurial.   An entrepreneurial spirit within a development organization is required to generate great products. In many regards, high performance results are not produced following cookbook approaches. A team focused on achieving great results for users and breaking the rules when necessary is sometimes required.

Market Driven.   Another way of being entrepreneurial is focusing on users and their real needs in an uncompromising way that cannot be achieved by competitors. A competitive spirit requires knowledge of the competition, its strengths and weaknesses, as well as a desire to match feature strengths and/or deliver features that exploit weaknesses.

Team Building.   A team leader and team management must ensure that the right things are done to build cohesiveness and effectiveness in a team—merely putting people together in a room does not a team make. Group dynamics is an extremely important consideration. There are many team building techniques designed to build trust, capitalize on individual differences, communicate effectively, and group problem solving. The most important factor leading to team effectiveness is having clear goals with certain accountability for achievement. Not far behind in importance is effective leadership from the technical and management leaders of a team.

> **Rule of Thumb**: Be sure to allocate sufficient time, energy, and effort to build a high performing user-centered product team.

Team Skill Building.   The technical skills of individuals on the team must be sufficient for the project. The experience of many development teams is legacy-based applications. A theme common to these customers is moving existing development and applications from current platforms to UIs based upon GUIs.

At a minimum, GUI-based applications bring at least three potentially new technologies (new hardware, new OS, new UI style) to a software development team moving from host- or mini-based systems to GUI-based applications. All technologies, either explicit or implicit, must be called out as separate line items in plans. Although humorously referred to as WIMP interfaces, development of GUI-based applications is not for the feint of heart, schedule, or cost. Highly skilled and disciplined development personnel are required to achieve the potential benefit of GUI-based applications.

Team Work.   The biggest responsibility of a UC product team is to achieve creativity and innovation sufficient to deliver required results. A team must work smoothly, do the required work, and share accountability for results.

Team Rules.   Each team must establish rules of behavior. Honesty, clear communication, and playing to win are very important factors. Be sure to do some research on how to build an effective technical team.

Teaming with Users.   Involving users in project development work is discussed in more detail in Chapter 6. Major considerations for user-developer teaming are learning a common language, learning each other's needs, and developing a working relationship that facilitates delivery of software that meets user, business, and development needs.

Required Development Skills

Based upon personal experiences and observations of multiple UI programming projects, let's begin a more detailed exploration of the skills required by a developer of GUI-based applications. Basics can be acquired in a week. Mastery takes time.

Programming Language.   Basic to all GUI-based systems is some variation of the C programming language. At a minimum, knowledge of ANSI C is a must for a UC product team faced with the possibility of porting a software application from one GUI-based system to another. For complex, web-based software, some variant of Java is needed. There are many classes that teach basic programming language concepts. Bare basics can be acquired in a week, but programming techniques take years to learn.

Native Operating System.   As with programming languages, there are classes that teach OS basics. Basic knowledge can be acquired in a one-week class. Mastery of any operating system takes time.

UI Basics. Before developing a GUI or Web-based or PDA-based application, a UC product team must learn how to design one. Platform design guides provide helpful information. There are also classes that teach UI basics and process-oriented development approaches. Again, basic knowledge is acquired in a week, with mastery and exploitation taking time. More than other types of UI styles, GUI-based applications have many more details for a developer to worry about.

Native Toolkit. A toolkit is the collection of facilities provided by an OS or hardware platform to an application for receiving user input, processing that input, and providing system output, such as keyboard or mouse input and outputs, to a display device. Typically, a one-week class is sufficient to introduce key points. Mastery of basics and exploitation takes time.

Advanced Programming Language. As with other programming languages, advanced techniques are available. As with other things to learn there are one-week classes on the topic, with more time required to learn basics and then exploit.

OOA/OOD/OOP. Knowledge of object-oriented technology can be acquired for three aspects of development: OO analysis (OOA), OO design (OOD), and OO programming (OOP). OOA skills are required to specify real world problems in an OO manner. OOD skills are required to transform the analysis into a design of objects, classes of objects, class hierarchies, and inheritance. OOP skills are required to transform the design into an implementation language. Potentially, a one-week class is sufficient to learn the basic terminology and constructs. However, programmers experienced in procedural techniques seem to experience difficulty in making the transition to OO. Two to three months may be required to transition to the OO software architecture style, not counting learning an OO language.

Cross-System UI Tool. A number of projects require the same software and UI-based application style to be ported for execution on multiple platforms. For example, there are some number of applications that must run on a Mac, Windows, and UNIX. For these situations, a multiplatform toolkit is recommended. In single platform development situations, use of the native toolkit is sufficient.

A cross-platform tool is basically UI-building software that has the added feature of facilitating porting the UI of an application from one environment to another. Usually, many of the UI elements are converted from one toolkit style to another. However, there is usually some variance in low-level details like font and color that must be manually adjusted. Again, provide a one-week class and time to learn and exploit.

Advanced UIs and Techniques.   Up to this point, basics have been discussed to get UI-based applications exposed to end users. However, there are advanced UI-based applications that demonstrate real exploitation not possible with only basic knowledge and skills. As a UC product team becomes more familiar with the basic tools and languages, exploitation becomes feasible. Classes are available for stretching basic UI knowledge into more creative designs and implementations.

People Skills.   Implicit in most software development organizations is the knowledge that people must know how to work together. However, little formal training is undertaken in either group dynamics or organizational behavior. Provide a week of classes and time to learn and apply.

Other Technologies and Skills.   If other technologies are incorporated in the project, remember to add formal time for training, learning, and applying the necessary skills. Other skills needed by a UC product team are derived from other disciplines and include graphic design, nontechnical writing, version control, testing, performance evaluation, human factors, software evaluation, and project management. These skills are obtained from other personnel supporting the UC product team. However, the entire software development team should be trained in the basics of these disciplines.

Adding It Up.   If you are starting from ground zero, just taking classes for the key areas easily requires 8 weeks (see Table 4.3). However, the subjects can be studied in chunks. Each chunk of knowledge can be learned and time given to assimilate and apply before going on to the next. If more languages and toolkits are added, the table only gets longer.

TABLE 4.3
Basic knowledge acquisition

Skill	Time (weeks)	Source
C or Java	1	
Native OS	1	
Native toolkit	1	

TABLE 4.3 *(continued)*
Basic knowledge acquisition

Skill	Time (weeks)	Source
UI basics	1	Graduate and postgraduate level
Advanced C or Java	1	
X-UI Tool	1	
Advanced UI	1	Graduate and postgraduate level
People	1	Postgraduate psychology/sociology
TOTAL	**8**	

Some classes can be taken in different order, and some topics can be studied at the graduate level in universities. Providing time to assimilate and internalize knowledge takes three to six months. Learning how to exploit the technology available to UI-based applications takes a year or two.

New UI styles and languages can be substituted for items in Table 4.3, such as HTML/DHTML, XML, JavaScript, and other operating systems. The classes listed do not include comparable classes for graphics, information, usability evaluation, human factors, or other computer science skills. The table gets longer if the team requires additional skills, technologies, and languages.

Rule of Thumb: Build the table and give time to learn and practice.

An Approach to Skill Building

Although seemingly a daunting task, climbing the mountain of skill building for UI-based application software development can be accomplished. If you start by first learning how to crawl, running and flying through implementation of other UI-based features comes naturally. There are several options for learning the how-to aspects of UI-based application software development.

Classes.   Depending upon personal learning style, formal courses are appropriate for quick learning. Depending upon needs, a one-week class may suffice. Where graduate-level classes are offered on a particular topic, this is a hint that a one-week class may not be sufficient. Consider allowing extra time to build skills or take the graduate-level classes. For most of these topics, workshop-oriented courses are the best.

Self-Study.   A self-study approach to obtaining needed skills can be taken. Many classes, complemented by other reading and exercises, are adequate for skill acquisition. Some books assist learning native toolkits. Learn by example when possible.

Start Small.   After initial learning, apply the basics by building a small UI-based application. For example, be sure that the following can be done for a GUI application:

- Design the UI-based elements of an application, such as a desktop icon, its window, menus, a dialog, and a help screen
- Implement the icon for the native desktop and open a window from the icon
- Display the menus of the window using the pointer and the keyboard
- Display the action dialog and help windows

Initial Results.   Very humble UI-based software should be planned initially. Slow response time, unreliability that crashes the system, hard to reproduce problems, and difficult testing may be encountered. It's part of the learning curve.

Iterate.   After building a basic UI-based application, attempt refinements in small incremental and evolutionary steps. Add UI controls to the application. Keep adding underlying software support for the menu choices. Continue building the application in stages. Try an OOD and implementation. Attempt more exotic design and implementation over time.

Practice! Practice!! Practice!!!   Once the basic skills are acquired, exploitation begins. Exploration and experimentation are key ingredients here. Learning from others is important; not everything must be learned in self-discovery. Workshops are possible avenues for developing common skills within a team environment. Once developed, an important point is to maintain the skills.

Skills for Managers

Better project management skills are required for UI-based application software. During the learning phase of a project, development personnel find it hard to estimate.

Better People/Team Management.   The key to success in UI-based software development is good people, many times working as good teams. Ensure that team building takes place, including interactions with other teams. Management must listen to the development team, especially its concerns and commitments.

> **Rule of Thumb**: Listen for personal commitments very carefully: "I'll do my best" versus "I'll do it!"

Finer Level of Plan Granularity.   Implementation   plans   should schedule and track work and milestones at a finer level of detail. As painful as it seems and in spite of likely resistance, each milestone represents work to do; for example, UI design, specification, usability test, iteration, implementation design, implementation, and software testing for each item.

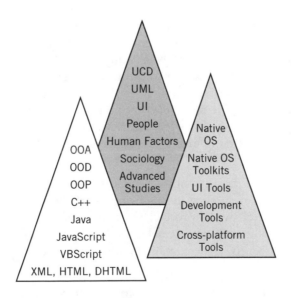

FIGURE 4.3
Skills for GUI-based software development (task, schedule, and resource needs).

Ensure Training Occurs.   UI-based application development is complex and requires skilled developers (see Figure 4.3). Management must carefully assess the skills of the development team and ensure that appropriate education and learning occurs. Part of the training includes planning UI-based software development. Although not discussed, extra time is needed for proper design and specification of a UI-based application.

Different Project Measures.   Because of complexity, productivity is hard to measure for UI-based applications. Higher user satisfaction and productivity over current software should be the goal, and it should be measured, tracked, and rewarded appropriately. If OO approaches are employed, different metrics may be needed to assess productivity. One of the big selling points of OO is reuse. Thus, an important point for a UC product team is to measure and reward efficient development and reuse of software.

Managing Technology Introduction.   Introducing too much technology into software development increases project risk. An important management task is to ensure that technology is introduced carefully and that skills and schedule are sufficient.

Organizational Behavior.   The behavior of formal and informal groups is organizational behavior. The group behavior noticed most is by formalized departments within an organization, where each department has specific charters and goals to achieve. Many times, the responsibilities and goals of groups within an organization are competing instead of complementary. Many times, individuals within these groups do not cooperate to achieve product goals. The result of competing goals, unclear responsibility, and uncooperative individuals is organizational conflict, which creates project risk. Conflict among groups and individuals within an organization causes many projects to fail.

Since large projects typically require people from multiple groups to contribute effectively, it is necessary to spell out clearly who is responsible and accountable for what. A UC product team must be appointed, responsible technical and management personnel must be appointed, and the team and leadership must be given clear responsibility and authority to achieve UI and usability results.

> **Rule of Thumb**: If there is confusion about who is in charge for a UC product development effort, the project will fail to deliver on goals.

Once the responsibilities, accountabilities, and assignments are made, management must monitor, track, and ensure that the right things are happening.

An Analogy _____

Skills development and team building is explored further with a sports analogy. For a software development team, the ultimate goal is to win a Software Superbowl. In software development, as in sporting events, the objective is to win. Players, coaches, and the team must commit to win, and the team must have the skills required to play and win. Table 4.4 lists several requirements for sporting teams relevant to software development.

Owner/General Manager.   There is only one owner and general manager, although there can be multiple partners. Certainly, an owner of a sports team must decide what game a team will play (the business we're in is . . .). An owner sets the goals and tone for an organization and communicates these clearly. If the objective is to win the big one, then a team needs to know by words and actions. Perhaps the most important job of an owner is selecting coaches.

Coaching Staff.   Although a team is likely to have a coaching staff, there is only one head coach. There are assistant coaches to handle subteams and specialized skills. There may be player-coaches who perform double duty. Coaching responsibilities include player selection, teaching players how to win, knowing how to use and improve player skills, and developing winning plays and strategies. Extending the analogy to software development, coaches must be identified and made responsible for ongoing and consistent training, conditioning, and team performance. Conditioning and support are especially important for large projects of long duration. Responsibility for these basics cannot be abdicated to infrequent and perhaps ill-suited educational experiences.

A coaching staff translates an owner's objectives into operational goals; that is, goals that each player can understand, relate to, and deliver. For example, if the goal is to win a Super Bowl, one of a quarterback's operational goals could be a 60 percent completion rate with no more than one interception per 50 completions. Extending the analogy to software developers, operational usability, UI, and other software metrics need to be established for any given component developed.

Players and Teams.   Depending on the game, players of different skills are needed with varying degrees of interplayer interaction. For downhill racing, players with different endurance and racing skills are needed, and interplayer interaction is low during competition. In soccer, similar skills are needed by all players (shoot, pass, dribble), and specialized skills are required for some (a goalie catches), but player interaction is very high in order to make the play.

The analogy applies to software teams, where high skills are needed and interplayer interaction can be low or high. For efforts requiring high interaction, simply putting people together on a project or in a room doesn't make a winning team. Some people are great running backs, centers, or quarterbacks, and some have temperaments and skills suited for greatness at other games. Coaches must ensure that skilled players are placed in the right position and that smooth interactions take place between team members.

The Player-Coach.   Perhaps the most demanding assignment for any sport is a coach who also plays the game. A player-coach must perform during a game, as well as evaluate the execution of others. A player-coach must focus on personal excellence as well as the excellence of others and must have skills other than execution. The position is so demanding that there are not many good player-coaches.

In software development, a player-coach can be the leader of a programming team (chief programmer) or one of its members. Responsibilities include design delivery and evaluation, writing code, reading the code of others, executing test cases, writing product information, and anything else needed to achieve a winning team and product.

Player Skills.   An extremely important ingredient to winning is a player with skills and endurance. A collective set of players must have a critical mass of skills required to achieve team goals. Superior team skills are achieved via dedication, exercise, training camps, conditioning, coaching, and practice, practice, practice.

A wide receiver must have individual and team skills, such as speed, and knowing how to run routes, catch a ball, and use blockers. But a team cannot rely on just one wide receiver. There must be balance among many players. The analogy applies to software development, where even small projects require skills in UI, data structures, algorithms, database, networking, information, and interaction with other team members.

TABLE 4.4
Software development as a game

Requirement	Explanation
Owner/General Manager	Single executive
Coaching staff (coach, assistants, player-coaches)	Teach players; develop game strategy; develop plays; set operational goals
Players (generalist, specialist, captain)	People who specialize in one position, or who can play multiple positions, or one who is "captain" to call signals (audibles)
Weight room	Task-relevant conditioning and development
Training camp	Practice skills and teamwork
Tryouts	Qualify for the team
Training film	View prior performance and see what competitors do
Playbook	Plays a team will use
Game plan (goals and plays)	Plays to execute during a specific game
Practice	Individual = basics + rehearse game plan; team = rehearse game plan
Game	Execute plays and game plan; keep statistics and scores; audibles and adjustments; win.

The Project and a User-Centered Product Team _____

At this point, you have probably started the second week of the project's overall schedule. The clock is ticking and major milestones are coming up. The project lead and senior management continue to be very excited about the project and its potential, especially with the information provided about UCD and users. These senior managers continue to ask for more details and presentations to other business areas, which has become a minor distraction in spite of the visibility it provides. The project lead, your teammate, and you have made very favorable impressions on senior management.

The senior management team wants to know what headcount and skills are needed for the project. Though serious planning has not yet occurred, senior management and the project lead need an early estimate of resources and cost, especially for the planning, requirements, design, and prototyping work. There are other projects that appear very important to the health and success of the organization, and they are competing for the same critical people and skills. The project lead has agreed to submit a preliminary request for people to start working with you immediately.

Because the parent organization is trying to respond more quickly to competitive threats and opportunities, the project lead has been asked to present skill and headcount needs through completion of a UCD-based high level design. The project lead must present this information at 7:30 a.m. tomorrow and has asked for your input. His parting words as he dashes out of your office are "You might have carte blanche, but make it reasonable! And, it has to include people to deal with everything that a user is going to deal with!"

It's 6 p.m., and you can spend no more than two hours on the assignment tonight. You need to brief the project lead at 7 a.m. tomorrow. You have not yet considered a project schedule, but management has agreed in principle with the user-centered process. The parent organization has good people with skills in current technologies, but very few people are likely to be available in any of the newer technologies.

Prepare briefing charts that address the following given the project as you understand it:

- Critical skills needed for the team
- What order the skills are needed
- How many people are likely needed by phase (e.g., planning, requirements, conceptual design, and high-level design)
- How gaps in team skills and training are to be addressed
- Likely assignments and how the team will work
- Management, organizational, and group considerations

Continue your research. You may want to include topics such as group dynamics, organizational behavior, leadership, team building, and so forth.

Any questions?

References

Nielsen, J., *Usability Engineering*, Academic Press: New York, 1993.

Pinchot, G., *Intrepreneuring*, Harper and Row: New York, 1985.

Rodgers, S.H., ed., *Ergonomic Design for People at Work*, Van Nostrand Reinhold: New York, 1983.

Rubin, J., *Handbook of Usability Testing*, John Wiley & Sons: New York, 1994.

Torres, R., "Graphical User Interfaces: Development Skills," Share 82 Conference, Aug. 1993.

Torres, R., et al., "The Rule Book: A Guided Rule-Building Expert System," IBM Technical Report TR 71.0039, April 1994.

Wegner, P., "Dimensions of Object-Based Language Design," *Proceedings of ACM Conference on Object Oriented Programming, Systems, and Languages*, 1987.

Popular UI Styles

5

There are several UI styles popular in the industry. You can argue that the absolute number of users on mainframe or minicomputer style interfaces is becoming more dominant. However, the trend for dominance is definitely in favor of GUIs and their derivatives. Not yet clear is what style of UI will dominate handheld devices, though you could argue that these are also variants of a GUI style.

GUIs dominate personal computers, and there are a small number of variations in style. WUIs, in their own right applications that use a GUI style, dominate access to Internets, extranets, and intranets. There are a small number of variations in style details of WUIs as evident in web browser windows. However, there is anarchy in the variation of application UI details. Handheld UI styles include GUI and non-GUI styles.

Topics that are discussed in this chapter are:

- GUIs
- WUIs
- Handheld user interface (HUI)

- An application UI
- Object-Oriented UIs
- Implications of UI styles on the project

Graphical User Interface (GUI)

A GUI is defined as a style of user-computer interaction employing four fundamental elements: windows, icons, menus, and pointers (see Figure 5.1). GUIs are sometimes called WIMP interfaces.

Important features implicit in the fundamental features of GUIs are direct manipulation, mouse or pointer support, graphics, and an area for application function and data. An initial discussion of fundamentals of GUI styles is kept separate from that of the application layer of GUI-based applications, which is discussed later.

Window. A window is an area of a display device used to view and interact with an object, information about an object, or actions that apply to an object. A window has a title bar, moving and sizing operations, menus, and an area for object information. Typically, windows are rectangular. An example of an application using a window is a GUI-based address book

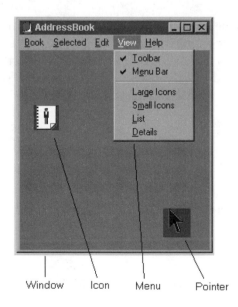

FIGURE 5.1
Major components of a GUI.

application on a computer display (see Figure 5.2). Other uses of windows are action dialogs, messages, and help.

Implicit in the definition of a window is that it displays information on a subset of a display device. Partial use of a display device allows viewing multiple windows for interacting with multiple objects or command dialogs concurrently, as in Figure 5.2. Also implicit in the definition of a window is the use of graphics or visualizations instead of textual information to indicate how much information is available; for example, the use of a scroll bar instead of Line 1 of 45.

Icons.   An icon is similar to a window in many respects although a formal definition is that an icon is an area of a display device used to pictorially rep-

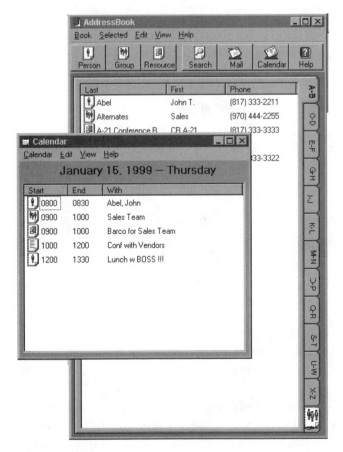

FIGURE 5.2

Concurrent display of multiple windows and icons.

resent an object. Typical features associated with icons include a graphic symbol to represent an object, a title or name, and direct manipulation operations. An example use of an icon is representing a person within an address book window or representing another application on a computer display. The most important action performed on an icon representing an object is Open to display a window containing detailed information about an object.

There are many graphic symbols used in GUIs that are not icons in a formal sense. Graphic symbols used to represent actions (minimize), an attribute of an object (color), or status (new mail indicator) may be thought of as icons by end users; however, these are considered graphic buttons by GUI and standards developers. We'll use the term icon or graphic interchangeably to represent all of these uses.

Menus.   A menu displays a collection of choices from which a user can select. Typically, choices in GUI-based menus are names of user-selectable commands for performing an action on an object. An example of a menu is File, and a command choice located in a File menu is Print. The full set of user commands is contained within menus. In contrast, non-graphical systems require that menus use the entire display via hierarchical dialog techniques.

Typically, menus are displayed within windows, although they can sometimes partially extend outside of the window area. There are several types of menus: bars, pulldown, popup, and cascade. For all intents and purposes, devices such as iconic toolbars are menus.

Pointers.   Graphical systems typically have pointing devices in the form of a mouse or trackball.

Associated with a pointing device is a location on the screen where a user can make input with the pointing device. A pointer is a graphic that visually depicts a location where pointing device input to the system is made. GUI pointers include the system arrow, graphics cross hair, and text I-beam. In many respects, a pointer is similar to a typing cursor, which represents the location on a display device where keyboard input is accepted. An example of using a pointer is for selection of an icon within an address book.

Application Client Area.   Not often considered a salient feature of a GUI, the client area is a subarea within a window where application information is displayed and where interaction with the application's information takes place. Examples include conceptual models, views, entry fields, selection lists, graphics, text, user assistance, and tables. Examples of inter-

action with application information include typing or selection of alphanu-
meric data.

Direct Manipulation.   Perhaps the most significant feature of a GUI is
direct manipulation, which allows user interaction with objects via use of a
pointer. For example, a window can be moved on the screen by moving the
mouse, pointing at the window title bar with the pointer, pressing and holding down a mouse button, and moving the mouse (this is sometimes called
grab and drag). Another example of direct manipulation via a pointer is
selection of text (swipe and type) or drawing directly in a graphic area using
the pointer and a graphics tool such as a paint brush.

Many actions performed using choices on menus are available via direct
manipulation. For example, dragging a document icon to a desktop printer
icon prints the document on many systems. Other actions performed via
direct manipulation include move, copy, delete, and link.

Other Features.   Clipboard, shortcut keys, access keys in menus and
dialogs, and mouse-keyboard augmentations are several other UI techniques available in GUIs. Although useful, these mechanisms are not considered essential features of GUIs.

Examples of GUI Styles.   Major GUI-based operating systems are
examined to demonstrate how WIMP features are supported. Major similarities and differences are highlighted to demonstrate the complexity of the
design and development challenge. From a GUI perspective, each system
supports windows, icons, menus, and pointers.

- **Similarities**. In many respects, the systems are very similar. It has been
  said that "From ten yards away, they look . . . pretty much the same"
  Windows are used to display object information. Icons are available to
  represent objects. Menus are provided for selection of commands for
  objects. Pointing devices are supported for such operations as selection, direct manipulation, window sizing, and moving windows and
  icons. There is a single pointer and a single input cursor on each system. There are graphic symbols for shortcut operations, e.g., Close,
  Maximize, Size, etc.

- **Differences**. There are distinctions in graphics. OSF/Motif uses 3-
  dimensional features in its windows and icons. Microsoft Windows
  uses a multiple document window style in its major applications. Macintosh has a single menu bar to support all application windows, while
  other systems allow a menu bar for each window. OSF/Motif, Macin-

tosh, and Windows follow the File-Edit-View model for mapping commands to menus.

OSF/Motif uses mouse button 1 for direct manipulation, Windows uses button 1 and button 2 for different direct manipulation results. Macintosh direct manipulation is performed with its single mouse button. Although the keyboard mappings are different, operations not supported by mouse clicks and movements are supported by mouse-keyboard augmentations (combined keyboard and mouse button presses).

- **Style guides**. Each major system has its own unique UI style guidelines. Applications are expected to follow these guidelines in order to implement a consistent UI style across applications that reside in the environment. Each style guide provides a set of design principles. The design intent for general look and feel is provided by descriptions of how common operations such as placement of commands in menus are accessed and performed. The system toolkit provides support for implementation of various style guide features.

Non-GUIs.   In contrast, there are systems that are not graphical. The most well known example is full screen MS-DOS and its applications. However, access to MS-DOS and other non-graphical applications is now available within windows with menus and limited pointer support.

Benefits.   GUIs certainly don't provide any free lunches. As with any UI, there are benefits with associated tradeoffs to consider. Each tradeoff depends on the GUI and the application using it. However, unpublished IBM usability tests with novice and expert users performing office tasks demonstrated that GUI-based applications can provide better usability than non-GUI applications (see Figure 5.3). Initial learning is faster and general productivity is better. Where platform standards are followed within an environment, transfer of learning across applications is achieved. Non-IBM sources have found similar results.

> **Rule of Thumb**: GUIs do not guarantee better usability, but well-designed GUI-based software applications can be better than non-GUI counterparts in user effectiveness and satisfaction, given the right tasks and skills. The initial challenge for a novice user is learning to use the pointing device and locating commands in menus.

Basic user understanding of GUI techniques occurs within an hour. However, long-term comfort with a pointing device takes longer due to deciding

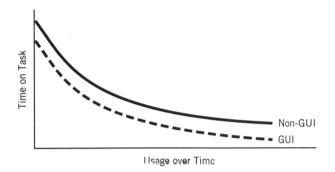

FIGURE 5.3
Time on task comparison (GUI and non-GUI applications).

something as simple as where to place a mouse on a desk. A user must develop a style of use that accommodates personal hand-eye coordination.

Over time, hidden and advanced features are learned to increase user productivity. However, once a user establishes a comfortable interaction approach, significant transfer of learning occurs across GUI-based applications and systems due to the similarity of GUI features across environments.

Web User Interface (WUI)

A basic WUI style is very similar to a hierarchical menu structure that a user experiences on a non-GUI environment, except for a more visual presentation and use of hyperlinks. Essential navigation is performed across one or more applications using textual or visual hyperlinks. Depending on the hyperlink structure of the application, navigation within a WUI displays web pages in an application hierarchy one page at a time in a linear or non-linear fashion within a single GUI window. In many respects, a WUI-based application is back to the future—or possibly worse, given the volume of e-paper and other stuff on the Web.

In an application using a WUI style:

- Information is typically displayed in a single GUI window called a browser, though multiple browser windows can be used by an application to display information.
- A browser provides menus for a web application.
  - Action choices are limited in that a menu is not readily available to applications for access of functionality.

- A web page has little inherent control over the client area for detection of specialized popup menus.
- Creation of specialized menus requires additional programming work.
- Application features must be mapped to techniques for invoking commands.
- There are no conventional icons within the application area.
  - Many applications use graphics and animation for aesthetic or navigation purposes. This has the potential downside of extraneous visual noise and longer response times for loading and expanding graphics files.
  - Browsers and applications provide features to disable web page graphics so as to display text-only versions.
- Pointer support is basically for 1-click selection of navigation choices. Drag and drop is not supported except by special programming in certain environments. Button 2 behavior is limited as well.

  Rule of Thumb: Web-based software is becoming more and more like GUI-based software (probably because users are consistently requesting popular and useful GUI features such as drag/drop and popup menus).

Figure 5.4 illustrates a web-based application.

Navigation.   Getting from one page to another using hyperlinks or a search mechanism is the most frequently performed function in a WUI. Pages that a user encounters exist within the same or other web sites.

A web browser provides the primary navigation features for movement across sites and within sites in a linear manner using Back and Forward toolbar buttons. Navigation from one application page to another within the same application site is performed using hyperlinks, site maps, buttons, and navigation bars.

Presentation and Behavior.   A primary purpose of a web page is to provide useful information including the navigational structure and organization of the site. Web pages are composed of one or more constructs in dazzling and myriad smorgasbords of colorful graphics combinations. More so than on GUIs, many WUI-based applications include significant amounts of behavior not invoked by a user, e.g., animations. It is literally UI anarchy on the Internet.

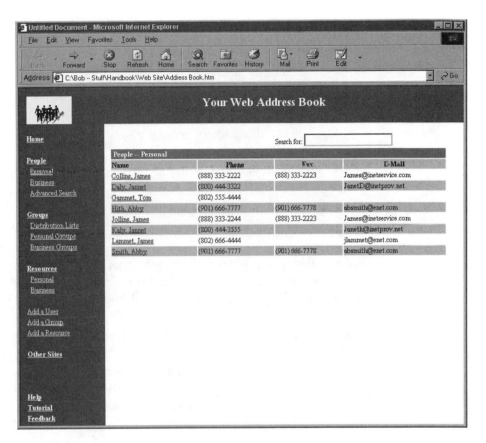

FIGURE 5.4
A web page within a web browser.

WUI Components. Common components are banners, navigation bars, and visual or textual hyperlinks arranged in many ways. Varied approaches to use of graphics, animation, and color are employed as well.

- A banner is a visual headline displayed at the top of a web page.
- A navigation bar is a list of hyperlink choices to information.
- A hyperlink is a selection that displays the next page of information or moves display focus to another area of the same page.

Page Layouts. Information is presented on pages using one or more layout and navigation styles:

- Browser. A browser is typified by having a header, a navigation bar, and a browse area displayed within a screen.

- Directory. A directory is a visual search mechanism that lists hyperlink choices used to navigate to additional choices until a desired result is found. A header and other types of navigation choices may be available.

- Search and search results. One or more controls for a user to type or select criteria for performing a search. Results of a search are displayed in the same or another web browser window.

- Document. Much like its conventional counterpart, a web document displays textual information together with links to additional sources or expansion of information.

- Notebook. Some sites present a visual notebook as a metaphor for organization of information. This is not significantly different from a navigation bar, other than a smaller number of choices.

Data Collection.   An additional purpose of some web pages is to collect names and addresses and other information from a user. Conventional GUI controls are used for this purpose, though sometimes with restrictions.

Design Challenges.   The critical success factors that influence the usability of an application using a web UI style are similar to mainframes—ease of navigating the information hierarchy, ease and speed of locating desired results, and response time. Other important factors include aesthetics and value of current information content.

Handheld User Interface (HUI)

There are two major classes of PDAs in use today—those using a true GUI style of appearance and behavior and those that use a GUI subset. Both classes of UIs employ a gestural style for user input with a stylus and touch screen.

In general, such devices have very small displays (see Figure 5.5). Each PDA display area is smaller than most GUI-based application windows on desktop and laptop systems. There is usually GUI-based software for a laptop or desktop to support the PDA.

GUI Subset.   A HUI provides some features of a GUI, namely, icons, menus, and pointer behavior. A single object is displayed at any one time without any window dressing. The general UI style can be called a SIMP (screen, icons, menu, pointer). Many GUI features are provided.

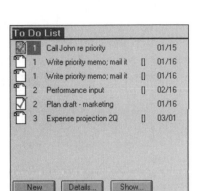
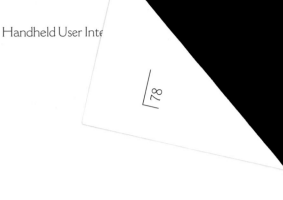

FIGURE 5.5
An example of a UI for a PDA.

- Icons are used on many PDAs, and their resolution varies with that of the display device. As in GUIs, icons are used to represent objects, actions, and attributes.
- A menu bar and menus are displayed on demand and have conventional behavior.
- A stylus serves as a pointer for mostly single-click interaction. Dialogs are displayed as windows that overlap a calling object. However, these windows do not have standard GUI window dressing and cannot be moved or sized.

Interaction.   Although keyboards can be attached to some PDAs, a user must learn pointer-based interaction and writing with a stylus to work directly with a PDA. Some commands can be performed with gestural shortcuts equivalent to shortcut keys of GUIs.

Design Challenges.   The major design challenges for a HUI-based application are:

- Simplifying the demands on a user for input and interaction
- Exploiting the constrained display area

Benefits.   The major benefits for PDA users are replacement of physical pocket organizers containing paper calendars, note pads, and address books with an electronic equivalent. The tasks performed with the physical equivalents are improved significantly when an integrated PDA-PC software package is considered.

Entry of large amounts of information using gestural or handwriting techniques is cumbersome. However, entry and subsequent maintenance of this information on a PC is fairly efficient. Minor changes of information on the PDA for subsequent synchronization with a PC is simple. Synchronization of information between the PC and PDA is a major functional usability improvement over integration of information between physical organizers and PCs today, including laptops.

Application Layer of a Software UI

Graphical, web, and PDA UIs are general styles. We'll now focus on an application that uses a GUI style for a user interaction technique. We'll then explore the same application user interface within other UI styles.

A GUI-based application is software implemented using GUI techniques for user-software interaction. Basic components of a GUI style contribute to the usability of an application. However, there are several factors independent of a particular GUI style that determine whether an application is usable and more usable than competing applications.

Some of the many application UI factors that influence usability include how the GUI style is used with application-level UI components. Figure 5.6 depicts the potential usability of an application as a function of components of a UI style and components of an application UI style. A UI-based application uses UI style components well or poorly. Similarly, a UI-based application uses application-level UI components well or poorly. The combination of GUI and application UI components leads to overall usability.

Application Layer.   There is more to a UI-based application than putting the information and interaction into a screen with menus and providing icons and pointers. The application layer of a UI-based application includes all features that go beyond the window dressing. The application layer includes all end-user visible features and interactions implemented using different UI styles.

The features of the application layer include:

- Conceptual design
- Object and command semantics and properties
- The visual presentation and behavioral style of the object within the client area

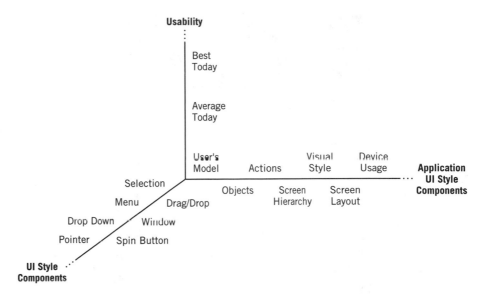

FIGURE 5.6
Components of UI and application UI style and usability.

- The syntax (structure) of the object—data formats, input ranges, and window flow
- Interaction techniques going beyond simple data entry and direct manipulation
- Unique actions
- Physical device usage

Examples—Address Books

Figure 5.7 depicts a GUI-based address book. The address book is displayed in a window and icons are used to represent people. Different types of menus are used, such as popups (one for the Address Book object and one for people icons), a toolbar, and a menu bar. A pointer is used for selection and direct manipulation of the window, the icons, and textual information. Keyboard input is valid for typing information into address book records, as well as for selection.

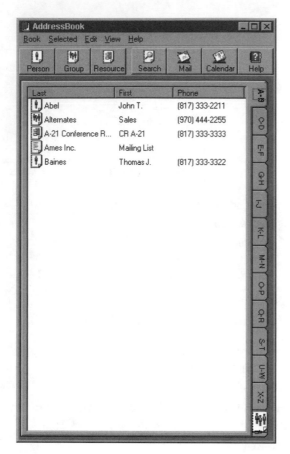

FIGURE 5.7
A GUI-based address book.

This address book is conceptually quite different from the one depicted in Figure 5.8. Both are GUI-based applications using the same WIMP features of the same basic GUI style. Assuming that both have the same features, performance, and other factors important to users, the address book in Figure 5.7 has a higher user preference because it looks like an indexed notebook that a user might have, because of how it uses the GUI style, and because of its application GUI components.

Comparing different GUI-based applications performing the same functions raises an interesting point—some GUI-based applications are better than others, and some are significantly better. One GUI-based program can be better than another in terms of time on task, requests for help, errors, user preference, and user satisfaction.

FIGURE 5.8
Another GUI-based address book.

In a WUI-based address book, the application layer of the address book UI is mapped to a web style as depicted in Figure 5.9. With the exception of a reduced feature set available through the browser menus, the look and feel of the WUI-based address book is very similar to that of the GUI-based address book in Figure 5.8.

On a PDA, the address book of Figure 5.8 is mapped to the HUI depicted in Figure 5.10. A very similar look and feel is provided except for window features and unavailability of a notebook control in today's environment. A somewhat more consistent UI might be achievable with some clever design and programming in the future.

Good Application User Interfaces

Recognizing a good UI when you see one, and knowing when one is better than another seems to be driven by a small number of salient characteristics evident on a half-hour tour of any application, regardless of UI style. The characteristics of good GUI-based or web-based or HUI-based applications are centered on five major principles with the acronym SAPCO: simple, aesthetic, productive, customizable, and other.

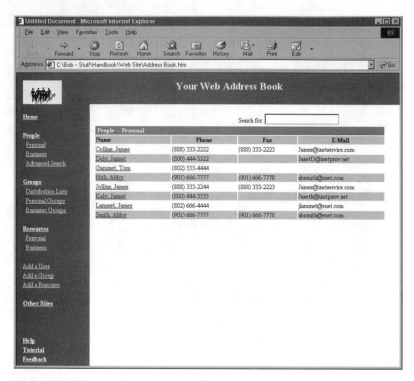

FIGURE 5.9
A web-based address book.

FIGURE 5.10
A conceptual HUI-based address book.

Simple.   Although some computerized user tasks are relatively complex and cumbersome, the real-world counterparts of software objects are relatively simple. Software objects provide productivity enhancements and augmentations without unnecessary complexity in a UI. Minimalism and layering are used extensively in an initial presentation and interaction style. Key guidelines influencing the principle of simplicity are:

- This is not rocket science
- Minimal and layered objects
- Err on the side of simplicity

This is contingent upon the complexity of an application domain and the requirements defined upon its UI and usability. For example, what if the application domain was rocket science and the task was computation of a spacecraft maneuver? Just because it is rocket science doesn't mean a UI to the function and information of the application has to behave like it.

> **Rule of Thumb:** A good application UI does not require use of a book or online help in order to get started with simple end-user tasks. In the worst case, a good application UI is intuitive (a user has to be told only once about how to achieve a result).

Aesthetic (Looks Good).   Drawing from the real world, popular physical objects have aesthetic and ergonomic appeal. Software objects are presented to users the same way. Graphics design and visualization are used extensively.

Key guidelines influencing the principle of aesthetics are:

- Look less like a computer artifact and more like a user object
- Be enticing (inviting, appealing)
- Visualized information

> **Rule of Thumb:** A good application UI looks nice.

Productive (Feels Good).   Use of software objects requires a minimal number of work steps to accomplish end-user tasks. A UI is implemented without large hierarchies of windows and/or screens and needless keyboard or mouse steps.

Key guidelines influencing the principle of productivity are:

- Be task sensitive
- Use the 80/20 rule for interface optimization
- Reduce work steps to the absolute minimum

- Provide convenience features
- Be forgiving, or, at a minimum, don't provide severe penalties for small mistakes

Rule of Thumb: A good application UI is basically fast to use and no worse than doing the work using physical counterparts. A good application UI avoids the most common pitfall of too many screens and too many steps (or its equivalents in various user interface styles).

Customizable.   Software objects are available in various forms in order to suit individual needs. Software UI objects, as well as end-user created objects, are tailorable.

Key guidelines that influence the principle of customization are:

- Follow a toolbox model in design
- Initial objects include entry level features
- Provide multiple views, fonts, and colors to select from
- Progressive disclosure gradually reveals all features

Rule of Thumb: A good application UI allows a user to select interaction techniques as well as layout and access methods for optimization to user needs.

Other.   Once beyond the principles of simplicity, aesthetics, productive, and customizable, there are countless other principles available. The majority are variants of the SAPC.

Object-Oriented UIs

Designing software objects provides an opportunity to deliver an application with an OO UI style and/or OO internals. Many real-world OO features are included in a UI appearance, behavior, interaction requirements, and functionality. Any computer-oriented enhancement or augmentation to a real-world object is clearly visible to an end user and does not necessarily conflict with learning or perceptions unless poorly designed or implemented. Although implicit in the design, notions of object classes, class hierarchies, and inheritance via the class hierarchy are kept transparent to a user.

An OO application UI should

- Have direct manipulation (drag anything anywhere)

- Have direct entry (write on anything)
- Be object-contextual (popup menus, help, consistency, etc.)

A good application UI that is OO is natural to use; that is, its user interface mechanisms are transparent.

Implications of UI Styles on the Project _____

Although still very early in the project (you are late in week 2), senior management is sensitive to the potential importance of the UI on the success of the project. They want to meet with the project lead and you about the project UI. Schedules, vacations, and other conflicts require that the briefing take place at 7:30 a.m. tomorrow. If the request is not met, it will be over a month before the senior management team is available again, which may create risk in obtaining approval for general direction. The project lead has agreed to the meeting.

The project lead asks you to develop a prototype or sketches to present to senior management tomorrow: "Whatever is handy, but it's got to be good! These people are starting to talk the talk! But, they are not above vending the entire project if the direction doesn't feel right or they lose confidence in us."

You have about two hours to work on the request. Because software tools for the project are not yet installed, you must develop a low-fidelity screen design using tools other than the likely implementation tools.

Provide design visualizations for one likely major object and one likely action related to the project (e.g., a conference agenda and a search action on an item on the agenda). For each of the possible UI styles to be used (GUI, WUI, HUI), design:

- A possible screen that displays a daily conference agenda
- A possible screen for performing searches on the agenda
- Examples of basic user interaction for each UI style

Anticipate some of the likely questions from the project lead and senior management. Be prepared to discuss questions about similarities and differences in UI styles across platforms, potential development approaches, reuse of software across platforms, tools, and so forth.

Be prepared to answer questions about how your design relates to what exists on the web today and what other conference web sites or competitors might provide. Be prepared to discuss the interaction techniques that must be supported on the project.

The project lead has become aware that the lab director uses the same very popular PDA that is proposed for the project—a windows-free environment. The project lead has advised you that one very influential senior manager is an avid web surfer who checks the competition regularly and that another senior manager is a heavy user and proponent of a PDA using a popular windowing platform. Although the windows-free PDA is the likely direction for the project, be prepared to discuss tradeoffs of using a windowing platform on a PDA.

In addition, for your own benefit, and even though it is early, document the major principles that will guide your design work. The effort is not a waste. The information gained will help in detailed project planning and requirements gathering.

Be sure to continue your research—you're going to need it!

Any questions?

References _____

Galitz, W., *User Interface Screen Design*, Wiley-QED: New York, 1993.

Mayhew, D., *Software User Interface Design*, Prentice-Hall: Englewood Cliffs, NJ, 1992.

Nielsen, J., *Designing Web Usability*, New Riders Publishing: Indianapolis, IN, 2000.

Rhodes, N., and McKeehan, J., *Palm Programming: The Developer's Guide*, O'Reilly: Cambridge, MA, 1999.

Shneiderman, B., *Designing the User Interface*, Addison-Wesley: Reading, MA, 1987.

Sprool, J., et al., *Web Site Usability: A Designer's Guide*, User Interface Engineering: North Andover, MA, 1997.

Torres, R. J., "Graphical User Interfaces: An Introduction," Share 81 Conference Proceedings, Aug. 1993.

Participatory Methods

6

One of the highest risk areas associated with product development is a lack of appropriate user involvement. Without involvement by users, a product team runs the risk of not understanding:

- Who users of a product are
- What a user is trying to accomplish
- How a user needs or likes to accomplish tasks
- User likes/dislikes about functional, UI, and information designs
- What is important to users when tradeoffs inevitably happen

A product development process can claim to be user-centered and have user involvement that is necessary but not sufficient. To eliminate the risk associated with lack of user involvement is to know what is necessary and sufficient to achieve product success. *Necessary* means that something must be done to achieve success; *sufficient* means that something is good enough to achieve success. So, necessary and sufficient means doing the right things well enough to achieve goals.

The most commonly used methods of user participation are employed during the requirements and evaluation tasks of a project. However, there are many simple and cost-effective techniques for user involvement early and often throughout a product's development. Participatory methods include techniques that allow a user to be a full partner with a user-centered product team. Even better, there are techniques that allow a product team to be a full partner with users.

Involving users early and often, and the use of participatory methods, is not a slam on the skills or abilities of a product team. If anything, use of these methods by a user-centered product team is indicative of a team's awareness and dedication to ensuring that a user's needs are met. It's just another set of tools and techniques to give a product team a chance to deliver the right product.

The following topics are discussed:

- Techniques to involve users in planning, requirements, design, construction, product evaluation, and deployment
- Involving users in the project

As in other areas of product development, there are many considerations for involving users and there are many techniques to do so. A participatory method (see Figure 6.1) is a technique that allows direct and proactive user involvement in product development tasks and decisions that determine system content, UI, graphics, information, usability, and other important product factors. An example of a participatory method includes JARs and JADs.

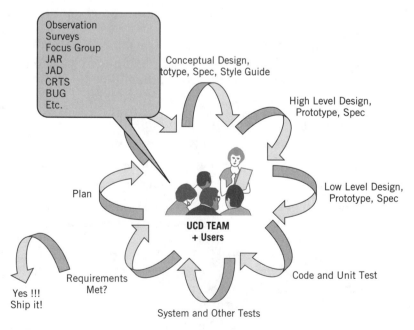

FIGURE 6.1
User-centered products and participatory methods.

Joint application requirements (JAR) and joint application design (JAD) are popular techniques for working with the vested interests of a product to gather requirements in highly structured and disciplined meetings. If early prototyping is employed, it is possible to supplement a product's requirements with a UI prototype and a logical data base model.

Many other techniques are available for a UC product team's tool kit. Use of a Business User Group (BUG) approach is described in more detail later in this chapter.

> **Rule of Thumb**: Employ participatory methods for projects that must succeed or meet stringent criteria.

Techniques for User Participation During Planning____

A user may not be able to help in the technical planning of a product. As a member of a user-centered product team, a user can help plan appropriate user participation in technical aspects of a product's development tasks. The right user advocate can work to involve the right people in the project at the right time (see Figure 6.2).

A user may not know what user-centered product development is, or the subtle distinctions made among techniques and deliverables. However, other members of the team can explain what is involved, suggest the goals of user participation, and provide examples of user participation.

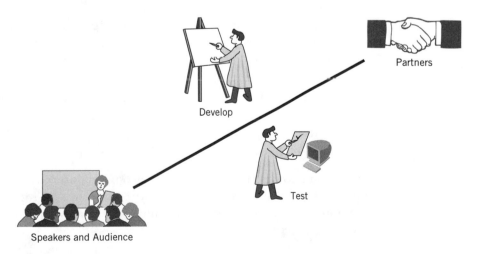

Partners

Develop

Test

Speakers and Audience

FIGURE 6.2
Spectrum of participatory roles and tasks.

Based upon this clarification, a participating user can provide insights into ways of being involved—including techniques not previously considered by the technical team members. To be most effective, participation by users must move from passive activities to active partnership in all phases of product development.

Many users are experts in their domain; for example, keeping a business running, helping their customers, and making money that supports development activities. Their insights into business tasks and how computers and software are used are extremely important.

During planning, a user can provide insight into:

- Skills and concerns of peers and managers
- Other users of the software who may need to be involved
- Pointers to sources of other users to involve and different sources of input
- Pointers to user-defined needs, data, procedures, and other information not known or prior to filtering within a development or business organization
- User perspective on priorities and requirements for the system

It may be surprising and humbling for experienced product personnel to hear what a user and business person thinks or says about needs and products and how they are used.

Rules of Thumb: Beware of arrogance throughout a product development process.

- Be sure that product and user management sponsor the approach taken to user participation. The cost of user involvement is measurable, as is the potential value of system improvements.
- Involve real users as quickly and as often as possible, beginning on the first day. Business needs may allow 1-2 hours per week. Development needs may allow 4-8 hours to support one meeting with users.
- Don't leave home without users involved.

It is also important to get real buy-in to ongoing user involvement throughout a project's lifetime. A UC product team must properly balance the amount of time spent working with users and what it takes to prepare meaningful participation information for users.

Techniques for User Participation During Requirements

There are many participatory techniques that are effective in different contexts and with specific scope of applicability.

The most important aspects of participatory methods are to

- Get real users involved and active within a product's development
- Keep users participating throughout a product's development process
- Extend the scope of participation beyond conventional evaluation of products
- Have a broad set of participatory techniques available to draw upon

Each technique has advantages and disadvantages and ease of use. However, if a single user group is available to a user-centered product team throughout a development life cycle, it is desirable to have a single, simple, and consistent approach that works well across all life-cycle tasks. Different specific techniques are utilized within the context of the overall approach. Such an approach is the BUG, which is a user participation technique that involves real and current system users in a new product's development process.

User participation in the development process begins during the requirements phase and continues through the design, construction, and test phases. However, user participation in a BUG can begin during product planning. Users participate with a product team using multiple mechanisms that include observation, surveys, presentation, demonstration, analysis, rapid design visualization and prototyping, scenario walk-throughs, alternatives exploration, usage work shops, and usability testing. The BUG technique complements other participation and evaluation methods, such as ongoing feedback from other users that complements lab-based usability tests.

Team Composition.   A BUG is an extension of a user-centered product team. The initial core members of a BUG team consist of a business representative or analyst, a UI designer and prototyper, and typical users from appropriate business areas. A graphic designer, training staff, other non-interface software personnel, and software development and business managers are members of the extended BUG team, and participate as appropriate.

Information to Obtain.   The objective is to work with real and active users to validate requirements and design for application functional and UI features, data, task flow, and the overall UI approach. The topic areas to cover explicitly include all aspects of a user's experience:

- User profile definitions
- Business context, task flow, patterns of work behavior
- High-frequency tasks and features
- Current process and system problems
- Wishes for improvements and anticipated business changes
- Screen flow and task interaction steps
- Information and data needs as well as organization and layout of information
- Features (function, UI, performance, information)
- Priorities and tradeoffs
- Order of features buttons and data on screens
- Graphic preferences and terminology preferences
- Change management implications

There is quite a bit of information to obtain, and it typically must be gotten in an iterative and evolutionary manner. Where information is not obtained, assumptions are made and designs are formulated. With user involvement, the assumptions are validated.

As important as what is needed is what is not needed in a software application. Where a business is moving from one environment to another (e.g., a mainframe to a workstation environment), designers find certain data and features have been implemented and fine tuned over a long period of time. Many features useful at one time are obsolete, or these features are staged beyond the initial software release. However some users and developers may resist change involving these features.

The Power of Observation.   Before starting BUG meetings, a team conducts a period of informal but structured observations of users doing work. In addition to a general sense of what users do and how they do it, a general feel for the automated and nonautomated aspects of a work environment is obtained. Common tasks, artifacts, pressures, needs, obstacles, and characteristics of work flow are identified, together with areas of potential improvements. Results of an observation period are analyzed and summarized for follow-on analysis and input to design. If nothing else, the observations are good to generate shock value in a product team.

Rule of Thumb: An appreciation for distinct learning, working, and using environments and styles is an excellent result of observation.

A Follow-on Survey. To ensure that a good sampling of tasks and relative frequency is known, a follow-on survey is administered to a larger user community. The survey asks users to identify their most frequent and important tasks, perceived needs, and attitudes. The survey is used to corroborate the results of team observations.

Invitations. Before each BUG meeting, an invitation is sent to business area managers. The invitation identifies the topics to be discussed and asks for business area end users as participants. Management is encouraged to send previous attendees in order to achieve a level of continuity, sometimes identifying specific users by name.

Source of Users. Users represent their work units and have diverse skill levels, tasks, working styles, and business rules. In many cases, users do not know each other or do not work together on a regular basis. Initially, users do not know members of the product team. This will continue to be a challenge in cases where there is turnover among team members or where participation is done remotely via video conferencing or using Internet or intranet methods.

> **Rule of Thumb**: Team building is an integral part of a BUG process. Trust and confidence are necessary to ensure quality input, feedback, and results.

Requirements Analysis. After the observations and surveys, initial analysis abstracts key requirements from the raw data. Requirements take the form of documented features for function, data, work flow, UI, information, usability, and other important product factors. These are used for initial discussions with a BUG.

A requirements-oriented design is a representation of features, data, flow, UI, desktop integration, feature and data access, and information. Requirements-oriented visualization is an instantiation of requirements design for a very concrete review with users. The design and visualization can be fairly crude and high level.

Visualize the requirements-oriented design on paper with the express intent of clarifying user needs—as opposed to providing an initial UI design. UI and usability features are represented and clarified in this manner without getting locked into a specific design too early. The information gained during a requirements phase is useful to gain insights for conceptual design (conceptual models and UI structures).

Rule of Thumb: Formulate, as quickly as possible, a requirements-oriented design and visualization that reflects a team understanding of required product features.

A key point about a requirements design and visualization is that its primary purpose is not to formalize or finalize a design approach for a UI, but rather to drive implicit or unstated requirements out into the open for subsequent documentation and review. Another very important purpose is to obtain user priorities on features and on speed of access for features and data, i.e., surfacing the most important features and data.

Rule of Thumb: Document the results and decisions of BUG meetings very clearly and distribute them for quick review and confirmation of understanding.

Techniques for User Participation During Design

From a design perspective, all aspects of a UI design are valid to expose to user participation, just as all aspects of a user's work are valid to expose to UC product team participation. A user has full access to all activities and deliverables that are traditionally the purview of product developers.

Rule of Thumb: The hardest job for a traditional UI designer is letting go and letting users guide!

Design and Prototype.   As requirements stabilize, a requirements-oriented design and visualization begins to evolve to interactive designs and prototypes. Construct an interactive prototype using the implementation language for the product and demonstrate it to users for feedback. Paper walkthroughs and reviews with BUG users continue. However, as a prototype becomes more robust, provide the prototype to non-BUG members for hands-on use in informal and formal contexts. User comments are documented as a design prototype is reviewed.

From a UI perspective, users are able to participate in the design of

- Desktop behavior, integration, and consistency
- Conceptual models, terminology, and icons
- Screen flow/steps/content, graphic style, and layout
- All the details involved in a UI and the total user's experience

Rule of Thumb: Make designs very specific and tangible via real user scenarios.

Selecting Alternatives.

Present options to a BUG, but do so objectively and in a scenario-oriented manner. Provide positive, negative, and neutral factors. Ask open-ended questions. Solicit user opinions. When team alternatives are not acceptable, invite users to brainstorm and codesign alternatives.

Rule of Thumb: Take care to not sell users a bill of goods by leading them to a place they shouldn't go (or letting them go to a place they shoudn't).

Review/Iterate/Evolve Rapidly.

Design changes are made as features, data, information, and UI mechanisms are added and as user requests are satisfied. Follow-up reviews are performed until convergence of user needs and system capabilities is obtained. The requirements visualization evolves to an interactive UI prototype, which has sufficient robustness to allow user interaction during hands-on workshops and usability tests with users. In some regards, a prototype may contain some functional aspects that represent how certain features are implementable.

Ongoing Task Analysis.

The BUG becomes a mechanism for ongoing task analysis. Task oriented considerations that might have been overlooked earlier surface. Some examples of things that might be overlooked are task variations due to date or seasonal situations. Stress or pathological stories surface to stress test the product during design.

BUG Meetings.

A typical user session can last about two hours. Each session is somewhat informal and consists of several phases with an agenda that includes

- Introductions (facilitator, designer, scribe, users, and topic)
- Rules of Engagement (open, honest, etc.)
- Distribute review materials (tasks, windows, questions, specifications, etc.)
- Overview the features and UI
- Walk through with sample tasks
- Conduct hands-on with a prototype if possible
- Document meeting results (decisions, questions, etc.)
- Schedule the follow-on meeting and topic

Meeting results are documented and distributed immediately after a BUG meeting. Documentation is used to influence several product deliverables including

- Product issues log (to document problems and work items) and resolution
- Product Plans (content, staging, priorities, etc.)
- Requirements (features, UI, information, and priorities)
- Use cases (scenarios)
- UI design/specification/prototype
- Product business object model

The meetings are repeated as often and as long as necessary.

Special Interest Groups.   In some cases, subgroups are needed to tackle very specific tasks or problems that are not efficient to handle during regular BUG meetings. Special interest groups (SIGs) are formed under the direction of the product BUG. Interim and final results are coordinated with the product BUG and team.

> **Rule of Thumb**: Meet with the BUG when a critical mass of meaningful review information is available. Early in a project, twice-weekly meetings may be required. Later in the project, meetings may occur every other week.

Work a Mile in a User's Shoes.   As a design proceeds and becomes more refined, attempt to use it as a user is doing real work. For example, as a user is performing a task using current tools and methods, perform the task in parallel using the design. As an alternative, analyze current and future tasks in a comparative work step manner. This should validate sufficiency of requirements, design, and work flow.

Techniques for User Participation During Construction _

The construction phase of development is usually full of surprises and "gotcha" types of work. Very low-level design decisions not handled or overlooked during high level or detailed design are dealt with. Many times, these surprises happen during coding and unit test activities as implementation challenges, constraints, or oversights are noticed. Such surprises or overlooked decisions include

- Readability of some graphics on some display devices or resolutions
- Number of items to return in a search results list
- Initial (first time) display response time
- Behavioral glitches
- Odd print formats

Many times, decisions are made quickly. Many times, a short period of time is available to think about and consider an appropriate solution to the challenge. In either case, the BUG is used to select from design options. If a snap decision must be made, the BUG confirms the answer as soon as possible. Otherwise, an electronic confirmation via e-mail or voting is an option. When time permits, options are reviewed at the next BUG meeting.

The key point is that a designer or user-centered product team does not need to make these decisions—many of which can be critical to low level usability—on their own. The BUG is there to participate and assist in decision making.

Techniques for User Participation During Product Evaluation

Product evaluation is basically testing. There are lots of different tests possible, including component and system testing. There are many ways to keep users participating during this phase of product development. Once again, BUG members are candidates to participate in these types of evaluations.

Complementary Evaluations.   A BUG technique is complementary to other forms of user evaluation. A team may still conduct requirements/design workshops with an extended set of business users to validate BUG results. Usability tests to validate the various components and the overall design approach are performed in parallel, with BUG members performing the role of experienced users.

System Test.   End users can be extremely effective software testers since, obviously, many use software quite a bit. A user can execute test cases for a product's system test team. Also, a user can perform ad hoc tests to see how the software handles unusual situations that are encountered in the real world of work.

Perhaps the best part of having an end user perform testing in both a scripted and ad hoc manner is when it is performed over a relatively long period of time. Real long-term usage problems not discovered during short usability tests begin to surface. If a user is involved with early design prototypes, long term usability impacts surface earlier rather than later. A user can verify that a system being delivered meets the expectations from earlier work.

Pilot Programs.   A pilot test uses fully tested software to perform live work prior to general availability. A pilot test is not a beta test per se, which uses software that has not completed its system testing. Having real users perform real work over a fairly long period of time in a somewhat controlled setting is extremely valuable—consider it a shakedown cruise to double check training, reliability, and procedures before going into a production environment.

Pilot programs are important. However, a project that has had no user inter-action before the pilot has a small chance of success. Care should be taken to involve users long before the pilot program begins.

Techniques for User Participation During Postdeployment

In many regards, postdeployment activities are a return to square one. The software is available to the entire user community and broader surveys are performed to gauge user satisfaction with the software at discrete points in time.

BUG members also participate in the survey and help analyze and explain results for follow on action by a product team. Important feedback to obtain includes user satisfaction with the system and specific applications, problem-atic tasks, usability defects, error-prone areas, and hard-to-use or learn areas.

Best Practices

There are several best practices that work well for a BUG team:

- Promote team building, teamwork, and joint responsibility for results
- Let go and let users guide
- Provide specific design visualizations quickly (rapid design and proto-typing)
- Solve user needs quickly (iterate/evolve effectively)

CHECK-OUT RECEIPT
University of Gloucestershire
Date: Thursday, April 26, 2012
Time: 8:55 PM

Item ID: 3700086105
Title: User interface design /
Due date: 03/05/2012 23:59

Item ID: 3702124467
Title: Human-computer interface design.
Due date: 03/05/2012 23:59

Item ID: 3703739812
Title: Designing interfaces /
Due date: 03/05/2012 23:59

Item ID: 3702987481
Title: Practitioners handbook for user interfa
ue date: 17/05/2012 23:59

items: 4
ou for using Self-Service
rk Learning Centre

- Communicate with each other (educate, listen, understand, and respond)
- Be honest and clear (needs, priorities, alternatives, possibilities)
- Always use open ended questions to get the right answers
- Document as you go

There are some meeting techniques that work better than others. For example, task walkthroughs using transparencies of screens or projecting an image of an interactive prototype running on a laptop are much more effective than window and flow reviews based upon hardcopy alone. In all cases, provide copies of screen images and scenarios to users.

A Lot of Attitude.   As a rule of thumb, you'll know you're successful when a BUG representative thanks you for listening. The attitude of the team has a lot to do with the likely success of the interactions with users; bad and arrogant attitudes show through.

The members of a team must listen and respond to the needs and concerns of their users, while users must listen and respond to the constraints of a UC product team. Many positive organizational and technical results are achievable.

Some Rules of Thumb

Although relatively simple, a BUG participatory method requires hard work on the part of a UC product team and users. There are many factors to consider in order to keep a user coming back for more.

Trust, attitude, responsiveness, and effectiveness are extremely important for a team to achieve involvement with users in sessions. Following are some tips for how to work with users during participatory meetings.

- **Don't ask "What do you want?"** Most users won't know how to answer and many users are put off by it. Instead, get users to express their needs by asking, What are your high frequency tasks?, What tasks are your hardest?, and What things do you wish could be improved?

  Users may not know how to express what they want/need in a way that is understood by designers and developers but they'll know it when they see it.

- **Don't underestimate user involvement.** Acknowledge the value of user input and thank them for their time and input, meet regularly (once or twice per week; two hours per meeting), and have a consistent set of users (core + others).

- **Don't walk into meetings with end users unprepared.** Be prepared and consistent (agenda, handouts, screens, transparencies, etc.), encourage the inquisitive nature of users, and keep things on track and under control.

A typical BUG cycle can take multiple days to perform correctly (see Figure 6.3).

- **Don't be abstract with business oriented users.** Instead, be specific and concrete, bring a real design (hand waving not allowed), and have a real scenario to demonstrate the design.

- **Focus beyond the component being designed.** Provide a system level view (display image, windows, and scenarios), provide realistic data in fields, and provide a view of help and training to be provided.

- **Don't overcommit to a design under review.** Instead, conduct scenario/task flow oriented reviews with multiple options, ask What do you think about this design? What do you like/dislike?, and listen and observe objectively.

- **Always implement what users want.** Sometimes, the product team may not perceive what user's want as right. When the wrong path is being suggested by a user, show the implications of a request, show alternative ways to achieve the desired result, and give users what they want if the tradeoffs are understood and acceptable.

- **Introduce change carefully.** Revolutionary change is hard to achieve. Instead, preserve the familiar when possible and make evolutionary improvement, provide a migration path to more radical and revolutionary change, and provide the change management framework to facilitate user acceptance.

- **Don't design on the fly.** Careful thought and implications must be understood. Instead, come back with a design proposal with alternatives if possible, show how the UI looks and feels and observe what

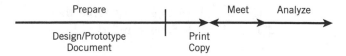

FIGURE 6.3
Typical BUG cycle.

must be explained, and provide a hands-on interactive simulation/ prototype and let users drive when possible.

- **Don't ignore user feedback.** Instead, allow plenty of time to review each topic, document user feedback and suggestions noting what users say/do and how they say/do it, and turn things around quickly (fixes or responses).

- **Don't oversell your ideas.** Instead, help users understand the value over current methods, help users understand tradeoffs (e.g., large information demands vs. screen space), and speak with one voice (i.e., all UC Product Team members convey a common message to users).

- **Don't abuse user availability.** Instead, use the user's time responsibly, add value to their software based upon their input, and try to build teamwork with the users.

Involving Users in the Project

No one on the team is experienced in the use of participatory methods of any kind. However, there are a small number of people on the project team who have attended large conferences. There are other people within the development laboratory who have also attended large conferences and do so regularly in support of marketing activities for the laboratory. For the project, decide which participatory methods to use and decide on when each specific technique should be used.

Decide the sources for users who will participate in the project. Estimate the likely costs and benefits to use such techniques over the course of the project's schedule.

So far, the project lead has been extremely supportive of all your recommendations, including use of participatory methods. The project lead is very open to use of participatory methods. In a process discussion with senior management, the project lead mentioned that such techniques were going to be employed. However, he was unable to explain or defend use of such methods in a manner that satisfied senior management.

The senior management team is extremely negative and skeptical. All the senior managers are from the old school of being responsible, taking charge, deciding on an intuitive sense of user needs, and pushing a product out the door and adjusting it later.

The senior management team told the project lead that they knew what users want and need in the conference companion and are more than happy to give guidance here. They are extremely concerned about using these methods and believe that the project schedule will be extended needlessly and that unnecessary costs will be incurred. The senior managers are so negative that they have threatened to not approve the expenditure of any resource for this activity.

The project lead came back from the meeting quite flustered. He asked you to put together a briefing for the senior management team. The topics to address include rationale for using these methods, contrasting these methods with conventional techniques for user involvement, benefits of using these methods, and impact to schedule and cost. Because of the intensity and severity of their concerns, a briefing must be scheduled ASAP. As usual, the only time available with senior management is at 7:30 a.m. tomorrow. It's 5 p.m., and you have about two hours to devote to the request.

It might be a good idea to do a little research before going in to face the music!

Any questions?

References

Beyer, H., and Holtzblatt, K., *Contextual Design*, Morgan-Kauffman: San Francisco, 1998.

Carmel, E., et al., "PD and Joint Application Design: A Transatlantic Comparison," *Communications of the ACM*, June 1993.

Muller, M., et al., "Taxonomy of PD Practices: A Brief Practitioner's Guide," *Communications of the ACM*, June 1993.

Torres, R., et al., "Case Study in Participatory Design," *UPA Conference Proceedings*, 1998.

A Word About Tools

7

Many tools are required to perform user-centered design and development tasks. Some tools are relatively low technology and are quite effective. Just having the best of high technology tools is not necessarily sufficient or productive.

Depending upon the team and task, many of these tools are more appropriate than others. Of course, user-centered development plans must account for these tools. The UC product team begins acquisition and evaluation of these tools very early and very quickly because of the lead time required to obtain and learn these tools.

Topics to be discussed in this chapter are:

- Software
- Hardware
- Facilities
- Materials
- Design/Prototype/Evaluation templates
- Tools needed for the project

Software

Aside from cost, acquisition, and training lead time, there are other reasons for early thought and action on software tools for the overall project and UI software. There may be legal and licensing issues to work through before some of the key software needs are resolved. These challenges are sometimes thorny and time consuming.

Project Management.   As with software for change management, project management tools will likely be decided at the overall project level. The project may also require that certain types of activities and milestones be tracked. However, because there is so much detailed work to do and so many interdependencies, a UC product team may choose to track activities and deliverables at a lower level of detail.

> **Rule of Thumb**: For new teams with moderate skill and experience in user-centered design and development, manage the project work at a fairly low level of detail. Don't make the plan so detailed that it is cumbersome rather than an aid.

Operating Systems.   The OSs upon which a software application will run must be obtained and installed very quickly. Hopefully, the OS is not undergoing significant development during the applications development cycle, which is likely to add significant instability to overall software development. The UC product team exercises the OS thoroughly in order to determine how the software application will integrate and be consistent with it. Any software development kits (SDKs) are obtained and tested for learning and understanding of constraints.

Design Aids.   There are many new technologies and methods with supporting design aids. For environments that benefit from use of standard design methods like the Unified Modeling Language (UML), there are tools available to facilitate design. A UC product team must explore what tools are available to help in all aspects of design.

Development Languages.   The software to be used for design, prototyping, and implementation is acquired very early. It is best if the languages are used as early as possible on the target OSs and hardware platforms. Any additional software packages with supporting widgetry or other features are added as soon as possible. It is most important to get the basic construction tools very early, when the team begins learning and testing to verify that expected results are achievable and to assess the amount of work required to reach these goals.

User Interface Builders.

Software that is used specifically for construction of a UI is considered a UI builder. In some cases, the implementation language has a visual UI development tool. In some cases, visual support is provided for construction of software algorithms, data structures, and logic.

> **Rule of Thumb**: Obtain visual UI builders whenever possible.

Criteria useful for selection of a UI design and development tool include:

- Cost
- Sufficiency for the platform being supported
- Sufficiency for the user interface style being planned
- Ease of use (tasks supported, learning time, productivity, etc.) for developers
- Footprint (development and run time memory and disk space requirements)
- Response time, reliability, quality, and other important software criteria

Cross-Platform Tools.

When a product is to be implemented on multiple hardware and operating systems, the UC product team must consider whether to obtain a single tool for cross-platform implementation, if at all feasible. Some software tools facilitate formulation of a single design that is portable to multiple platforms.

If more than one platform is supported, there may be advantages to the use of a single tool and the need to live with the constraints imposed by it.

> **Rule of Thumb**: If two platforms are supported, it may be a toss-up as to whether to use a single tool or two. If three or more platforms are supported, try to acquire tools that facilitate cross-platform design and development.

Graphics.

Software for design, construction, and editing of graphic images used in animations, icons, bitmaps, and other graphic needs is part of many SDKs. Some software packages may be better than others for creation of these graphics and must be evaluated.

Samples Library.

There are many reusable deliverables on any project. Examples include templates for software modules or routines, icons and bitmaps, and test plans. It is worthwhile to explore reusable components and examples in order to build on examples and save time during design and implementation.

> **Rule of Thumb**: Create a reuse library for the project to include the most reasonable starting points for various types of deliverables and activities. Actual templates and deliverables are a part of the library.

Screen Capture.   Probably the next most important software tool is for obtaining screen captures. The captured images of a UI are used in presentations and product documentation. Many OSs provide mechanisms for capturing screen images in real time and automatically placing them on the clipboard. In some cases, better screen capture and manipulation software may be appropriate.

Change Management.   Change control software is used to manage and control change to product software and artifacts as they are being developed. The software package is usually decided at the project level. However, the UC product team decides what is placed under change control.

Virtually all user-centered deliverables are candidates for change control—plans, requirements, specifications, style guides, prototypes, product code, graphics, test plans, scenarios, and so forth. As with other project-related items, the team uses good judgment for what is essential to place under change control and when to do it.

Document Processor.   Aside from software development tools, the next most basic tool for a user-centered product team is a very good document processor. The document tool is used to produce requirements, specifications, style guides, test plans, test cases, and test reports. Templates are created and used for many documents of the same type.

Presentation.   There is another class of graphic software very useful for giving demonstrations of intended product behavior. In addition to its use for presentation of software designs, software for presentation graphics is used for low-fidelity prototyping, storyboard flows of software, and slide shows. Some software is easy to use for creating graphic images for web pages as well. A very good software package should be acquired.

Performance Evaluation.   Software to monitor and time low-level internal behavior of other software is extremely important because it is increasingly complex. Such software can trace the execution of modules or instructions, time execution speed, and follow execution paths. Along with helping to debug response time and memory leak problems, such software helps debug functional problems.

Spreadsheets.   Spreadsheet software is useful for tracking and organizing user profiles, use case lists, and so forth. If tables are created and used properly, the software can sort and display results in different formats.

Team Related Software.   Software packages fundamental to teams working together include email, scheduling, and other forms of groupware for sharing information quickly. This is very important for teams that are becoming increasingly separated by time and space.

Competitive/Predecessor Software.   For projects intended to deliver software better than competitive, model, or legacy products, be sure to have these products available for hands-on evaluation and competitive testing. There may be other software that is good to have available as reference points (e.g., best practice types of software), even though they are not direct competitors. It's always good to see how another team is handling similar problems.

Other Software of Interest.   There are other software packages that may be of interest (e.g., computer-aided software engineering (CASE), decision support, or user interface management system (UIMS) software). These products may not have worked out for general use. However, there may be specific cases where these tools may prove beneficial.

Hardware

Another critical set of resources for the project hardware for which the software is being developed. Team needs include hardware required for development, testing, and for team end use.

Target Hardware Devices.   Each developer should have free and easy access to at least one instance of each target hardware platform for testing of software and UI features. Each hardware platform must have the target OS and other needed tools installed. Testing is important prior to deployment in order to validate that no timing issues exist.

Development Machines.   Each developer should have the most powerful development platform possible for speed of development. These high power devices may not be available to end users—but that is all right. Speed of development is the goal for developers. For web-based development, a web server is required as well.

Test Machines.   The test team needs multiple instances of the intended hardware and operating system combinations. These devices range from low-end to high-end machines. The test team includes those who verify functional, UI, usability, integration, consistency, performance, and reliability. Competitive and legacy systems may require special installations. This facilitates frequent testing of the hardware with minimal scheduling conflict.

End-Use Hardware.   Each member of the UC product team should have a machine used solely for email, administrative work, and so forth. The end-use machine is not a development machine subjected to multiple software installations that may yield an unstable environment because of the nature of the software being installed. These development machines sometimes become corrupted.

Disk Space on LAN.   There is lots of information to deliver for a UI. There are myriad documents with lots of graphics, images, code, and versions of software and documentation. Be sure to reserve plenty of space on a local area network (LAN).

Printers and Plotters.   Along with electronic distribution of software and documentation, there are many opportunities for distribution of hardcopy versions of documentation for reviews. High-speed and high-resolution printers are required for these needs. For presentations, there is the need to display color versions of the key portions of the UI. Again, high-speed and high-resolution devices are required.

Projection Devices.   Typically many presentations of the UI and other product information are given. The audience includes senior management, potential customers, and other development groups that have an interest or need to know. Projectors for transparencies are essential. Transparency projectors are also useful for recording notes during UI team meetings and walk-throughs. LCD projection devices of high resolution are also essential to display product UIs directly from a prototype or the product.

Cameras.   A usability lab requires video recording and editing equipment. Polaroid cameras are good for immediate recording of information that may be written on white boards. Other photographic equipment may be needed for creation of graphic images.

Audio/Visual Recorders.   Recording and editing equipment may be needed for the usability lab and audio clips that may become part of the product.

Whiteboards (With Print Capability).   Design thoughts and plans are frequently recorded on whiteboards. Polaroid cameras can capture this information. However, a whiteboard with print capability is even better.

Facilities

Although a product team can get by using conference rooms, a more effective technique is providing permanent design and test facilities. Construction of these rooms is a high priority for effective support of a user-centered product team.

Design Laboratory.   A design laboratory is a room where a team meets to perform its primary task. The design laboratory is dedicated to the UC product team. There is plenty of room to write ideas on white boards or flip chart paper hanging on the walls; sufficient space for equipment with competitive, legacy, prototyping, and design tools; and wall space to hang posters, pin charts, and screen prints. There is plenty of room for team members to spread out and work. If designed well, the Design Lab is useful for holding participatory sessions with users. The Design Lab is not a replacement for office space for team members.

Usability Test Laboratory.   A usability laboratory is a room where personnel conduct and evaluate test results. There is plenty of room for white boards, test monitoring equipment, and test equipment for users. The area for user evaluation is comfortable, spacious, and comparable to conventional office work areas.

Decision Support Center.   An approach for capturing information from multiple users at the same time is a decision support center (DSC). Multiple workstations are set up and connected by networking software and hardware. Decision support software collects and consolidates input from the collected users. Typically, a DSC is used for requirements gathering. However, it can be used for participatory methods during planning, design, implementation, and evaluation.

Materials

Though not as time or cost critical as other resources, it is always good to start getting other design materials together to ensure availability in a timely manner.

Flipcharts and Stands.   These are always useful for capturing design thoughts during team meetings. Flipchart paper can always be taped or pinned to walls and carried to other rooms when needed.

White Boards.   Each work room and work area should have a white board to capture design thoughts and actions. Be sure to have plenty of markers of different colors.

Writing Materials.   Plenty of paper, rulers, tape, pushpins, transparencies, pens, pencils, and markers are needed. A coin is useful for tie-breaking situations.

Sticky Pads.   An essential design tool, sticky pads have proven useful in all aspects of the UI development cycle. All sizes—from small to flip chart size—and colors are useful.

Notebooks.   Lots of writing materials should be available. In particular, a design notebook for recording design decisions should be readily available in the design lab. Each meeting of the product team is dated, signed, recorded, attendees listed, and key decisions and work items documented.

> **Rule of Thumb**: A useful technique to employ is to construct a design notebook with favorite or interesting screen images or techniques that may serve as part of the UI playbook for the project.

Even though no one has all the answers, it is good to obtain reference information about UI, human factors, tools, and the industry. Here are some general topics of source information that may be required on any UI project. Though more and more information can be found on the web, there are many journals and texts that provide valuable insight into UI and usability oriented projects.

- General UI
- General human factors
- GUI

- WUI
- HUI
- Graphical and visual design
- User assistance design
- Performance support
- Web sites
- Key books
- Key articles

The volume of information in any of these areas is extensive and growing exponentially.

> **Rule of Thumb**: Select three to five references from each category appropriate for the product being worked on.

Find the authors that you respect, are respected by others, who develop usable products, and make practical and theoretical sense. In particular, look for common themes among the sources as a form of corroboration of ideas.

Tools needed for the Project

It's budget time as the project is getting under way. The project lead has asked you to identify what resources are needed for the project so that capital and other expense requests can be made quickly and available funds not lost.

Even though detailed planning has not begun, decide what tools, facilities, and materials are required. Update your project plan notes to reflect how long it might take to secure the required tools. Reflect the order in which these tools will be secured and applied. Keep in mind that some tools will take longer to acquire than others.

As usual, the request has to be submitted quickly. You have one hour to get input to the project lead. Luckily, he'll carry the message forward to senior management and the budget process.

If you haven't done so, now is a good time to perform a fairly rigorous search of the Web to get information about UI, usability engineering, user-centered design, techniques, software templates, examples, and tools for each of the operating system platforms supported.

Any questions?

Part 2

Getting Started

A tour of some of early product tasks follows. These tasks could be considered the first major iteration of a user-centered product development effort.

Chapter 8. Planning a UI Design and Development Effort

Chapter 9. Requirements

Chapter 10. Users, Their Work Environment, and Tasks

Chapter 11. Conceptual Design and Architecture

Chapter 12. Principles, Guidelines, and Style Guides

Chapter 13. Mockups, Simulations, and Prototypes

Chapter 14. Usability Evaluation

Chapter 15. Iteration

Even though discussed in a linear manner, remember that user interface design is nonorthogonal and nonlinear.

Planning a UI Design and Development Effort

8

Product end UIs are receiving increased attention and importance as a feature with competitive advantage. As product feature lists grow longer, users responsible for product purchases look to the UI. If a product's UI appears simple to learn and use, the product may gain competitive advantage, especially if claims of reduced training costs and productivity gains are real.

However, achieving a product with real advantage over competitive or legacy software doesn't happen by fiat, art, or magic. Concerted, systematic, and hard work is required on the part of management and technical personnel. The process for design and development of products (for both UI and non-UI elements) includes: plan, gather requirements, conceptual design, design, implement (system design, code design, code, and unit test), test (systems, integration), iterate (until requirements are met), and follow-through into deployment.

There are different ways of representing the essential development process elements. However, each step is performed explicitly and consciously—or each step will be performed implicitly and unconsciously. A critical mass of work must be performed efficiently and effectively. The work must be performed in some fashion even for rapid application development (RAD) or web speed projects.

Successful traversal of essential process steps is more than painting by the numbers. Tough, hard, and committed work is required and focused on achieving results (or else it's just lip service).

The best way to begin dealing with a highly complex, error-prone, and high-risk endeavor is with planning that includes risk management activities. This chapter discusses:

- Planning a UI design and development effort
- Schedules and iterative processes
- Staffing, skills, and other resources
- Planning for the major usability factors
- Planning for the projects

Planning a UI Design and Development Effort _____

The first step in the journey for a user-centered product is planning. Depiction of a user-centered process is typically linear in fashion. However, it is definitely nonlinear. Subsequent development steps are traversed in a potentially nonlinear and nonorthogonal manner. Central to each step of the

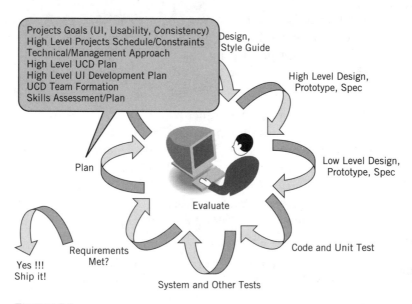

FIGURE 8.1
Planning for user-centered product development.

development process is at least one evaluation of product compliance to requirements with end users.

In an ideal case, users participate directly with members of a user-centered product team throughout a product development effort. As discussed in Chapter 6, user-centered product teams abandon the notion that restricts user participation to only product evaluation tasks.

If a development team is extremely lucky, one iteration is sufficient to meet requirements. For the rest of the design mortals in the world, multiple iterations are required to achieve requirements. The essential process is similar to what a gourmet chef does to generate great recipes. The basic steps lead to many recipes as variations in ingredients and implementation details are made. Not all of the recipes are great. However, a gourmet chef knows which recipes to keep and offer to customers, as well as which recipes to throw away.

Rule of Thumb: 30–50 percent of software code bulk is UI related.

This statistic should give software developers pause. As a development manager asked once upon a time, "Why is GUI software so hard?" Part of the answer is that there is so much of it. The design and implementation of application software using a GUI or its derivatives is detail-oriented, knowledge intensive, and labor intensive in application, UI, and implementation domains. The task is even more challenging if stringent requirements for usability, consistency, integration, cross-platform considerations, and competitiveness are levied upon the product. However, the most difficult aspect of UI work is usually people oriented—people skills, group dynamics, and organizational behavior.

Today there is a major conceptual chasm between graphical and visual UI designs and the character-based software by which the intended design is instantiated. As an example, enabling and disabling a menu choice based upon selections is a trivial feature of a UI. However, this small feature requires software design, code, and test to instantiate for each usage. Figure 8.2 depicts some VB code—five instructions to enable and disable a single menu choice based upon a single situation.

```
'Disable MenuChoice A
If Condition A = True Then
        MenuChoice A.Enabled = False
        Else
        MenuChoice A.Enabled = True
End if
```

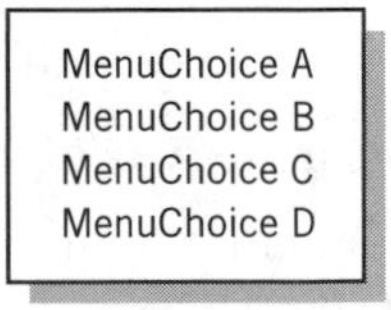

```
MenuChoice A
MenuChoice B
MenuChoice C
MenuChoice D
```

FIGURE 8.2
Code listing example for enabling/disabling a menu choice.

This code *is* easy. However, what makes it so difficult is that so much of it requires design, specification, code, and documentation for test personnel and end users, and testing for even a simple application. When multiple conditions and related choices are involved in determining what is enabled and disabled, complexity increases exponentially.

A First Step.   Given a very difficult (but not impossible) task, what can management and technical personnel do to ensure a success? Considering the magnitude, cost, and risk associated with developing a product with high UI content or high usability risk, putting a fairly solid plan together seems like a reasonable first step. Although engineering approaches to UIs are popular, more is possible from the perspective of a user-centered product team.

A product plan focused on UI process elements in a fairly detailed and measurable way helps take some of the art, magic, and blind trust in luck out of the process, as well as containing some of the risk. In order to achieve success:

- A product plan must specifically account for the essential schedule milestones of each process step and its UI and usability deliverables
- Execution of a plan must specifically account for and track the quality of UI and usability deliverables with respect to plan
- Tracking and reporting status on the plan accounts for managing the risk elements associated with the many sensitive tasks
- Compliance to requirements is explicitly evaluated and reported at each process step

    Rule of Thumb: Never begin a project without a plan.

Selection of a Software Development Model

There are many criticisms of the waterfall model of software development, which is usually depicted as a downstream flow of work. There is a perception on the part of many that it only gets easier as each step of the process is executed. The converse is more accurate. The volume of work and barriers to overcome becomes larger over time. The analogy is closer to that of salmon trying to navigate upstream to achieve delivery.

The salmon analogy is meaningful from a number of perspectives.

- The amount of time, effort, and energy spent in planning, requirements, and design is smaller than that spent during the construction and test phases. It is easy to begin the journey but not always easy to complete it successfully.

- The early work is more conceptual and abstract in nature, while the upstream work is very specific and concrete. It is easier to overlook things earlier rather than later. These efforts must have a solid start and effective finish.

- Along with construction work, design efforts continue all the way through delivery. There are many potential surprises and compromises during construction that lay waste to even the best of intentions and designs.

- Unless rejected by users, a product that survives the upstream climb will certainly be around much longer than its initial development time. The fruit of development must yield long-term benefits for the sponsoring business and user community.

- Not all products make the jump successfully on the first try. This is the concept of iteration—keep trying until requirements are met (or the project is terminated or requirements adjusted).

Rule of Thumb: Selecting some form of iterative and/or evolutionary model is a best practice from a software and UI design and development point of view. Iteration with user participation is an even better practice. There are many flavors of iterative and participatory processes—pick one that works for your organization and project and stick with it.

Iteration with user participation is a best practice because no one knows all the answers to the multitude of questions and problems arising in software UI design intended to meet business and user needs. The experts recommend an iterative approach.

- There is complexity in UI software. It may take numerous iterations to work out the details of a specific approach in order to meet ergonomic, user, and business needs.

- There is still more to learn about people and how they interact with computers and software applications. Iteration with user participation helps tune a specific approach to a particular user group and task.

The notion of a single-try (one-shot) approach to developing a product and meeting all objectives seems foolhardy—needlessly adding unnecessary risk to an already high risk endeavor. If a general development model used by a project is other than some form of iterative or evolutionary model, it is strongly advised to employ an iterative model for the user interface at a minimum.

All designers and developers of software UIs should approach the task with humility and involve and ask users as often as possible. Iteration prior to release of a software product gives the development team a chance to be right in private. Otherwise, sometimes embarrassing iteration in public is required.

Even though many web-based projects follow an evolutionary model in the field, most cannot survive this approach. However, not all products using an iterative approach are necessarily successful. There are many variables to take into account.

Goals.   From a user-driven perspective, the most important step for management is ensuring that product objectives and criteria for the UI, usability, consistency, integration, and other relevant factors are set. Knowledge of the technology, skills of the product team, and competition is essential to set the bar at the right place.

Management sets the goal at conventional user satisfaction (the historical result is just about average results), which is achievable with conventional techniques. Setting aggressive goals requires deviating from well-known and comfortable development paths (conventional techniques and designs are rejected to pursue a great UI).

Details, Details, Details.   The next biggest risk area is related to the skills and knowledge required for designing and implementing applications using current UI styles. Aside from the application domain functionality of the software, there are myriad UI features and techniques. A short list of features includes drag and drop, clipboard enabling, window memory (of size, location, state), multiple views, and print.

It is sometimes surprising how many developers are not aware of all that is involved. However, a plan and schedule for a project must take into account learning the details of the technology, the implicit and explicit requirements for the UI, and the tools that support the implementation of the requirements.

Requirements.   Another area of high risk on projects is a lack of knowledge of project requirements. A plan provides for adequate time and methods to collect, understand, and prioritize essential product requirements. One area that needs special focus: requirements for UI, usability, consistency, training, and integration.

Many UI details are never mentioned explicitly during requirements gathering. Many users are not even aware of the details in a UI. Requirements like conforming to platform user-interface standards or suite level consistency and integration have significant implications to a UC product team.

Requirements for product usability and consistency must be measurable and compliance verifiable. For example, time on task 25 percent better than the legacy system is a very real and measurable requirement. More detail on requirements for the UI, usability, training, and consistency is discussed later. Once established, the requirements must be committed and supported by management and technical personnel. Measurement, tracking, and reporting methods must be established.

Management Approach.   Management must be proactive in the process of UI design and development. Empowerment is a good thing—but management cannot abdicate responsibility and accountability nor remove itself from the hook of achieving success or failure. Along with other management tasks, setting up the right team with the right skills is extremely important.

Clear responsibility must be assigned, a technical lead and responsible manager must be appointed, measurable plans are required and tracked, performance to requirements is tracked, and accountability and rewards are established. In addition, management must support, protect, and keep the focus on deliverables and quality.

Technical Approach.   Technical personnel establish the technical approach for the project. Decisions include selection of the amount and form of user participation, UI technology, styles, standards, implementation technology and tools, non-UI relations and staging, prototype approach, and evaluation and iteration approach.

> **Rule of Thumb**: From a UI and non-UI viewpoint, plan to start small, design an entry-level product, prototype quickly, test against competition with real end users, and incrementally evolve the design and prototype to full product level software.

Another way of looking at some of the technical tradeoffs is:

- UI technology (OO or procedural) and tools (4GL or 5GL)
- UI-non-UI relationship (integrated or separated)
- Evaluation (comparative or standalone)

Schedule.   A product plan is not complete unless it is measurable and documents milestones and deliverables on a schedule. Milestones are measurable events on a schedule. Deliverables are tangible work products associated with an activity or milestone and against which quality criteria are established.

> **Rule of Thumb**: Activities that do not generate required product deliverables must be challenged before expenditure of precious project resources on tight schedules. *If it doesn't improve the product, don't do it.*

Deliverables for each milestone are evaluated for satisfaction of quality criteria; tracking and reporting performance against a plan is required. Deviations from interim milestones on a plan are not necessarily bad since recovery from some deviations is manageable. However, consistent and major departures from an expected plan are useful for predicting whether product schedule and quality criteria are achievable or whether alternatives are required, including adjusting schedule, adding resource, or reducing features.

> **Rule of Thumb**: A project plan is like a sports game plan—adjustments and audibles are sometimes required in order to achieve goals.

The major milestones are completion of requirements, design, construction, and testing. Interim milestones for each of these major milestones are included on a schedule in a measurable manner. For example, requirements for a product are not finished without completion of UI requirements, user profiles, environment analyses, task analyses, and criteria for usability and consistency. Along with content, requirements are reviewed, approved, and managed with respect to a plan. Similarly, milestones for design and construction are not complete without usability evaluations demonstrating compliance to requirements.

> **Rule of Thumb:** Fifty percent of a development schedule for the initial release of a software product is used for construction, unit test, and system and integration testing beyond conventional design. This means that early planning, design, prototyping, and evaluation must be very effective. In addition, some flexibility for refinement of the product once in system test is planned.

A User-Centered Product Plan.

What is a user-centered product plan? Look for the following in a scheduled and measurable plan:

- Formation of a multidisciplinary team to design a user's experience
- Establishing a user-centered plan of activities for the product
- User participation throughout the process—including requirements, design, and test
- Early and rapid design and prototyping milestones—starting with early visualization of requirements
- Early and rapid usability evaluations—fast and effective user-based testing of interim designs and the product relative to requirements

- Planned design iteration—fix what's broken and improve what's right until requirements are met. At a minimum, three user-based iterations are planned
- Tracking and reporting of interim performance to schedule and requirements

An example of a schedule for an iterative approach to an UI is depicted in Figure 8.3. Each process step is represented, as are measurable UI milestones for the key deliverables of each step. Deliverables include UI objectives, specification, market research, business case, development (for simulators, prototypes, and product drivers), and test reports. The example depicts three planned design iterations (I_1, I_2, I_3) during the design, prototyping, specification, and evaluation tasks for a medium- to large-scale project. Smaller projects follow a similar model with some variation.

Plans are defined early. In successful projects, milestones are fairly granular, tracked, and status reported frequently. During successful development efforts, requirements are defined and subsequently managed and controlled. UI decisions and tradeoffs are made throughout the product development cycle, not just during the specification period.

Rule of Thumb: Provide three views of the UI schedule details.
1. Project duration (high-level milestones)
2. Ninety-day look ahead
3. Two-week detailed (especially during design, code, unit test (DCUT))

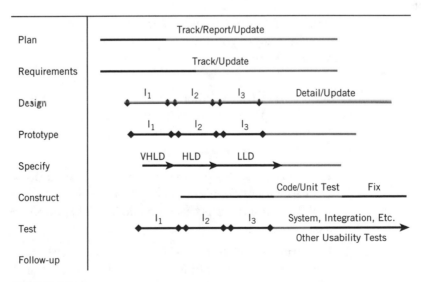

FIGURE 8.3

Example of a user-centered product plan.

A project-duration view gives a big picture, one-page orientation of an entire project's life cycle and critical milestones. Since projects with a relatively long schedule have more risk and are harder to predict, it is advisable to formulate 90-day chunks of work and milestones in more detail. Regardless of project duration, a two-week lookahead is easy to comprehend, predict, lay out, execute, and track.

Multiple milestones are defined for designing, prototyping, developing, and testing. Each iteration provides additional refinement and incremental growth of features. Based on test results or direct user feedback, modifications are made to the design, prototype, and product. Iteration continues until requirements are met. Tracking and reporting performance against a plan is required.

Chunking the Plan.   As with actual design and development, there are many unknowns associated with any UI plan. A good approach is to know first where you want to end up. From the start, start small and grow smart. Plan small bite-sized chunks, define deliverables and responsibility and quality clearly, and expand the plan and schedule as unknowns are resolved.

Examples of bite-sized design chunks include entry-level design and non-entry level system components delivered via multiple design drivers, or full system staged in design drivers. Drivers (interim drops or builds) for specifications, simulators, prototypes, and product software are helpful from many perspectives.

> **Rule of Thumb**: Chunk project feature content into builds of software composed of windows, pages, or screens and supporting components and techniques.

Design Growth.   Another approach to chunking a plan is staging delivery of design content by scheduled iteration as depicted in Figure 8.4. An iterative user-centered plan defines at least three major iterations whose content is defined as:

- I_1 = **conceptual design**. Design for main-line, high-use, high-risk, and critical elements; exploration of alternatives, tradeoffs, and constraints; tool validation. This is based on a low-fidelity approach to prototyping and evaluation.

- I_2 = **20 percent design**. Design repair and/or enhancements to I_1; addition of the 20 percent of features used 80 percent of the time; addition of other areas of design concern. This is based on a high-fidelity approach to prototyping and evaluation.

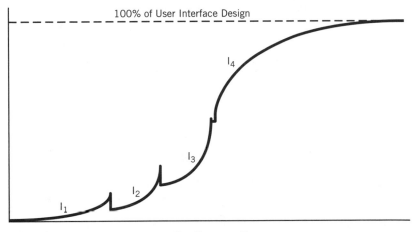

FIGURE 8.4
Conceptual design growth during iterations during the design phase.

- **I_3 = next 20 percent**. Design repair and/or enhancements to I_2; addition of the next 20 percent of features and other areas of design concern (problematic user tasks).

- **I_{4+} = design complete**. Design repair and/or enhancements to I_3; addition of the remainder of product features that are of lesser importance and will likely be iterated upon very little during the remainder of development. Examples of these types of product features include messages, low-use function, and so forth. These items are specified, reviewed, and implemented.

Design enhancement means change to areas of the design in order to improve software performance relative to UI, usability, and other criteria. Enhancement is typically opportunistic in nature (new ideas to make design features quantitatively or qualitatively better evolve over time, and that are not necessarily driven by users or testing).

Design repair means correction of areas that cause criteria failure, UI or usability problems, or other problems encountered by real users. A hope is that by completion of I_3, criteria satisfaction is achieved with confidence and major problems are resolved. Subsequent iterations are used for design refinement, polishing, and correcting previously detected or undetected problems of a less severe nature.

Another hope is that as each successive iteration proceeds, the amount of design repair becomes smaller. As required, additional iterations are scheduled. If criteria are very stringent, more iteration are explicitly planned.

$I_1 - I_3$ define major iterations of features. Within each major iteration, there are many iterations of a smaller and more granular nature.

> **Rule of Thumb**: Iteration is only for those serious about meeting criteria. Don't do it otherwise.
> - Plan on at least three with a conventional process
> - 7 +/- 2 iterations is better
> - Better yet is 100-plus iterations

Schedules and Iterative Processes

A major lesson about UIs is that aggressive criteria are rarely achieved in one iteration—multiple iterations are typically required to achieve tough criteria with an acceptable residual usability and UI error rate. However, how many iterations are required to achieve a user satisfaction target of better than six on a three-month schedule?

Multiple iterations improve UIs with the right process, measurements, tests, and skills. More importantly, iteration is manageable if planned. At a minimum, three solid user-based iterations are desirable. If criteria are not achieved, it may be back to the design drawing board.

> **Rule of Thumb**: Iteration is a trial-and-error approach.

Iteration Impacts to Schedule.   Iteration does not necessarily add to the schedule (see Figure 8.4). The only portion of design that needs to change is that which causes criteria failures or major usability problems. For these cases, there is a drop in effective design that must be made up.

The schedule cost of change at this point is relatively inexpensive in comparison to conventional processes that delay finding such problems until late in design, very late in construction, or very late during deployment. In many cases, early detection of such defects is made up easily over the course of typical development schedules. Corrective costs become exponentially higher over time.

Requirements.   A major area of project risk is requirements—they must be right after the initial period of requirement collection. Then, the requirements are managed as time goes on and other users, project personnel, and situations change. This is especially true with long duration projects.

Rule of Thumb: Focus on a few critical measurements that are the critical success factors for the product.

Requirements for UIs are typical weak spots. A possible remedy is for UI personnel to visit real customer end users in their work environment. Informal visits to perform structured observations allow a UC product team to gain insight into real users, their social environments and tasks, and competition within the user environment. More formal techniques are employed to conduct real market research into what users want and need.

Business Cases.   When product comparisons are based on feature lists, a new product typically does not compare well against older established products. However, if new UIs and product features do indeed reduce learning time and improve productivity (reduce time on task), a user-centered business demonstrates the value of a new UI/product vis-a-vis current technology. Usability test results demonstrate product value.

Rule of Thumb: Base tough design decisions on measurable and comparative business value and user preference.

Design.   Employ software and UI design best practices. Code can always be made better—but know when what has been implemented suffices.

Rule of Thumb: Beware of providing the best possible design. In many ways, the search for a best possible design is like a search for the Holy Grail. A design that meets product requirements and business/ user needs within schedule and resource constraints is what is required. How would one know that the best possible is ever achieved?

Prototype.   Always keep the purpose of prototyping in mind. It is a means to an end, and the end is to meet requirements as quickly, efficiently, and effectively as possible. Plan on keeping it around to evaluate design alternatives that surface during implementation or follow-on releases.

Rule of Thumb: Move from low-fidelity to high-fidelity design, prototype, and evaluation techniques as soon as possible.

Specification.   Describing a design in a specification is just another form of design instantiation. Multiple levels of detail discussed later—conceptual (architecture), high-level (all windows/pages identified and key ones designed), and low-level (nearly all the details written down and/or understood).

Code/Unit Test.

Writing the actual software and performing unit testing results in code that is tested sufficiently well to go into System Test with a high degree of confidence. An exit criterion for unit test is performing a UI certification. The intent of this milestone is to demonstrate that all low-level appearance and behavior of the UI is correct. The low-level detail includes things that may not be in the spec (e.g., cursor placement and initial selections when a window is opened). Much standard platform behavior does not need to be written down.

Systems and Other Testing.

A major criticism of usability testing is that it only evaluates short-term initial usage. This is true if test vehicles and test designs do not support long-term usage. A way to solve this is to have end users perform planned and ad hoc testing during the entire system test step. Surveys and usability test scripts are administered throughout the system test period to gather long-term usability assessments of the product. It may be possible to correct some problems late in the test cycle, but these items are certainly considered for the next release.

Custom Controls.

For most efforts, standard UI controls are sufficient to achieve desired usability results. However, if specialized and/or custom controls are desired or needed, they are specifically and explicitly spelled out in the UI development plan. Typically, developers underestimate the amount of work required to design and implement a custom control, which must provide all the standard appearance and behavior associated with standard controls.

Other Work Typically Forgotten.

Many things typically happen during development efforts that are not explicitly planned for. Each organization has its own unique set of surprises. Examples include product presentations and demonstrations to customers and executives, trade show participation, changing development versions or tools in mid-stream, major networking problems, vacation and holidays.

Be sure that the known unknowns and unknown unknowns are anticipated and accounted for. An example of an unknown is that a LAN-based development environment is likely to crash during a project's life cycle. An example of a different type of unknown is whether a key person will be ill for an extended period of time during a project's life cycle. Project schedules and assignments are adjustable for containing the risk of some unkowns.

Estimating.   Table 8.1 shows factors for GUI-based software that must be taken into account. Web-based and PDA-based UIs have some of these elements as well as others.

TABLE 8.1

Typical sizing factors for a GUI-based application

Major factors	Characteristics
Functional features	Domain features of objects, commands, and their properties
UI features	Menu bar, popup menu, menu choices, toolbars, toolbar choices, drag/drop operations, clipboard operations, shortcut keys, access keys, etc.
Number of objects	Icons and bitmaps of various sizes and resolutions, data types; desktop behavior; system features; print formats
Number of object windows/pages	Basics, window memory (size, position, state)
Number of views per object	View layouts; keyboard behavior, mouse behavior
Number of settings per object	Customization features per object and for the user interface in general
Number of action windows per object	Application unique; system common; graying behavior
Number of controls per object window	Dropdowns, entry fields, spin buttons, etc.
Number of controls per action window	Same as above
Number of user feedback operations	Hourglass, progress indicators, etc.

TABLE 8.1
Typical sizing factors for a GUI-based application *(continued)*

Major factors	Characteristics
Number of unique print formats	Print and preview layouts
Number of help and tutorial screens	Including the organization of such user assistance into a UI flow
Number of performance support panels	Including the various techniques employed
Number of messages per object window	Feedback, errors, messages
Number of messages per action window	Same as above
Number of unique appearances/ behaviors	Special features of appearance and behavior requiring software design and development
Number of custom controls	Nonstandard and specialized UI controls requiring software design and development
Install/Uninstall/Upgrade Features	Special software required to install, update, and remove an application from a user's system
Unique keyboard, mouse, and other device operations	Shortcut keys, access keys, gestures, button behaviors, etc.

Rule of Thumb: Provide a detailed work breakdown structure for each window/page of the UI. This technique is especially good for developers or teams new to UI work and its detail.

Scheduling Rules of Thumb.
The following calendar durations can be used for schedule estimates of moderately large and complex software:

- 8 weeks for conceptual design
- 6-8 weeks per early iteration using a prototype
  - 6 weeks for design, prototype, and test prep
  - 2 weeks for test, analysis, and planning the next iteration
- 1-2 months for high-level design/prototype/evaluate/specify

- 2-3 months for low-level design/prototype/evaluate/specify
- 2-3 months for each custom control (may require one full time programmer per control; includes design/prototype/evaluate/specify)

Table 8.2 is based on project duration.

TABLE 8.2

Time per task by number of developme schedule months

Task	Schedule Months						
	24	18	15	12	9	6	3
Plan	2	1	1	1	1	1	2 wk
Requirements	3	3	2	1	1	1	2 wk
Design	7	5	4	4	2	1	2 wk
Construct	4	3	3	2	1	1	3 wk
Test	8	6	5	4	4	2	3 wk

Rule of Thumb: The shorter the schedule, the higher the risk because of the shorter amount of time to do the work required. The longer the schedule the higher the risk because of challenges in predicting and scheduling the volume of work.

Repeatable Process. The basic steps to UI design and development and usability engineering are certainly repeatable. Some standard UI ingredients such as controls and tools are constant. However, variation in the greatness of a recipe occurs as skills, ingredients, or implementation details vary. For example, design and development skills vary from project to project, as does commitment to achieve stated UI and usability goals. Sometimes the perceived need to announce and ship a recipe outweighs its quality. Consistency is achieved only by expert use of ingredients and true commitment to results.

Cycle Time Reduction. Reducing development time and cost is very important within any development project but even more so in consumer software and web environments. An approach to reduce software cycle time is avoiding requirements, design, or coding errors. UI and usability is significantly less scientific than non-UI design and development. In the long term, cycle times required to achieve great UIs decrease as UI skills increase and ingredients improve. In the short term, commitment to objectives is required to iterate UIs with user participation until requirements are met. A comparable goal for performance is reducing the number of module rewrites to achieve subsecond response time and memory targets.

Listen Throughout.   Throughout execution of a plan leading to delivery and follow-up on a recipe, *listen to users*. A consumer of a UI recipe is a final judge of its quality. For more details on techniques for effectively listening to users, refer to Chapter 6.

Staffing, Skills, and Other Resources

UI design and development and usability engineering for software using current *UI styles* requires strong skills and teamwork. No one individual has all the skills to perform all the different tasks. The required skill set of a user-centered product team is described in Chapter 5. In addition, the team requires clear goals, the right management support, tools, facilities, and attitude to tackle a tough job.

> **Rule of Thumb**: The importance of the appropriate number of each type of skill should not be underestimated.

The skills needed for a project are mapped to specific roles within a user-centered product team. One person can perform multiple roles but there must be close working relationships among the members of the team to ensure success.

> **Rule of Thumb**: Each person should have sufficient skills and be able to perform more than one role. If some individual just does not fit in, rotation to another project is appropriate. The schedule should be adjusted to accommodate skill and team building as needed.

Refer to Chapter 4 for more details on technical and people skills required for effective delivery of a product that meets requirements for usability, UI, consistency, and so forth.

Organizational Considerations.   Just as there are different development models to choose from, there are different organizational models to use on a user-centered product development. Factory approaches to development can be employed:

- One team formulates requirements and hands off to a team that builds an architecture

- The architecture team performs a handoff to one or more design teams
- Each design team performs a handoff to one or more construction teams
- Each construction team performs a handoff to a build and test team

Needless to say, much is lost in the various handoffs.

An alternate approach is a single user-centered product team that follows a product from planning and requirements all the way through deployment. A single design is formulated, prototyped, specified, and tested under the leadership of the same team.

> **Rule of Thumb**: Small team processes and approaches seem to work the best for delivering high usability results.

Leadership.   A single manager is made responsible for a user-centered product team and delivery of a UI that meets requirements. A single technical person is made responsible for leading a user-centered product team and delivery of a product that meets UI and usability requirements. The focus is kept on responsibility and accountability.

> **Rule of Thumb**: When there is a product success, there is enough success to spread around to an entire team. When a product fails, it should be clear who is responsible, accountable, and appropriately rewarded.

Implementation Tools.   From the earlier discussion of tools, there are many tools and facilities to secure. The earlier that needed tools are secured the better.

Constraints.   There are usually many limitations imposed on a UC product team due to tools and OSs. Once the tools are secured, a team determines what the limitations are and begins to work around them.

Planning for the Major Usability Factors _____

Things will always go wrong. Whether it is stability of the system, performance, or the nagging quality problems, a schedule contingency should be considered depending upon the confidence one has in the ability to solve problems.

Rule of Thumb: For each area of schedule concern, assign at least two weeks of additional calendar time.

Sizing Estimates.   As the work is broken down and further refined, the implementation team is asked to provide estimates of how long it will take for features to be designed, coded, and unit tested.

Rule of Thumb: Have the programming team provide estimates in terms of SMOPs (small matter of programming units), where

- 1 SMOP = one-half a programming day (4 hours)
- 1 week = 32 programming hours

Implementation Assignments.   When scheduling the UDCUT milestone, plan some form of high-level design and specification review. Ask a product team for real UDCUT dates. This makes an implementation team think in terms of completion of solid

- design for UI and implementation (UD)
- implementation (C ~ Construction ~ Code)
- unit testing (UT)

Table 8.3 depicts a possible table for layout assignments for the tasks associated with design and deployment of a single screen. Alternatively, the table could be used at the application level, though much of the work detail would be lost.

TABLE 8.3
Product assignments

Task	UI and implementation design/spec	CUT	System test
Install			
UI base			
UI screens (a list)			
UI support			
UI controls			
Print			
Help			
Training			
Graphics			
Usability			

TABLE 8.3
Product assignments *(continued)*

Task	UI and implementation design/spec	CUT	System test
Database			
APIs			
Communications			
Build/distribute			
Test			
Technical lead			
Manager			

Rule of Thumb: Overlapping design tasks are possible. However, plan on sequential implementation tasks.

Plan a project checkpoint to confirm schedule upon completion of conceptual design, high-level design, and low-level design.

Planning for the Project

You're in week two of the project and the hectic pace continues. The project lead has committed to provide a preliminary assessment, project schedule, and likely resource estimates for the project. You have total responsibility for the UI, usability, and the team of people involved in its development. Your assignment is to develop the UI and UCD plan and schedule for the entire project.

The plan and schedule for the non-UI software is being formulated by your teammate, and he has assured you that the requirements will be supported without question by his part of the plan. Assume that his intent and commitment are real.

Senior management has asked for estimates and a schedule for an early delivery of some web-based portions of the overall project. The remainder of the project software can be staged over time. It's up to you to recommend a schedule.

As usual, the resource needs and schedule must be reported to senior management early tomorrow morning. You have about two hours to work on the request. You will brief the project lead as soon as you are done. Provide a preliminary assessment of

- Needed resources and skills

- A likely schedule (next two weeks, next 90 days, through project duration)
- Potential staging of features, including the early web delivery
- Areas of product, user interface, and usability risk
- Likely number of iterations and when each is scheduled

Remember to reflect key tasks and milestones in some view of the project schedule (e.g., completion of recruiting for the UCD team, completion of recruiting for the user participation approach, and identifying major project features for early design and prototyping).

Be sure to conduct a search of the Web for information of potential assistance to your planning and project.

Any questions?

References

Brooks, F., *The Mythical Man Month*, Addision-Wesley: New York, 1995.

Cantor, M.R., *Object -Oriented Project Management*, Wiley & Sons: New York, 1998.

Gould, J., et al., "Making Usable, Useful, and Productivity Enhancing Computer Applications," *Communications of the ACM*, Jan. 1991.

A Guide to Software Usability, IBM Corporation: Purchase, NY, SC26-3000.

Karat, C., "Cost-Benefit Analysis of Iterative Usability Testing," ACM/SIGCHI Tutorial, May 1991.

McConnell, S., *Rapid Development*, Microsoft Press: Redmond, WA, 1996.

Mayhew, D., "Managing the Design of the User Interface," ACM/SIGCHI Tutorial, May 1991.

Nielsen, J., "The Usability Engineering Life Cycle," *Computer Magazine*, Mar. 1992.

Rettig, M., "Interface Design When You Don't Know How," *Communications of the ACM*, Jan. 1992.

Torres, R.J., "User Interface Design and Development," Westlake Reflections, 1991.

Requirements

9

Two frequently cited reasons for product failure are related to requirements: the lack of clear, specific, and measurable requirements and the lack of controlling requirements during development. There is possibly a third reason for project failure related to requirements that is not well recognized—the lack of clear requirements for usability, UI, consistency, integration, user, and business-related needs and expectations.

Aside from gathering information specific to UI, usability, consistency, integration, response time, and learning, there is nothing unique or intrinsic to the gathering of these requirements that is not experienced in the gathering of functional requirements. The same methods are useful for addressing these topics as well as gathering functional requirements. The major difference is one of focus and perspective to ensure that the right requirements are obtained.

A difficult part of requirements gathering is working with people to determine what is really wanted and needed. Requirements are obtained throughout the development of any product. Reasons for this are that the needs of a user change, the needs of a business change, and the perceptions and awareness of needs change. A major challenge for a product under development (regardless of stage) is to collect and manage the introduction of new requirements into an ongoing development effort.

There are technical and social considerations that apply to requirements gathering. Depending upon the magnitude of change, technical considerations result from introduction of new features into unreliable and unstable software during a test cycle. There are social considerations that impact tired and harried development teams trying to stabilize ill behaving software during the late and hectic construction and test phases of product development. "What now?" and "Why now?" are frequently asked.

The following topics are discussed in this chapter.

- Key features
- Requirements gathering approach
- UI requirements
- Usability requirements
- Making requirements visible and measurable
- Requirements for the project

Focus is kept on identifying key UI, usability, user, and business information and its sources as opposed to the methods for gathering such requirements.

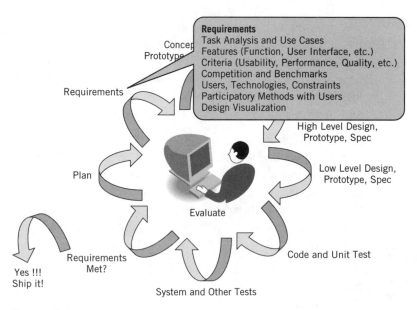

FIGURE 9.1

Planning for user-centered product development.

Key Features

Product usability and UIs are receiving increased attention and importance as a feature of competitive advantage. As product feature lists grow longer (to the point of being unfathomable and not implementable with palatable schedule or cost), users responsible for product purchases look to a UI. If a product's UI appears simple to learn and use, the product may gain competitive advantage, especially if claims of reduced training costs and productivity gains are real.

Now that the general types of information needed are known, the next step is to understand where to find the requirements for UI and usability. Typically, such requirements are not written down except at a very abstract level. So a user-centered product team formulates requirements from many sources that include the current business, users, and systems (see Figure 9.1).

Question: How would you recognize necessary and sufficient requirements if you tripped over them?

Existing Documentation.   Use cases, functional requirements, functional specifications, and business training manuals are sources of explicit and implicit requirements. Customer presentations, strategy documents,

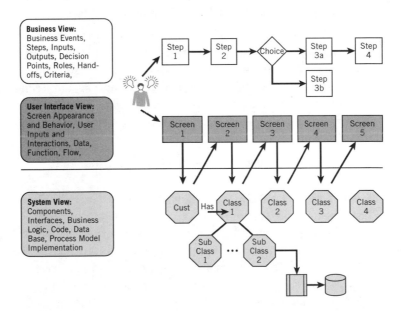

FIGURE 9.2
A business, user, and system view.

and process documents are examples of very good sources of other information.

Requirements for application UIs are typically very high level and lacking in specificity. Typically, requirements for product UIs include statements like:

- A GUI must be provided
- The UI must conform to the OS platform and corporate styles
- The interface must be simple to learn and easy to use

In comparison to requirements for functional features, UI requirements leave a lot to interpretation and the imagination. However, existing documents are a good starting point for understanding product needs.

User Tasks and Business Procedures.   End user tasks require good descriptions, together with the frequency distribution of tasks. For example, use of the 80/20 rule helps to keep focus on categories and priorities of requirements. The 20 percent tasks include those performed infrequently or which have minimal importance or priority for users, a business, or its customers. The 80 percent tasks are those performed most often, the most error-prone or costly, and/or have the most impact to a business, its users, and its customers. Given this information, an approach that focuses on optimizing a system for best effect is possible, and this avoids building an average system targeted for average impact across all tasks and users.

In addition to knowing what tasks users perform, the procedures followed by end users in completing work are useful to know. Related to procedures are end-user protocols, which are social practices and conventions that influence how work is performed. Software UIs and systems can be responsive to protocols, as well as procedures and tasks. This type of information is obtained through use of participatory methods such as observation, interviews, and focus groups.

More detail about user tasks is discussed in Chapter 10.

User Descriptions.   Along with feature descriptions, detailed information about end users is required. End users are not monolithic collections. Each user is an individual with uniqueness in skills, attitudes, and knowledge about a job and about a computer and its software. A UC product team describes the variability in skills, attitudes, and knowledge for a target user group. User descriptions must be sufficient to give UI designers and developers an understanding of the likely users and the variance in skills and attitudes. The requirements must also describe the same information for users in each country for which a product is being developed. This information is obtained via surveys and during observations and other participatory techniques.

Users are discussed in further detail in Chapter 10.

Current Product Evaluation. Use of reverse engineering techniques allows formulation of requirements based upon existing systems. Feature lists, data needed, response time, task flow, current information, and UI techniques are derivable. Business and user needs are added to the requirements and reviewed for completeness and priority.

Assessing the usability of current systems helps to understand and assess an overall current environment. Key system and business usability information is obtained to establish metrics and success criteria. A requirement for a UI and overall system helps ascertain benchmark values for productivity and satisfaction given current methods. At a high level, key criteria include:

- User performance in current environments
- User satisfaction with current systems
- User attitudes (likes and dislikes) toward current systems
- What users want and need instead of what is available

Formal and informal methods are applicable to understanding the current environment in a qualitative and quantitative manner.

One thing to remember about current systems is that they include other software that is in use by users. Other software packages available on a user's system including office suites and other programs supporting a user's work.

> **Rule of Thumb**: Be sure to understand all software in use by a user and how the various packages interact.

Competitive Evaluation. Along with current products in use, other sources of features, information, UI, and usability information include real competitors and like products. Competitive and like products are evaluated using the same techniques as for evaluation of current products.

> **Rule of Thumb**: As requirements are gathered, document and validate against current and other systems for completeness, importance, and need.

Industry Evaluations. There are many sources of published information in the industry. Techniques and details are sometimes difficult to understand and have confidence in. However, the information is another important source for validating the importance or the usability of features.

Industry journals, industry organizations, web sites, and consulting organizations provide volumes of information useful for evaluating concepts.

Users and Sponsors.   When in doubt, ask a user. User groups are important sources of requirements. User groups in most forms are excellent for validating usage and priority of features and characteristics. Remember to keep project sponsors and key vested interests involved in the requirements process. Participatory methods are ideal for requirements gathering and validation.

UI Features.   In order for user, business, and customer needs to be met, requirements for software UIs must be more specific. Here are examples of UI features common in graphical, web, and handheld device UIs.

- Graphical support (windows, icons, graphical controls, etc.)
- Menus (menu bar and pulldown menus, popup menus, cascade menus, toolbars)
- Views (layout, outline, etc.)
- Navigation aids (site maps, bread crumb trails, etc.)
- Shortcut keys and access key characters in menus and dialogs
- Direct manipulation (move, copy, and other commands)
- Specific operations (e.g., save, print, clipboard, undo/redo, etc.)
- Minimalism (product and information)
- Customization (keyboard, mouse, progressive disclosure, etc.)
- Alternative input and output devices

Understanding the usage distribution of these features is important since many UI designers believe that some of these techniques are rarely used. Implementing infrequently used techniques reduces the ability of products to deliver other more useful UI features.

Visual and Media Features.   Requirements for software graphic, visual, and other media support must be specific about needed features. Examples of visual and media features are:

- Static graphics used in icons, banners, and other visual cues
- Animated graphics used for messages, signals, and other purposes
- Audible information used for messages, signals, and other cues

Understanding the distribution of use for these features is important since many of these techniques are perceived as gratuitous and not adding direct business value to an end user's task at hand.

Information Features.   Requirements for software informational support must be more specific about needed features. Examples of information features are:

- Hardcopy references and work aids
- Classroom training, online tutorials
- Help, wizards, cue cards, prompts, Tooltips

Understanding the distribution of use for these features is important since many of these techniques are used rarely due to lack of effectiveness of current methods. Implementing infrequently used techniques reduces the ability of UC product teams to deliver more useful or effective information features.

Constraints.   Many organizations have limitations that constrain the organization or its people during efforts to achieve certain goals. It is extremely important to know what freedoms and flexibility exist, as well as any constraining boundaries. An example of a freedom is "pulling all the stops," while an example of a constraint is "five people for six months."

Trends.   Knowing how the industry is evolving is more important than knowing where it is, since the industry is moving very rapidly. Evolution occurs in technology, in the install base, and in what users know. Social trends are important, but more subtle than technical ones. Requirement documentation must consider change leading up to the timeframe in which a software UI is targeted.

Requirements-Gathering Approach _____

In a typical requirement-gathering scenario:

- An end user talks to a supervisor
- The end user's supervisor talks to an I/S representative
- The I/S representative talks to the I/S manager
- The I/S manager talks to a product planner
- A product planner talks to a development team

This is a very indirect form of requirements gathering that loses significant information in the handoffs. A more direct form of requirements gathering by a UC product team is needed in order to be more market driven. Current processes involve too many layers of definition and interpretation to the point where real needs are lost in the shuffle.

JARs/JADs, decision support facilities, focus groups, observation, contextual interviews, competitive evaluation, questionnaires, task analysis, use cases, scenarios, UI prototyping, and other participatory methods are useful for collecting, structuring, documenting, and validating requirements. Requirements must take current and future user, business, and customer processes and needs into account. Change management actions must anticipate the needs of people in the future environment.

> **Rule of Thumb**: As with other areas of a product, requirements are subject to an 80/20 rule for significance and completeness. Twenty percent of the requirements define the essential features of a system and its UI and are the most critical for design and development. The other 80 percent of requirements are important but not essential or core business or development needs.

The most important aspects of the task are to approach the product requirements gathering with discipline, to interact with future real users of the software, to interact with the business sponsors, and to gain agreement on the requirements. The result of such an effort is a set of requirements that meet the needs of users, sponsors, and developers.

> **Rule of Thumb**: You'll know a requirement is well understood when it is reflected as discrete commands and screens in a UI prototype, and users can evaluate and agree with its features and usability.

Tables to collect, structure, and prioritize the business needs are extremely useful. Sometimes, a simple spreadsheet is sufficient for capturing and sorting the needed information. Each row in the spreadsheet describes a very simple and discrete requirement that an end user perceives and which is mappable to a UI. It is useful to identify the source and date of all requirements for subsequent tracking. Project requirements are evaluated by a UC product team to ensure necessary development skills, cost, risks, and schedules.

> **Rule of Thumb**: Requirements tables are useful throughout a project's lifetime because columns can be added for mapping where features are visible in a UI and how the requirement is tested.

Signing Off.   Agreement with and approval of requirements by users and a development team are important for software projects. Users, sponsors, and development organizations must stabilize requirements so that product planning, design, and development proceeds to an acceptable conclusion.

Rule of Thumb: Remember the 80/20 rule during the approval phase.

It is always uncomfortable for business users to approve system requirements—no one wants to be locked in or blamed for something that may lead to an unacceptable product. On the one hand, developers don't want to build a product based upon unapproved requirements. On the other hand, everyone wants to deliver a product at a point in time that meets business and user needs in an acceptable manner.

Tracking Change.   Here is where a UC product team working in partnership with business and development organizations helps foster the trust needed in today's fast-paced business and development environments. Managing change is the real issue once a baseline set of requirements is defined.

Rule of Thumb: Be sure to track changes in requirements with more discipline than the original capture of requirements.

Change in and of itself is not bad. Most changes are simple and relatively inexpensive. However, unmanaged change, regardless of cost, is a business and project killer. A UC product team works with all vested interests to identify:

- Changes to product requirements, benefits, potential losses of not making a change, and business risk.
- Potential impacts to project cost, schedule, resource, and risk.

Change to a product under development is then assessed as a business risk proposition—tradeoffs for the vested interests to weigh and then decide upon.

UI Requirements _____

Aside from identifying key features of a UI, certain key behaviors and appearance characteristics are required. If UI heuristics are known, these are incorporated into the requirements—it's only giving a hint about success criteria!

Rule of Thumb: Define a UI feature or characteristic as part of a product's requirement if it were going to be measured, reported, acted upon, and tracked.

Some areas tend to be surprises or common problems in UIs. Items to identify clearly in requirements are:

- UI style
- Platform and other UI standards for the application
- Consistency with leading software on the platform (e.g., application X or suite Y)
- Screen content (e.g., data and features needed at key points during tasks)
- Screen behavior (e.g., input focus on the first control of a screen when it is displayed)
- Screen appearance features (e.g., use of graphics for data, views, and aesthetics)
- User interaction techniques (e.g., command access, shortcut techniques, etc.)
- Keyboard enabling, including tabbing behavior and cycling of the tab key
- User feedback on system status and response time
- User control of various features
- Memory of window placement and sizing operations as well as data, state, and context
- Navigation features for the application
- Saving user data during navigation
- Memory of interim user data during navigation
- Online training, performance support, and help
- Error prevention and recovery
- Direct entry techniques to avoid dialogs
- Field validation and identification of required fields
- Standard use of colors, indicators, graphics, and so forth
- Accessibility features for users with physical challenges

Many UI items like these are not documented clearly or specifically in UI style guides, requirements documents, or product specifications. However, this is not sufficient given how often you encounter such problems.

Major Usability Requirements

Usability requirements are easy to state in an ambiguous and difficult to measure manner, e.g., "provide an easy to use system" or "provide an intuitive system." Not all members of a UC product team or users of the system are likely to agree on the meaning of these requirements or whether they have been achieved. Usability, ease of use, and intuitiveness are ultimately in the perceptions of a user and business sponsor. However, it is possible to make these requirements more tangible, understood, and measurable.

Table 9.1 lists standard or frequently used metrics useful to capture for software usability. Again, the goal is to take implicit requirements and make them explicit and measurable. Other requirements can be added to the list.

TABLE 9.1

Examples of usability requirements

Type of goal	Example
Installation or upgrade	Successful installation within 15 minutes
Learning	Successfully complete a list of basic tasks within 20 minutes after a 15 minute overview of the system
Performance	8 tasks per hour at the end of the first day of use
Productivity	15% better than current system
Consistency	90% of users are satisfied with UI consistency
Error-free task completion	90% of tasks are error free
Help-free task completion	15% fewer than current system
Help	90% of accesses to Help generate a successful answer and 90% user satisfaction with Help
Visuals and Media	90% positive satisfaction with graphics, animation, media
Defects	0 Severity 1 or 2 usability defects relative to requirements or standards
Satisfaction with system	90% positive satisfaction after first hour of use
Preference	90% of users prefer new system over predecessor and competition

Further classification of errors—based on business or customer impact—is possible. For example, some user errors impact a business without impacting the clients of a business, while some errors impact a business and its clients. These are quantifiable in terms of severity driven by cost to the business or client.

> **Rule of Thumb:** Define a usability characteristic as a requirement if it is going to be measured, reported, acted upon, and tracked.

Task and Workflow Support.

Certainly, software products must support each user task within requirements and constraints. However, it is very typical for a user to perform tasks that are interrupted by other tasks. Typically, a user puts the interrupted task aside, performs the interrupting task, and then returns to and completes the interrupted task.

It is important to define requirements associated with environments where users must perform multitasking with the same application. Important user-oriented task and workflow features include:

- Number of task interrupts to support

- Features to support during interrupts or navigation

- UI support during interrupts

> **Rule of Thumb**: Multitasking requirements usually have implications on the number of perceived or actual instances of the same application open in separate windows or browsers.

Consistency.

A software application or suite is expected to be consistent within itself and other software on the same platform in a few key areas. Consistency applies to concepts, terminology, graphics, and visual style and appearance of screens. Consistency also applies to interaction behaviors and use of UI controls (e.g., dropdowns within a base operating system platform and the application software). Consistency is a major area of implicit and ambiguous expectations that is made explicit and measurable with a few criteria:

- There are no arbitrary deviations from platform standards (e.g., keyboard and mouse behavior on screens or standard and custom UI controls)

- There are no arbitrary differences across applications

- User satisfaction with consistency is better than 90 percent

Rule of Thumb: An arbitrary difference is one that does not need to exist (i.e., a consistent solution is available and satisfactory relative to consistency and other usability requirements).

Integration.   Another major requirement is smooth integration with other software. Conventional data integration is typically provided across application software using Clipboard commands (Cut, Copy, Paste), direct manipulation, or other commands that perform data interchange or meaningful launching of other applications with data passing. Specific and measurable criteria are used for qualitative and quantitative requirements in a testable and verifiable manner.

Competitors.   A useful technique in certain environments is to identify the current internal and external competitors. Then, quantitative and qualitative measurable goals are set for the product relative to the competition. An example of a quantitative goal is time on task 15 percent better than a competitor. An example of a qualitative goal is user preference of 10 to 1 over the predecessor.

Other Important Requirements.   Recall that overall satisfaction and usability is a function of several parameters. Response time, reliability, and overall system quality are important to meeting satisfaction and usability goals for users. A factor important to a software development organization is software maintainability. These are sometimes called nonfunctional requirements.

Making Requirements Visible and Measurable

Essential to the success of a project and achieving key goals is crisp communication between project sponsors, users, and a development team. Once understood and agreed upon, requirements are mapped to high level and detailed product development plans and schedules. Subsequently, requirements and schedule items are mapped to a UI and its supporting software. Team skills are evaluated for sufficiency and any dependent actions scheduled.

Visible Requirements.   Functional requirements are easily mapped to many forms useful for tracking. A simple spreadsheet or project plan is sufficient for listing functional requirements. Other columns of the spreadsheet are used to map completion of specific requirement to a specific version of product software or a date when a requirement is implemented.

Similarly, UI or usability features are mapped to a spreadsheet or project plan. However, tracking UI requirements is usually more complex. For example, an application of a suite UI may have a general requirement of window memory of user actions and state, and this requirement is mapped to each window or page of an application. Complexity increases when requirements change and are remapped to each window or screen that requires change.

Broader system-level requirements are also made visible. At a minimum, checkpoints that validate performance to requirements for information, graphics, usability, consistency, performance, integration, and other factors are added to a project plan.

Publishing Requirements.

Requirements are made readily available to all vested interests. Availability takes the form of hardcopy documentation, electronic documentation, requirement prototypes and storyboards, and presentations. Multiple forms of communication are usually required.

> **Rule of Thumb**: Provide tracking information on all information for change control purposes.

Prioritizing Requirements.

It is not unusual to have many more requirements than the capacity to implement in a reasonable time frame. Lists of feature-oriented requirements have a tendency to be very long. In these cases, it is important to establish priorities for incremental and evolutionary implementation.

> **Rule of Thumb**: A useful exercise for setting priorities is asking, "If I can do only one thing, what is it? If two things can be done, what are they?" The goal is to determine which features can be delayed or avoided altogether, "Would it hurt the project if I didn't do this?"

Approval of Requirements.

As with product plans and other product deliverables, the requirements for a product undergo visible approval and commitment. Project sponsors and developers are the key approvers. However, all participating vested interests are responsible for obtaining approved requirements of sufficient quality. Approvals are tracked in project plans and completion done visibly and measurably. Once approved, requirements are subject to change control procedures as business needs change.

> **Rule of Thumb**: Don't allow any wiggle room in obtaining approvals nor commitments.

Measuring and Tracking.   Once a requirement is defined, approved, and committed it is mapped to a development schedule with committed resources. Each work item on a development schedule maps to an item in requirement documentation. Each task performed by a developer maps to a requirement and development schedule. Design, build, and test are formulated against the committed requirements. As development proceeds, it is easy to see when requirements are achieved.

Requirements for the Project_____

Your meeting with senior management to review the high level plan went extremely well. The plan was approved but you walked out with several action items: provide an estimate of the number of windows, web pages, and screens; provide a rough estimate of number of hours per window, page, and screen; and explain the tradeoffs involved in use of OO and techniques such as UML. The clock is definitely ticking for delivery of the project.

The project is large and seems to be growing in functionality, complexity, and abstract demands with each day. Feature lists are received verbally and via email from potential purchasers of the product and senior management. The potential purchasers include very prestigious and large professional organizations with regular conferences worldwide.

One of the early tasks on the project plan is formulating requirements. You must address how requirements are to be gathered and validated, as well as determine a likely order of delivery. Senior management continues to be under fiscal pressures and is seeking a very early release of the product. However, the project lead has indicated that senior management also wants major delivery of functionality and state-of-the-art usability across additional platforms on the first release.

There is pressure on the schedule as well. Contacts with the potential purchasers of the software have indicated that several customers could use the product as early as nine months from today.

Potential new technologies applicable to the product include wireless e-books and e-appliances that are able to download and hold large amounts of information and which allow impressive user interaction.

The project lead has come to you with the following requests:

1. Prepare a short briefing for senior management about how requirements for the project are to be collected, documented, approved, prioritized,

and scheduled into the work plan for the project. As usual, the briefing is tomorrow and you have about 30 minutes to prepare. The project manager emphasizes the importance of schedule and correctness.

2. Prepare and document the most important features of the product as you perceive them up to this point. Prioritize and stage the features for implementation purposes. Do this in no more than one hour.

3. Prepare and document requirements for product UI, integration, information, graphics, usability, response time, and reliability. Describe how you will ensure that the product is going to be competitive as well as better than current and anticipated methods when the product deploys. Do this in no more than 30 minutes.

4. Based upon the requirements collected so far, revisit the likely content and schedule for the initial release of the product. Continue to assume a web-based delivery in no more than nine months from today. Consider what skills are required to deliver the product and when these skills are needed.

5. Prepare your answers to the action items given to you by senior management. You have one hour to prepare this information.

The requirements are the basis for future work on the product.

Be sure to conduct an Internet search to locate information related to requirements gathering techniques, as well as requirements related to your project.

You have about four hours to work on the request.

Any questions?

References

Schneider, G., and Winters, J., *Applying Use Cases: A Practical Guide*, Addison-Wesley: New York, 2001.

Torres, R.J., "User Interface Requirements," Westlake Reflections, Apr. 1992.

Wiegers, K., *Software Requirements*, Microsoft Press: Redmond, WA, 1999.

Users, Their Work Environment, and Tasks

One of the major causes of product failure is lack of user involvement. Perhaps there is a similarly important corollary to lack of user involvement—lack of understanding of the real user(s) of a product, environment(s) of usage, and the usage task(s). Some products have very well-defined user sets with very well-defined environments and tasks. Other products have many diverse sets of users with major differences in environments and tasks. Regardless of whether a UC product team faces a homogeneous or heterogeneous set of users, environments, and tasks, there is essential information to obtain.

The essential information about users, environments, and tasks helps establish a framework for a design direction for a product's UI and usability. There are a few very useful techniques applicable to gathering the essential user, environment, and task information.

Along with UI and usability requirements, the critical information about users, environments, and tasks makes it easier for a development team to hit the mark on what real users want or need in a product. The information about users and what they will be doing is critical for the appropriate selection of UI techniques and design approaches for an overall application style.

The following topics are discussed in this chapter:

- Understanding a product's users, work, and environment
- Methods
- Example questions
- Communicating the analysis
- Users, tasks, and environments for the project

Understanding a Product's Users, Work, and Environment

As in any relationship, an individual brings a set of characteristics, skills, and attitudes to a computer and its software. Examples of salient aspects of a user relative to work on a computer and its software include:

- Prior knowledge and experience with the computer hardware and software being used
- Prior knowledge and experience with the task domain being supported
- Physical and personality characteristics
- Characteristics of the physical and social work environment

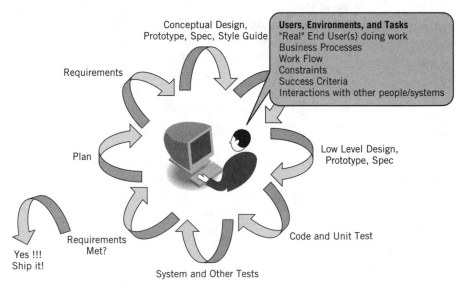

FIGURE 10.1
Planning for user-centered product development.

Even if you were designing software for a single user in a single environment, it is a major challenge to address all factors satisfactorily. Because of the enormous variability in individual characteristics, designing for a larger collection of users within a single environment is an even more daunting task.

> **Rule of Thumb**: You can't please everyone. A software product and its UI cannot be all things to all users.

A UC product team strives to design and develop a system that meets requirements with sufficient scope and flexibility to accommodate business needs, the basic needs of any individual user, known requirements, and do all that with acceptable user attitudes. To that end, a UC product team must understand the intended set of users, the environments in which users are intended to work with the system, and the work that users are intended to perform with the system.

Contrasting Examples.

It is easy to assume that most audiences are uniform in skills and attitudes. It is also very easy to assume what users want in a product. So, it is good to explore some examples to demonstrate contrasts.

1. Consider the characteristics of a young population in the United States, age group of pre-school through kindergarten. Consider key aspects of such an audience that have implications on a design of a simple computer game to run on a conventional PC that is located on school premises. Consider the characteristics of a young population that is worldwide and the implications on design of the same computer game.

2. Consider the characteristics of an older population, living in an assisted living or nursing home environment. Consider the key aspects of such an audience that have implications on the design of a computer game intended to test a user's visual and auditory acuity.

3. Consider the characteristics of the user groups described in items 1 and 2 for a single application designed for simple PC-based email and telephone communication.

4. Consider the characteristics of an office workforce in the United States, ages 18-65 with a large number of supplemental part-time workers aged 14-17. Consider the key aspects of such an audience that have implications on the design of an office application for a conventional PC.

5. Consider the characteristics of a manufacturing workforce in a worldwide environment, where the age ranges from 10 to 75 and effective

grade level ranges from 4th grade to postgraduate. Different languages are spoken, and various cultural factors come into play.

- Consider the key aspects of such an audience that have implications on the design of an application that provides assembly instruction on the manufacturing floor as well as quality monitoring on the manufacturing floor and management offices.

- Consider further if the application runs on a conventional PC and specialized hardware, and where the assembled product competes in a highly price sensitive market and the assembly process is highly sensitive to work steps.

Rule of Thumb: Avoid making too many assumptions about any groups of users and the physical and social conditions under which work is performed.

Implications.

By contrasting these user groups, their environments, and tasks, it is easy to speculate that the more homogeneous the users and working environment, the better defined implications are to a design. The more diverse and general the audience and environments, the more problematic the implications on a design.

Rule of Thumb: The more general an audience, environment, and tasks that an application must support, the more important it is to plan for flexibility and customization features in a product.

The implications of diversity in tasks and environments are similar (i.e., larger differences have bigger implications on a design). However, forewarned is forearmed. Planning on flexibility and customization in a product is critical even in productivity-oriented software. Examples of design options that may be required instead of optional include:

- Novice, casual, and expert interfaces
- Progressive disclosure of features
- Multiple performance support techniques
- Features for selection of user preferences
- Multiple views

In other words, more work is required to support more diverse audiences with diverse tasks, especially if there are stringent requirements for UI, usability, and other factors. This is counter to what is experienced in web-based software, which is basically a one-size-fits-all approach.

General User Characteristics

End users are not monolithic collections with the same characteristics. Each user is an individual with uniqueness in skills, attitudes, and knowledge about a job and computer hardware and software. In addition, each user has unique preferences, likes, and dislikes. Prior to design, knowledge of the variability in user skills, attitudes, and knowledge for the target market being served is obtained.

For example, aside from education and years on the job, critical information about users includes the statistical distributions for:

- Knowledge and experience with computer systems and software, computer software applications, and the domain that is being supported
- Attitudes toward the job, business procedures, and the tasks performed
- Attitudes toward supporting computer hardware and software
- Physical and personality characteristics
- Characteristics of the social and physical work environment

However, there are even more factors to consider when understanding a user relative to software being provided:

- Reading level and education
- Primary language
- Typing skill and pointer usage skill
- Vision, hearing, speech, and other physical limitations relative to use of computer hardware devices
- Age and gender
- Learning preference and style
- Perceived skill and comfort level with computer hardware and software
- Motivation

It is very good to know distributions for these factors, as no one single number or range is sufficient to characterize a heterogeneous collection of users. For example, experience level in a work force may vary from beginner to expert, and usage of a system may vary from infrequent to frequent. If the vast majority of users are beginners who use the system infrequently, a UC product team may need to formulate a beginner-oriented design. If the users are distributed normally from beginner to expert and the system is to be used frequently, a more flexible design is likely required.

Physical Environment Descriptions

As with users, there are certain features that characterize a working environment in terms of physical factors. Examples of physical factors include a user's physical workspace, layout of a work area for an organization, lighting, noise, distractions, and other physical ergonomic elements that influence how a user interacts with a computer system and its software. A UC product team must understand and deal with any physical factors that might impact achieving usability and UI goals. For example:

- A factory worker may use an application while standing in a noisy environment
- An office worker may use the same software at a desk or in a mobile environment

Current and future work environments are quite varied. Work is performed in centralized work locations on company premises, in mobile environments, and at home environments. Support of user tasks is likely to be quite different in each environment. For example, someone working in an office may have the benefit of a high-speed LAN while someone working remotely may have only a relatively low-speed modem. Even within a single business environment, the technology supporting users is usually not uniform. The key variables must be accounted for and understood.

Social Environment Descriptions.   Several features characterize a working environment in terms of social factors. Examples include proximity to others, privacy, task interruption, and work that involves others. A UC product team must understand and deal with any social factors that might impact achieving usability and UI goals. For example:

- A customer service representative (CSR) may need to interact with an external client using a telephone headset in an environment where privacy is needed but not possible.
- Another CSR may need to interact with one or more associates while placing the customer on hold at least once.

The amount of change in business processes and computer systems is another major factor to understand and consider during design. The degree to which users are comfortable with change is important to understand as well. However, there are other factors like:

- Business pressures and demands
- Pressures from management, supervisors, associates, and customers
- Group dynamics and organizational behavior

- Expected work hours
- Task interruptions
- Tone of the overall work environment, motivators, and measures of success

Again, it is good to establish a distribution of answers for workers, supervisors, and managers for these factors.

Task Descriptions

The next critical input to obtain is specific knowledge of work performed by a user or group of users. End-user tasks require good descriptions, together with the frequency distribution. For example, tasks can be described and categorized via an 80/20 rule. Again, around 20 percent of tasks are performed 80 percent of the time and are those around which a system is optimized for end-user productivity and satisfaction. Other categorization schemes can be used to assess and contrast the importance of tasks.

In addition to knowing what tasks users perform, the procedures followed by end users in completing their work tasks must be known. Related to procedures are end-user protocols. Protocols are social practices and conventions that influence how work is performed. Software UIs and systems must be responsive to protocols, as well as procedures and tasks.

A task has discrete starting and ending points. However, some tasks are:

- Relatively short in duration (seconds or minutes), while others are relatively long (months or years)
- Very structured, while others are unstructured or ad hoc in nature
- Deterministic and linear, while others are unpredictable in results
- Performed by a single person, while others are completed by a series of people
- Ongoing, while others occur seasonally

The list of differences in tasks is quite large. Regardless of the situation, knowledge of the task is essential. Examples of other factors that characterize a task include:

- Goals, frequency, importance, constraints, and cost
- Beginning and completion criteria
- Preparation, work aids, and tools
- Dependencies on user knowledge and skill
- Inputs, outputs, and sources of information

- Degree of risk and resulting impact on users, customers, or a business
- Degree of being error-prone and resulting impact on users, customers, or a business
- Order of work steps
- Interactions with other individuals or any legacy systems
- Degree of satisfaction

Performing a complete analysis of a user's tasks is a very large and costly effort that most organizations are unwilling to perform. However, a critical mass of essential knowledge is required to build the right tools for performing tasks that meet requirements.

> **Rule of Thumb**: The cost of performing an analysis of a product's users, physical environment, social environment, and tasks is small in comparison to the total cost of total task time spent doing the work.

Methods

There are several techniques available to collect information about users, the work environment, and tasks. None of these methods are necessarily sophisticated or costly. Some might argue that these are just common sense, but the exercising of such common sense is not evident across the industry today. However, the right information is obtainable if the methods are applied with diligence.

Use of these methods confirms or corrects intuitions of known information. In addition, the methods invariably uncover potential things that are candidates for process improvement or software features. Supervisors or users forget about, or are insensitive to these things for a variety of reasons. For example:

- Users in certain jobs may keep informal written notes or logs to track work or interactions with clients, and this may not be documented in any business process. A user's informal task may be to count the number of interactions per day or to refer to notes about prior interactions with a client.
- A user may search the notes and logs often and update them with supplemental information over time.
- A software work aid may augment and make more efficient this informal aspect of a task that is not documented anywhere.

Rule of Thumb: A major goal of the analysis is to see what's going on and to determine how software can really help.

Participatory Methods.

Ask the UC team members and participating users to perform a self-assessment of skills, knowledge, and experience. An effective technique is to use a questionnaire that solicits answers to the key questions.

A supplemental technique is to ask UC team members and participating users to "guesstimate" the likely answer for the entire user set being represented. The real answers obtained using other techniques help to get everyone on the same page about actual user skills, knowledge, and work performed.

Observation Method.

Along with surveys, a very useful technique is for a UC product team to observe several real users in a variety of roles doing real work. Observations supplement what questionnaires reveal about users, the environment, and tasks. In many environments, it is useful and practical to unobtrusively observe users working. In addition, a questionnaire to calibrate a user's self-assessment, with observations of that user, is handy.

Rule of Thumb: Observe real users doing real work very early in the project.

In practice, members of a UC product team will view a user on their own versus viewing a user as a team. A data collection protocol and form are constructed to capture the essence of a user's real interaction with a system for specific tasks, as well as the overall work environment. A data collection protocol describes how an observer is to interact with users in a structured and consistent manner and what information to gather. A data collection form is used to obtain information in a consistent and structured manner.

Among other things, information to record during observations includes:

- Task name, description, and duration
- Perceived user skill level and role
- Actual user work steps including use of systems, printers, fax machines, and copiers
- System features, screens, and supplemental work aids used
- Information needs
- Difficulties with the current processes and system and errors performed
- Current system performance and reliability
- Current satisfaction

- Follow-up questions
- Answers to questions to better understand task frequency, perceived difficulty, and what was done and why
- Sample input, screen captures, and interim and final work products

The observed tasks serve as design points or test cases and validate earlier assumptions about user needs. As appropriate, the task is repeatable during design and in test environments to verify that real improvement is being achieved, problems are being solved, and requirements are being met.

Survey Method.   Well-constructed and objective questionnaires are excellent tools for gathering the essential information from a large number of users. Along with specific questions that are answered on a discrete and quantified scale, some open-ended questions are provided to solicit user suggestions about potential improvements in software, systems, and procedures. Such a questionnaire can be answered in 15 minutes or less and distributed in hardcopy or electronic format.

General guidelines for selecting and structuring a meaningful questionnaire include:

- Ask only questions to which answers are not known and to which answers are needed
- Ask questions that are not leading or biased
- Ask questions in a clear, simple, and easy to read manner
- Ask questions in a way that provides a numeric answer

When it is impractical or too costly to distribute a questionnaire to an entire user community, a statistical sample of users is used. However, the sample must be sufficient to cover all significant groups of users and roles.

> **Rule of Thumb**: Along with real users, ask others in the task mix or environment (supervisors and real customers) to answer the questionnaire.

The questionnaires are analyzed, distributions constructed, and an interpretive report distributed to the UC product team and other appropriate individuals.

Individual Interview Method.   Another useful technique is an informal interview with a real user. In some cases, real work is conducted as a user talks about what is being done and why. Alternatively, a user may perform the task first and then explain it. In other cases, an interview during real work is not possible. An alternate approach is to record the client interaction and then follow-up with the user about what happened and why. As with an observation approach, a data collection protocol and form is constructed to ensure a structured manner to obtain information in a consistent manner.

Team Interview Method.   Another useful technique is a formal or informal interview with a team or set of real users. In most cases, real work is not conducted during team interviews. However, differences in management methods, business rules, constraints, and other style or preference oriented approaches to work may surface during interviews. Of course, a UC product team must account for this variability in a product.

Other Sources of Information.   Along with the participating users, many major organizations have human resource (HR) or training departments with answers to key questions. Some questions such as those about age or gender may be perceived as inappropriate in sensitive environments.

> **Rule of Thumb**: There is no substitute for the real thing!

Industry sources are also a good place to obtain benchmarking type of information. However, other sources only supplement information gathered directly from users.

Analysis and Results.   All members of a UC product team participate in the data gathering as individuals. The team works together on the sharing of individual results and analysis. Individual questionnaires and observation forms are gathered and results are summarized during team meetings. A common understanding of users, their environments, and tasks is achieved.

The key deliverable from the summary analysis includes:

- Distributions for user skills
- A salient description of the social and physical environment
- Descriptions and distributions for tasks

Tasks, work steps, and work products are provided independent of current systems and in end user and business terms. For example, a common and frequent task is to write a monthly status report which consists of steps like gather data, contact associates, review calendar, write draft, print and edit draft, and finally distribute and file report. How a task relates to current systems is important to know since many techniques should carry over to a new system. However, the essential user task must be described crisply. Potential interaction with a future system is described in use cases, which are updated as the analysis of users, tasks, environments, and requirements is completed.

> **Rule of Thumb**: Follow up observations and interviews with actual hands-on users of current systems and walk through perceived workflows and processes.

Example Questions

There is a lot of information to obtain. However, it may need to be gathered and refined in stages over the course of a project. It is easy to formulate over 50 questions when constructing questionnaires or trying to understand users, environments, and tasks. There are probably over 100 questions to be answered. The following are some examples of questions to ask users about themselves, their environment, and their work.

Questions About Users.   Here are three questions to answer about users.

How would you rate your computer experience?

Novice			Intermediate			Expert
1	2	3	4	5	6	7

How long have you used computers? _____ years

How would you rate your experience with your current system?

Novice			Intermediate			Expert
1	2	3	4	5	6	7

Questions About the Current Systems.   Here are three questions to answer about systems used, frequency, and user attitudes to these systems.

What hardware do you use and how often? (Hourly, Daily, Weekly, Rarely, Never)

Desktop System_____   Laptop_____   Handheld_____   Other _____

What operating system do you use? How often? (Hourly, Daily, Weekly, Rarely, Never)

X _____   Y _____   Z_____

What is your satisfaction with your current system?

Very dissatisfied			Neutral			Very satisfied
1	2	3	4	5	6	7

Questions About the Work Environment. Here are three questions to answer about the work environment.

How would you describe your work environment?

Very noisy   Neutral   Quiet

         1   2   3   4   5   6   7

How would you describe the privacy of your work environment?

Not private at all   Neutral   Sufficiently private

         1   2   3   4   5   6   7

What is your satisfaction with your work environment?

Very dissatisfied   Neutral   Very satisfied

         1   2   3   4   5   6   7

Questions About Work. Here are three questions to ask users about work.

How often does this task happen? Hourly___ Daily___ Weekly___ Rarely___ Never___

How difficult is this task?

Very difficult   Neutral   Very easy

         1   2   3   4   5   6   7

What is your satisfaction with how this task is performed?

Very dissatisfied   Neutral   Very satisfied

         1   2   3   4   5   6   7

Open Ended Questions.

What changes to the computer systems would make your job easier or more efficient?

What business process changes would make your job easier or more efficient?

Communicating the Analysis

By the time the initial data gathering is complete, there is a large amount of information to review. Original data collection forms and interview notes and forms are filed in a notebook with the summary documentation. The summary is communicated with all appropriate individuals and teams. It is good to provide feedback to organizations participating in observations and interviews.

> **Rule of Thumb**: Continue building and refining the analysis over time.

The workbook should have sections to describe the environments, work process and flows, users, and individual tasks. Specific scenarios and stories of particular interest are included in the summary.

Results are used to validate use cases and other documents developed during requirements gathering. The need for new system features or enhancements not discovered during requirements gathering is included in the requirements documentation.

Users, Tasks, and Environments for the Project _____

The project lead comes into your office in his usual hurry. The status meetings with senior management continue to go well, and the senior managers continue to grow in awareness of user-centered design. As a result, there is growing concern as the requirements for the product continue to grow and the word about the conference companion gets out to other potential customers. In particular, there is growing awareness of the diversity of the audience that is to use the product.

Other conferences have been approached about the product, and the attendees are not necessarily users of the originally intended computer hardware and software. For example, new major conferences and events that require conference-scheduling support include the State Fair of Texas, Electrical Workers of America, American Medical Association, Human Factors Association, and American Association of Retired People (AARP). There is even an inquiry from a major European air show being held in a country with major UI standards that have not been reviewed. Note that two of these new events include a large number of outside activities.

Senior management has requested a presentation to elaborate on the users, environments, and tasks that the product will support. In addition, although the same basic tasks seem to apply across the various conferences and potential users, senior management wants to validate the tasks and product implications given the various user groups. In addition, senior management needs a briefing on one other user group—namely, users who create schedules of events and administer the system.

The project lead says that you have a little bit more time to work on this—the next meeting of senior managers is the day after tomorrow. However, due to other commitments, you have about two hours to describe the

- likely user groups
- tasks
- environments
- implications to the product

In addition, the project lead acknowledges that you haven't had much time to work on getting the user and task information. As part of the presentation, he wants you to discuss how the more detailed information is to be obtained, validated, and reviewed with senior management. Be sure to include a discussion of how you intend to validate with real users in the task environment. You'll have about 15 minutes to present all this information.

Again, conduct a web-based search for information to guide your analysis and evaluation of users, tasks, and environments.

Any questions?

References

Beyer, H., Holtzblatt, K., *Contextual Design*, Morgan-Kauffman: San Francisco, 1998.

Mayhew, D., *Software User Interface Design*, Prentice-Hall: Englewood Cliffs, NJ, 1992.

Nielsen, J., "The Usability Engineering Life Cycle," *Computer Magazine*, Mar. 1992.

Conceptual Design and Architecture

11

All tasks that are related to product UI and usability design and development are extremely important. The first specific design task is conceptual and intended to get the right project design fundamentals in place. In many regards, a conceptual design of a UI is its architecture. Progressive layers of design add increasing definition and detail to appearance, behavior, information, and user interaction during later project stages.

All design steps are equally important. Conceptual design, which deals with conceptual models, UI style, and navigational structures, does not go into the appearance, behavior, interaction, and feature details of a product. A good first step is essential to improve chances of a minimalist and less painful journey to achieve project objectives for a project's UI, usability, consistency, information, response time, reliability, and other factors.

On the up side, alternative conceptual designs are formulated, evaluated, and iterated very quickly and inexpensively—at a conceptual level. Techniques for generating alternatives are extremely important, as are those for rapid prototyping, evaluation, and iteration. The most promising design paths are tested, selected, and refined in later stages of product development. Good decision making—early and late—is essential to success.

On the down side, a conceptual design defect not noted during the early design stage of development is propagated to the next stage and potentially affects many screens, interactions, user assistance, code, training, testing, schedule, and cost. As with other software defects, the cost of repair becomes higher the longer an error remains undetected.

The following topics are discussed in this chapter:

- Vision setting
- Distributing the components of work
- The intended user's model
- UI architecture—a very high-level design
- Conceptual design for the project

Although a style guide is a deliverable of a conceptual design milestone, it is discussed in the next chapter of the text.

A Conceptual Design (see Figure 11.1) is literally a preliminary sketch, outline, and blueprint showing the main functional, UI, visual, informational, or other features of a product's design. It is a potential view of what the

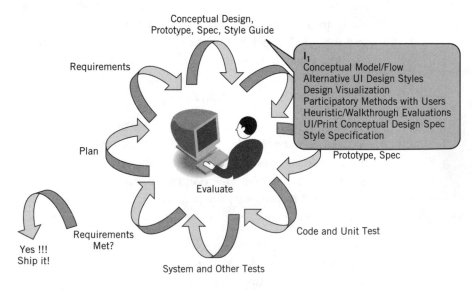

FIGURE 11.1
Conceptual design.

intended product is—a representation of the hopes and dreams of business sponsors and a UC product team.

Using a classical definition, architecture identifies a system's components, distributes system features to the various components, and defines the interfaces between the system components. With a user in interaction with a system, UI architecture is literally the distribution of work between a system and a user and a UI between them.

> **Rule of Thumb**: Based upon analysis of users, requirements, tasks, and business needs, an underlying visual and interaction design motif, organizing principles and structure, and behavioral patterns of the software are made explicit and visible.

The components of a conceptual design include

- General UI style
- Application UI style
- End user entities and artifacts
- Intended user's model
- Organization, structure, flow, and relationships among end user entities
- Key principles of operation

The scope of conceptual design deliverables is not limited to UI only. Members of a user-centered product team are on the hook for delivery of a conceptual design for their respective area of responsibility and accountability. For example,

- A team member responsible for training delivers a conceptual design and a prototype of the preusage materials (training, performance support, and work aids), as well as in-use help, just-in-time (JIT) training, and work aids.
- A team member responsible for usability evaluation delivers heuristic and user-based assessments of a conceptual design relative to requirements.
- A team member responsible for marketing oriented information delivers a conceptual design and prototype material.

All end user deliverables are subjected to the same design, prototyping, evaluation, and iteration as a UI component. Usability and effectiveness of all product deliverables is essential.

Vision Setting

The most important aspect of a conceptual design is its potential for vision setting. A conceptual design sets the stage for a product's look and feel, as well as for identifying what is designed and constructed under the covers to support the vision. The vision sets the tone for how a product hangs together and flows in support of user tasks:

- Conceptual design options are visualized in a specification and prototype
- Participatory methods are utilized to obtain end user input
- Usability evaluation techniques are employed to predict promising design paths

The most promising design path is selected and documented in a conceptual design specification. The intended UI style is described as well.

Preliminary Analysis.   A user-centered product team understands and analyzes user requirements, profiles, tasks, and environments. Existing user training, artifacts, work aids, documentation, and legacy software are analyzed as well.

Participatory Methods.   Participatory methods are extremely valuable in gaining insight from users about what is done, how it's done, and why. Involve users in conceptualizing the current tasks and how a system could improve tasks, visualizing solutions, and brainstorming alternative solutions.

> **Rule of Thumb**: Begin formulating a conceptual design as quickly as possible (once a critical mass of prerequisite information is available).

Design Iteration 1 (I_1).   For all intents, conceptual design is the first of many design iterations. Although labeled I_1, a UC product team performs many iterations rapidly during this design phase. Iterations within conceptual design are labeled I_{11}, I_{12}, and so forth.

Just as there are more ways than one to skin a cat, there are numerous ways to skin a UI. However, at some point, a user-centered product team decides which design path to follow based upon users. I_1 is the timeframe to make a decision.

Initial iteration takes place in the:

- Formulation of many design options
- Depiction of each design option

- Evaluation of each option relative to requirements, environments, and users
- Selection of promising options and discarding those that are undesirable
- Repetition, if appropriate, until requirements are met

A primary goal of a first iteration is to select the best design options for further consideration and refinement (see Figure 11.2). The best case for I_1 is to identify a single design option to carry forward and explore in more detail. Usually, there is insufficient time or resources to explore multiple design options during subsequent phases of design, which require more detailed design, prototype, evaluation, and iteration work.

Many times there are other design options that have promise. These are held back as alternate design paths or customization features if the primary path proves problematic as design is clarified and expanded. Typically other options present themselves in an opportunistic fashion later.

> **Rule of Thumb**: Evaluate many design options during conceptual design, but pick the one that has the most promise for achieving goals and meeting user needs to move into high-level design.

Alternative Usage of Basic UI Features

A user-centered product team also explores alternative uses of the basic UI styles to be employed and presents UI appearance and behavioral models of user interaction. Examples of alternative forms for use of basic GUI features include selection of options to have available to users and which are avail-

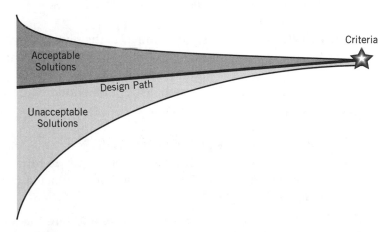

FIGURE 11.2
Narrowing acceptable options during design.

able by default (e.g., Menu Bar (on), Toolbar (on and displayed below the Menu Bar), and Toolbar icons (large with text)). There are myriad features and options to work with for GUIs, WUIs, and HUIs.

Alternative Application UI Styles

A user-centered product team formulates and visualizes design models for an application software user interface that supports five to seven high-impact tasks. These tasks easily represent the 20 percent of a design that has 80 percent of usage, impact, and value. Examples of alternative application UI styles include representations of user software artifacts in at least three forms:

- Electronic
- Physical
- Visual

Electronic Style.   An electronic style is conceptually similar to an electronic spreadsheet or document. These types of applications depict computer entities to users without physical bounds. An example is a computerized directory listing without pages (as opposed to an address book).

Physical Style.   A physical style presents computer entities using concepts derived from appearance in a real world but within the constraints of UI artifacts like windows. An example is an indexed address book with pages displayed in a GUI window.

Visual Style.   A visual style is similar to the physical style with one step forward—GUI window dressing is removed. A physical entity is available for end-user interaction without window features. The visual entity appears as it does in the real world, though it supports windowing features for closing and menus for access of commands.

Other Styles.   Another UI style to consider is a game-oriented approach which turns a problem on its head and seeks a way to turn a computer artifact into a computer game. For example, Find Francine might serve as a game model for an address book.

An architectural style for organizing features and information for a UI is an object (or OO) style. Product features are represented as objects, classes of objects, a class hierarchy, actions, and the properties of each. The style is not very distinct from a physical style except that an underlying OO programming language may be involved. Examples of objects include an address book and a directory, while an example of an action is Add a Person.

Another architectural style is a procedural style. Product features are represented as tasks from which a user makes choices and provides further information. An example is a wizard.

Observation.   In many ways, these styles are complementary and are often integrated in interesting ways (e.g., a procedural electronic task flow). Each provides a basis for selection of a basic style for an application's UI. There are other approaches that are appropriate to apply to a design problem in a meaningful or idea-generating manner.

Merging the Permutations and Combinations.   A UC product team must converge many variations in style. Approaches to generation of design alternatives vary from team brainstorming to individual design and subsequent team integration of ideas. Regardless of approach, idea generation is essential. A UC product team agrees on how to pursue this effort and then goes for it.

> **Rule of Thumb**: At a minimum, create three design alternatives using variations of UI style and application UI style—a conventional design, a really far-out design that pushes the limits, and a design somewhere in between (see Figure 11.3).

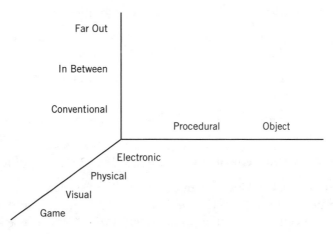

FIGURE 11.3
Dimensions of conceptual design.

A conventional design is representative of the current state of the art as reflected in current popular products. As with engineering tasks, a conventional design is a known commodity in terms of its known technology, techniques, and user acceptance.

A far-out design includes features that are blue sky, wish lists, or revolutionary. Far-out features may quantitatively or qualitatively improve, automate, or augment portions of user tasks or perceptions. A far-out design may be very difficult or costly to implement. A range of options derived from such a design helps determine limits of a likely design and consequent implementation challenges.

An in-between design pushes the envelope, is somewhat known in terms of design and implementation, and is a quantitative and/or qualitative step forward. If a project is evolutionary, an in-between design may be what is needed. A far-out design is used as a strategic beacon if usability results validate the direction.

Distributing the Components of Work

A major task associated with conceptual design is establishing what a user does and what a system does. The outcome of this task is determined by:

- Tasks to be performed
- Users performing tasks
- Strengths and limitations of user capabilities
- Strengths and limitations of the hardware, system, UI tools, application, and interaction styles relative to the tasks
- Likely software features that improve, augment, or automate portions of a user's tasks
- Likely path of least resistance to achieve schedule and cost within constraints
- Likely achievement of requirements for UI and usability

In general, a UC product team distributes appropriate task components to a system and a user. A system receives all work that is heavy lifting for users and reasonable for a system to do, while a user receives work that is a challenge for computer software. This is balanced by what is achievable by a development team.

An Intended User's Model

A user's perception of how a system works is called a user's model (see Figure 11.4). It is a user's view of what appears to happen, and it is a common property of people and how they learn and predict the behavior of software. An important aspect of a conceptual design task is leveraging this feature of user learning and behavior for intentional formulation of a UI to evoke a user's model that matches a design's intent.

Sometimes called a designer's model, an intended user's model is a user-centered product team's version of conceptual knowledge that a user must acquire in order to successfully learn and use a system. The goal of the team is to explicitly and consciously design and implement an intended user's model that elicits an appropriate user's model from an end user. An intended user's model conveys what is and is not supported in a product, as well as how a user interacts with a system. The degree to which the models match directly influences learning and ease of use.

Components.   Components of an intended user's model include:

- Concepts. General notions or ideas, constructs, or themes that represent a design

- Features. Capabilities provided by the functionality and UI. An example of a functional capability is Add a Person to an address book. An

FIGURE 11.4
Intended user's model.

example of a UI capability integrated with functionality is Drag a Person from an address book to a calendar event.

- Analogies and metaphors. Similarities between like features or concepts not literally related—both of which invite comparison.
- System and user objects. A representation of computer and user objects for a user. For example, a system object includes such entities as a desktop while a user object includes items such as a document.
- Appearance. The visual or graphic representation of an object or action on a display contributes conceptual information about the nature of the entity.
- Behavior, flows, and relationships. Explicit behavior of an entity during user interaction is an important conceptual component. Relationships between entities and availability of actions for like objects also provide important conceptual reinforcement.
- Interactions. Associated with each entity is the protocol that a user must follow in order to interact with it.

Criteria for Success.   The goal of a user-centered product team is to formulate a model that meets several criteria:

- User oriented. An intended user's model is described in end-user terms and visuals. Computer-oriented terms and concepts are avoided or are expressed in a user-oriented manner.
- Natural. An intended user's model is an abstraction and reflection of a user's environment. Objects, actions, and interaction styles are familiar and comfortable to end users.
- Big picture view. A high-level overview of a system is provided by an intended user's model. Critical OO and UI features of a system are described via an intended user's model.
- Integrated. The models for components (object, actions, widgets, etc.) work well when together. Classes of objects and actions, together with class hierarchy and inheritance structures, form an integral and complementary whole.
- Consistent. The components of an intended user's model are consistent with an intended system level model and with each other. Similarly, system components are consistent with a user's environment and needs.
- Simple. While sufficiently comprehensive to describe what a user must know for proper interaction with the system, an intended user's model is simple and concise. Complex and convoluted interactions and rela-

tionships among system entities do not exist or are no worse than real-world equivalents.

- Productive. Implementation of a design based upon an intended user's model maps to what users want to do. Artificial or extra work steps are not added, while automation and augmentation of user tasks is achieved.

- Intuitive. A user is able to figure out easily how to carry out unknown or infrequent tasks. In the worst case, a user must be told only once about how to perform a task.

Types of Intended User's Models. Several candidate approaches can serve as starting points for intended user models. Some of the more frequent models seen in software UIs have been discussed previously, namely electronic, physical, visual, and game. Two other options—search-based models and hybrids—are combinations of the various styles. Figure 11.5 depicts three models for addressing information: a search-based model, a directory of address books, and a more physical model that allows direct entry of information at all levels.

Design Principles for an Intended User's Model. Several principles and guidelines influence how an intended user's model is formulated.

- Provide a single system level model. One overriding intended user's model for a system reflects the key concepts and analogies that a team

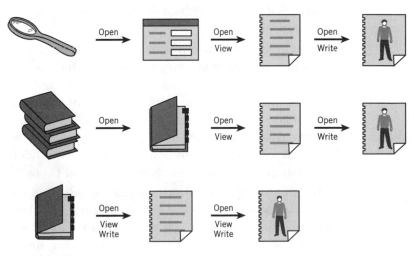

FIGURE 11.5
Alternative models for an address book.

wants a user to perceive for an entire system. A system level model provides an integrating framework for models of components within the system.

- Model a user's environment. Build an intended user's model that is natural and obvious to the target audience of the system. An intended user's model is consistent with the physical environment and experiences of users. Users transfer knowledge from the environment to a system by drawing on what they have learned.

- Complement a user's model for performing work. A user has models for performing work. A UC product team understands a user's model of how work and tasks are performed. Work products, processes, data, information, and knowledge are understood and modeled. Job-related concepts, objects, and actions complement a user's model of a system. Based upon an initial intended user's model, assume a user's view of a proposed design. Extend and enhance initial models to support automation and augmentation of user tasks, but preserve the natural features of a user's environment.

- Represent the system being developed. An intended user's model matches the reality of a system provided. It is an entrée into a system and represents a system for what it is and what it is not. An intended user's model facilitates initial user learning as well as complements functional and UI extensions beyond any metaphors provided by a UC product team. When designed properly, an intended user's model facilitates user learning and the exploitation of a system beyond initial and casual use, and keeps a user from viewing a system with conceptual blinders.

- Provide environment-consistent dialog and presentation. An intended user's model includes the manner in which a user interacts with objects on a system (i.e., interaction styles and display techniques employed). Environment-consistent presentation styles include use of visual and graphic analogs of objects and interactions. A UC product team strives to provide techniques that easily map to interaction and appearance in a user's environment. Conceptual fidelity between computerized and physical objects is an important consideration.

- Provide a flexible model. An intended user's model is flexible enough to allow for system growth and extension. Careful thought is given to the full capability that a system provides, and the model is chosen accordingly for each major component being designed. Models for actions are defined as well as models for objects. Visualizations for essential system features are formulated to the point where user capabilities, dialogs, and interaction paradigms are understood. Refinements may require developing models for primitives of objects, actions, and interactions.

- Iterate on a model. Invariably a first design is not necessarily the best to move forward with. Discuss an intended model with users to verify appropriateness. As with other design components, there are many possible options. Identify many within project constraints and select at least three alternatives to explore in more detail based upon user feedback. Simple and natural models are formulated—even for abstract user tasks. The challenge for a user-centered product team is to formulate a model that works for intended users.

- Follow through. Once an intended user's model is chosen, it is adhered to rigorously in all aspects of design and construction. Communicate an intended user's model to all product personnel. The concepts constitute fundamental principles that influence other aspects of system and object design and implementation. A shared model facilitates decisions made by a larger team. Training strategies to teach shared models are extended into an end user's social environment.

Rule of Thumb: You are working on an intended user's model when you describe a system entity *like* something else.

UI Architecture—A Very High-Level Design _____

All conceptual UI information is integrated to form a conceptual design, which includes a high-level specification, an early visualization of product materials, and evaluation materials.

Conceptual Flow.   The organizational hierarchy of windows/pages/screens for a software application is depicted visually. This is a high-level structure of UI software (i.e., how it is organized from a user's view). Conceptual flows are literally trees of screens traversed during task completion. A user must access one or more screens in a tree to input data, make selections, and review results of requests made to the software. Potentially, several flow styles are possible.

Rule of Thumb: Depict a screen hierarchy of a UI that includes access from the desktop and any action dialogs.

Conceptual Screens.   Some screens are unique within an application, and others are generic and offer design patterns or reusable components. An example of a generic screen is an object list, while an example of a specific screen is a layout for a business object.

> **Rule of Thumb**: Identify generic and specific screens and any unique types of widgets that require development.

Conceptual Visualization.
Key screens and behaviors are instantiated in a conceptual design prototype. Graphics, concepts, UI style, graphic style, and interactions are represented. The whole idea is to get a somewhat realistic design instantiation in front of real users for hands-on feedback.

> **Rule of Thumb**: Beware of visualizations that are too pretty, too fancy, or interactions that are too smooth. They may be too far out with respect to the implementation tools and custom widgets anticipated for availability within product constraints. For example, early visualization prototypes may include really neat techniques that are quick to do in a limited and prototypical manner by highly motivated people. Sometimes these techniques are costly and time consuming to implement consistently across large products.

Principles of Operation.
The basic and fundamental rules of software operation are described. Implicit behavior and expectations are made explicit. Some typical expectations of software include:

- Direct entry on all screens. An example is updating a record of an address book without having to perform a specific request to edit, waiting for a screen to display, providing input on an edit screen, selecting OK, and waiting to regain control with or without seeing the change automatically reflected.

- Perfect save. For example, remember what is input by a user without having to deal with a specific command to save or a dialog that asks Would you like to save?

- Window memory. For example, remember the last size, position, and view of a window that has been adjusted by a user.

Design Evaluation.
Heuristic reviews, demonstrations, walkthroughs, usability tests, and frequent reviews using participatory methods are good, as are desk check activities. Evaluation of the design with users, tasks, requirements, competition, and benchmarks is always good. Development inspection techniques are employed to validate the feasibility of implementation with the whole team.

Design Iteration.   When requirements are not met or the schedule allows, perform an iteration of the designs, visualize, and evaluate.

Make the Call.   Based upon the results of the design evaluation and how well requirements are met, a user-centered product team picks a design direction. Many times, it may be difficult to choose between the last two competing designs. Only one design is going to be explored in depth and implemented. During serious product development, decisiveness is needed to meet requirements within constraints.

> **Rule of Thumb**: Make a decision, but always have a fall back plan and design.

Documentation.   Two forms of documentation are important during a design process. Informal documentation is recorded in a design notebook. A formal document for recording and acting upon a design is a conceptual design specification.

A design notebook is a record of ideas, options, questions, and decisions made by a user-centered product team during team meetings. It is literally a collection of design notes, summaries of team meetings, alternatives considered, design sketches and ideas, and design questions and answers. It is a chronological record of design decisions that lead to a design direction. It includes design information for competitive or legacy software.

> **Rule of Thumb**: Construct a design notebook as an idea book that includes the best design plays of a product relative to what it is evaluated against or compared to.

A user-centered product team documents an intended design in a conceptual design specification, which is a very high-level design document—minimalist in nature and giving an outline of an intended design. The conceptual design specification is similar to a design overview document of 10-12 pages. The outline provides a subset of a UI specification and includes:

- Design goals, design principles, intended users, and user tasks
- Major product features—function, UI, information
- UI overview including
  - Intended user's model
  - Desktop features and behavior
  - General UI style and application UI styles
  - Graphic and visual style

- UI flow and major screens
- Performance support, training, and help
- Unique widgets
- Customization features
- Consistency and integration considerations
- Response time considerations
- Assessment of usability and participatory evaluation relative to requirements
- Work items and things that typically happen in the next phase of design

Rule of Thumb: A conceptual design specification explicitly documents the key design points. Otherwise, others may reverse engineer and abstract an intended design from an incomplete conceptual prototype. Invariably, key information is missed or wrong.

Design Review and Control.

A conceptual design specification is distributed to a larger audience, including members of the product team responsible for providing infrastructure, non-UI support, or widgets. A conceptual design specification receives normal project management control (e.g., design reviews, updates, and approval).

Once finalized, a conceptual design is placed under change control to manage modifications to the conceptual direction of a project. Although there is work yet to do, there is no need for arbitrary change in design direction. A project plan and schedule is reviewed to verify that schedule and resource constraints are not impacted.

Rule of Thumb: Just because change control is applied doesn't mean that things get slowed down—they just are more organized.

Update the Plan.

There are many details about the project not yet known. However, there are many things that are known and others that can be assumed. The initial requirements, screens, and UI flow give a UC product team a good idea of how much work is required. For example, an estimate of the number of objects, commands, techniques, and screens is available. Complexity of components can also be estimated.

Rule of Thumb: Look at existing complementary applications to be sure that key features and commands are reflected in the conceptual design and architecture.

Closure of Conceptual Design.   Conceptual   design   is   complete when the following are available:

- A conceptual design specification and visualization
- Documented participatory feedback and usability results
- A comparative analysis of legacy, proposed, and competitive task flows and screens
- An updated project plan
- The overall approach is fairly rigorous with measurable footsteps and accountability.

Conceptual Design for the Project

You're in week four of the project. Luckily, the project lead and senior management team are out of the office this week. However, they will be back next week. In the meantime, it's time to begin formulating a conceptual UI design for the project so as to select a design direction. It is to be documented in a UI design overview and style description. A usability assessment is expected, together with participatory feedback and confirmation of implementability.

Completion of this milestone is scheduled for three weeks from today. In the meantime, alternatives must be designed, prototyped, and evaluated. A review with a user group is scheduled for two weeks from today and a usability test the week after. The user-centered product team must begin working quickly and effectively. You have a review with the project lead and your peer for infrastructure design in one week to discuss design alternatives and potential implications to the supporting infrastructure.

With your team and available users, formulate as many options for the conceptual design as can be accomplished in one day. Design and visualize at least three conceptual design alternatives. Be sure to include the general UI style, the application UI, distribution of features between a user and a system, intended user's models, graphics, performance support, training, and help. Document design tradeoffs among the options that are explored.

Along with an intended user's model for the conference companion:

- Provide an intended user's model for one component level object and one action.
- Identify any possible new widgets that require more design and development time. Provide an intended user's model for any new widgets.

- Provide an intended user's model if any design patterns are identified.
- Conduct a design review with at least three potential users.
- Conduct a design feasibility review with at least one potential developer.
- Defer a heuristic review of design options until after usability evaluation techniques are discussed.
- Recommend a design option to pursue during follow-on design activities.
- Begin a design notebook.
- Construct and begin to fill in the outline for documentation of the conceptual design.

Prepare a presentation for the project lead and senior management for their return. Be sure to revisit the project plan, skills, and staffing needs.

Continue your research over the Internet.

You have about 20 hours to work on the conceptual design and its visualization.

Any questions?

References _____

Brooks, F., *The Mythical Man Month*, Addison-Wesley: New York, 1995.

Hix, D., and Hartson, H.R., *Developing User Interfaces*, Wiley and Sons: New York, 1993.

Sibert, J.L., and Foley, J.D., "User Computer Interface Design," *CHI '91 Tutorial*, Conference on Human Factors in Computing Systems, Apr. 1991.

Torres, R.J. and Karat, J., "Designing to Influence a User's Model: Some Practical Guidelines," IBM Technical Report TR 71.0004, Sep. 1991.

Principles, Guidelines, and Style Guides

12

Principles, standards, guidelines, and style guides for usability and UIs are typically not discussed in process documents or accounted for in most product planning. Development of a style guide is usually an afterthought that results in work that is absorbed by a product team and its existing resources and schedule. However, a UI style guide in either documentation or software form is a key deliverable resulting from a conceptual design task.

Many companies spend significant effort developing internal UI style guides to offset deficiencies in generic guidelines, although many of these efforts do not yield desired usability, consistency, or integration across products developed by independent teams. The impact of these problems is increased training cost, lowered productivity, and high frustration by users, designers, developers, and managers.

The following topics are addressed:

- Good things to do—principles, standards, guidelines, and style guides
- Some definitions
- Prescriptive style guides

- Prescriptive solutions for common problems
- Prescriptive style guide development
- A management view
- Useful techniques
- Principles and guidelines for the project

In this chapter we will describe what a UC product team needs to know about the selection and use of design principles and guidelines. Distinctions are made between the notions of principles, guidelines, and standards. A UI style guide is defined and characteristics of an effective style guide and techniques are provided for how to develop one for a product's UI, information, visuals, and other artifacts. Use of UCD-based techniques is recommended when developing a style guide, only the users are the project team.

A prescriptive style guide is described in detail. Techniques are provided for how to develop one from a technical and management perspective. Very specific examples of a prescriptive style are provided for use of GUI, WUI, and HUI elements, functional features, consistency, and integration. Processes are described for prescriptive style guide development, as well as processes for usage by UI developers and managers.

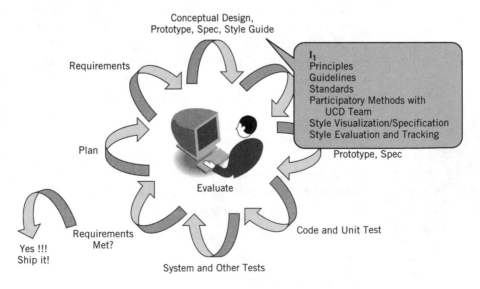

FIGURE 12.1
UI style guide considerations.

Good Things to Do—Principles, Standards, Guidelines, and Style Guides

There are a few UI style guides authored by vendors of OS and/or browser platforms. These platform style guides are generic in that there is no guidance to achieve specific and consistent high level results in any application or suite of applications or heterogeneous collection of applications on a platform. For example:

- There is a tendency to provide guidance for consistency in use of low-level controls and menu structures.

- There is limited guidance for consistency in conceptual and layout models, UI and functional features, and cross-application integration techniques.

- Use of such style guides leads to significant cross-application inconsistency.

Many companies spend significant effort developing internal UI style guides to offset the limitations of generic guidelines. Many of these efforts do not yield desired usability, consistency, or integration across products developed by independent teams. The impact of the problems in generic and internal style guides includes increased training costs, lowered development and usage productivity, and high frustration by users, designers, developers, and managers.

> **Rule of Thumb:** Even with the best of intentions, we tend to be inconsistent (even with ourselves). The goal of a style guide is to help ourselves be consistent.

Some Definitions

Before delving into details, a few definitions are offered so as to reach a common understanding.

Principles. Principles are general design guidance of a qualitative nature that falls in the category of good things to do. An example of a frequently stated design principle is keep it simple. Achieving simplicity is generally in the eye of a software user, developer, evaluator, or other beholder. Assessing actual compliance to a principle is hard to measure directly, subjective, and a matter of degree. With minimal effort, it is very easy to create a very long list of principles that is very difficult to use.

> **Rule of Thumb**: Select no more than 10 significant principles, then create measurable guidelines to make them operational and usable.

Aside from simple, principles mentioned earlier include aesthetic, productive, and customizable.

Guidelines.   A guideline is a design rule that is good to implement and easy to measure in terms of compliance. An example: "Use red (RGB 255, 0, 0) for the color of warning message text, which is displayed on a white background."

This guideline is easy to measure directly, objective, and specific. In many style guides, guidelines are written as rules while others are written as recommendations.

> **Rule of Thumb**: Write only guidelines that are required for design and implementation.

Standards.   A standard is a guideline that is reflected directly in an OS UI or followed by a large number of industry leading software applications or sponsoring organizations like the International Standards Organization (ISO). An example of a platform-based UI standard is use of the term Edit to name a menu containing clipboard commands.

> **Rule of Thumb**: Follow industry standards unless there is solid user-based evidence and agreement that deviation is appropriate.

Style Guide.   A UI style guide is a conceptual and very high-level specification of the overall appearance, behavior, and user interactions for a product's UI. General UI appearance, behavior, and user interaction are described, while unique details of an application's UI are avoided.

> **Rule of Thumb**: Develop a style guide based upon project needs, but insure project buy-in from sponsors, project users, and users.

Think of a UI style guide as a high-level overview or user's manual describing how to use a product or suite of applications. A UI style guide contains the principles, standards, and guidelines employed in a product's design.

> **Rule of Thumb**: Principles, standards, guidelines, and style guides are necessary but not sufficient for delivering excellent UI software. In

general, the best approach is to validate use of any guidance as applied to a specific product with the project team and end users.

Some examples of general elements of UI style include the use of color, terms, fonts, graphics, sounds, common conceptual models, layout models, common features, design patterns, and common formats for specific types of data. In contrast, examples of application specific information include field lengths and ranges, sources of data, specific tabbing order, and unique features.

The Problem.   Conventional UI style guides are descriptive (i.e., general guidance is provided without specific suggested direction). A descriptive style guideline advises a UI developer to use windows for various purposes, like displaying objects or actions. However, a descriptive style guide gives little specific guidance or direction about how to display an object, or an action within a window, or the desired interaction behavior.

A developer must abstract or surmise specific details by reading through the entire style guide, formulate a desired style, then define specific application details beyond the UI basics. The typical complexity of style for a UI is depicted in Figure 12.2, where a UC product team must build upon:

- Base UI components (a list control)
- Custom controls or techniques for specific application needs (breadcrumb trail)
- Integration of specific UI elements (placement of lists on pages)

Given the large number of details associated with the application layer of a UI and how UI controls are used, it is not surprising that different developers within the same application domain use the same descriptive informa-

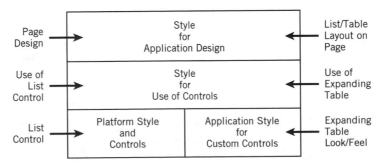

FIGURE 12.2
Style guide components and layers.

tion to achieve vastly different results. A critical fault of descriptive Style Guides is that subjective interpretation of compliance is required.

Current UI Styles.   Even though GUI, WUI, and HUI styles are well known in the industry, there are still many enterprises moving host-based applications to these styles. In addition, many new applications are being created by developers with little experience in these technologies and UI design. Current style guides are insufficient to help these new developers avoid the common pitfalls that lead to unusable applications and interfaces. Additionally, conventional style guides do not assist new developers in exploiting the opportunities that exist with current styles.

A Matter of Focus.   Developers of applications are focused on using UI components to good effect and ensuring that the application layer of a UI is usable and internally consistent. Developers of GUI-, WUI-, or HUI-based applications are not focused on developing UI components for appearance and behavior unless absolutely necessary.

Developers of UI-based applications focus on:

- Proper use of the UI style (controls, lists, menus, fields, etc.)

- Application UI (intended user model, installation, desktop behavior, UI and domain features to employ, object models, presentation models, user assistance models, command models, task flow models, effective use of the hardware, etc.)

- Usability (avoidance of common problems, e.g., too many screens/steps)

- Consistency (cross-application commonality beyond the base UI)

- Integration (use of direct manipulation, clipboard, etc.)

A Challenge.   A major challenge for a UC product team is to speak the language of users and developers. Another is to anticipate and avoid the common problems of UI-based applications.

Given the numerous details associated with the UI application layer and how controls are used, it is not surprising that UI developers use the same descriptive information to achieve vastly different results. An entire axis of user interface components is not discussed in any manner (see Figure 12.3). UI style and application UI style components influence how much usability and consistency is achieved.

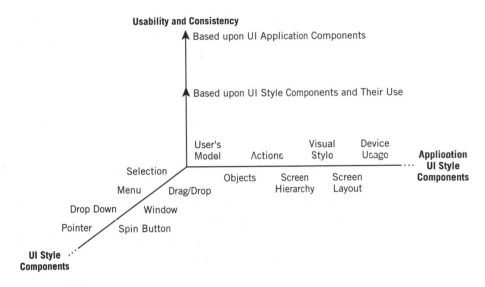

FIGURE 12.3

Contribution of UI and application UI style components.

Prescriptive Style Guides

Obviously, one solution to the problem of usability, consistency, and integration across applications is to create a single systems-level design for the application set. However, this may not be practical for large organizations with a large number of existing applications used by a common user set. There are cases where a single, system level design is not necessary to achieve organizational goals for schedule, cost, UI, and user performance and satisfaction. For these cases, prescriptive style guides are a necessary and sufficient answer.

Using a medical concept, a prescriptive style guide provides precise design and experience-based guidance to address specific problems or achieve specific results. A prescriptive style guide addresses both axes of UI components and offers a solution to many of the problems encountered with OS- or internally-produced UI style guides. Use of the guidance leads to usable, consistent, and integrated products. The guidance comes in the form of use of UI controls, design and use of application UI elements, and techniques that lead to consistent and integrated applications.

Prescriptive style guides provide rules and directions designed to achieve specific results for an application or collection of applications.

The scope of prescriptive style guides is sufficiently broad to handle UI usage, application domain characteristics, UI, consistency, and integration results. Used prior to development, a prescriptive style guide leads designers to achieve specific results. Such an approach is used after the fact to provide corrective guidance for applications that do not meet intended goals or those that experience usability problems. A critical element to the success of prescriptive style guides is objective and testable determination of compliance.

Rule of Thumb: Include all major UI design patterns of behavior, appearance, and user interaction in a prescriptive style guide.

An Example for Lists and Tables.

Let's discuss an example of a prescriptive model for simple lists of objects displayed in a web browser window, where simplicity is determined by the size of the action set possible on the list or its entries (see Figure 12.4).

A subset of possible prescriptive guidelines is provided:

- Use a table for displaying lists of objects and tabular information
  - If required for clarity, place a title left aligned above the table
  - Fields that control table content are displayed above the table and below the title
- The table is centered on the page and has white space around it
  - The first column heading is left aligned
  - Other column headings are centered over columns
  - Textual information is left aligned in a column
  - Numeric information is right aligned in a column
- Use of color
  - Display white text over dark blue (#336699) in the header row
  - Except for links, the first row in the table is black text over white
  - Alternating rows are displayed as black text over light blue (#9999FF)

Column Header	Heading	Heading
Linked information	Textual info	Numeric info
Alternating bands for ease of reading	Textual info	Numeric info
Linked information	Textual info	Numeric info
Alternating bands for ease of reading	Textual info	Numeric info

FIGURE 12.4
Example of prescriptive guidelines for lists and tables.

- Display white separator lines between columns
- Accessing commands
  - Open is the default command for table items via the Enter key (single-click the mouse)
  - Popup menus are provided for the List object and List entry objects
  - When pushbuttons are used for the command set of a list, they are grouped below the list and grayed when not valid

Prescriptive guidelines describe exactly how an application uses UI components. The number of possible prescriptive guidelines can be quite large. However, each project must determine what is needed in order to meet goals.

Rule of Thumb: Think about prescriptive guidelines as better components of UI recipes.

An Example for an Object.   Many   application   domain   objects require prescriptive guidance as well. This example provides a web-based example of an object using the metaphor of a real-world notebook, as opposed to the notebooks of conventional UIs.

- Use a notebook metaphor to represent an object that naturally organizes a small, related collection of data or other objects into index tabs
- Index tabs are displayed along the top
- The notebook uses a small number of nonoverlapped tabs that do not require horizontal page or tab scrolling on the default page size
- No minor tabs are used
- No visual binding is used at the bottom of the notebook
- The notebook is centered on a page and white space is displayed around it
- In order to have equal sized tabs, use brief terms, abbreviations, or icons for tab labels (in order of preference)
- There is one page of information per tab

Aside from the prescriptions for use of standard UI elements, there are prescriptions for how to use a notebook metaphor. A visual depicts the layout model for the notebook. The notebook is displayed visually and with white space around the graphic area. Data is displayed on the body of each notebook.

Prescriptive Solutions for Common Problems_____

For each problem that is common to UI-based applications or unique to a particular application, prescriptive guidelines are defined. Examples of common problems and prescriptive solutions include:

Screen Size.   Many developers have a tendency to design very large screens, almost to the point of being full-display windows or browser pages, when not necessary. For multipage or multiwindow applications, the impact is a large amount of window management and navigation.

   Prescription: The initial screen size for the client area is equivalent to a 5x7" or 4x6" area on a 17" monitor.

Number of Screens/Steps.   Many applications have a tendency to implement a conventional menu hierarchy using windows or within a browser. The impact is a large number of work steps opening, closing, and manipulating windows or browsers.

   Prescription: The maximum number of object windows/pages traversed in high use tasks is three: List, Object, Subobject.

Object Models.   Applications are developed with implicit or explicit intended user models, object structures, and layout models. For the most part, applications within an organization seem to be developed with widely varying models. The impact to an end user is more difficult learning and inconsistent patterns of presentation, usage, and support.

   Prescription: Use a physical object model with visual representations equivalent to their real-world counterparts.

Command Access Models.   Many applications have common functions, and many applications that should have these common functions do not. An example of a common function is sort a list in ascending and descending order. Even when a common function is available, a user does not always have common access techniques for the feature across applications. A function may be accessed using the menu bar and pulldowns, toolbars, popup menus, shortcut keys, and clicking in list column headers. The impact to users is more difficult learning and formulation of work habits.

   Prescription: Each action is accessed by menu bar, pulldown, and popup menu. High-use functions are also accessed by Shortcut key and Toolbar button. No action is available only through pointer inter-action.

An Example Outline.   Figure 12.5 depicts an outline for a prescriptive style guide. The outline content is extremely broad and comprehensive. Different approaches to outlines are possible (e.g., outlines closer to that of a UI specification or a process-oriented view of how a UI is designed and developed. The most important point is to provide needed information in a manner easy to use by a UC product team.

Guidance provided in each section is specific and directive. A benefit of such an approach is to eliminate a large amount of low-level decision making by

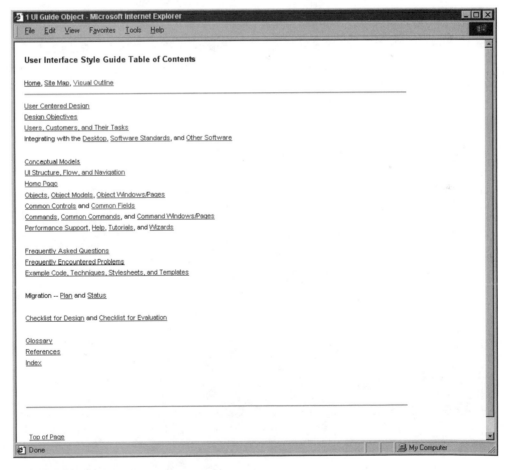

FIGURE 12.5

Example of a high-level style guide outline.

large numbers of independent project personnel. Many low-level decisions are relatively unimportant in the overall scheme of UI usability. However, the sum total of decisions is extremely important relative to overall usability, consistency, and the appearance of integration. By and large, many developers do not care about this type of detail; they simply want to know what is required.

An Example Outline for a Guideline.   Prescriptive guidelines are written using a consistent outline. Where appropriate, a graphic depicts the essence of a guideline with absolute compliance to other relevant guidelines. Figure 12.6 depicts a subset of the relevant guidelines for use of an access key character in a GUI-based application.

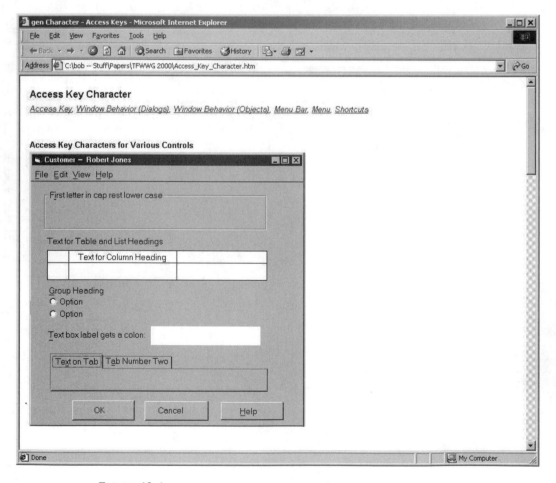

FIGURE 12.6

Graphic example for use of access key characters.

In general, an outline for a prescriptive guideline includes:

- A definition of the term, concept, or feature
- A visual or graphic depicting the topic
- Example(s)
- Measurable and required rules of use
- Predefined or reserved items based upon a system or suite of applications
- Tips and techniques of usage
- Rationale
- References, templates, and example code

Prescriptive Style Guide Development _____

Developing a UI style guide for an application is expensive, regardless of the approach used. Usually, several people are involved over an extended period of time during which negotiations and debates are common in attempts to reach consensus on points of style. Many times, compromises that water down any guidelines to achieve usability, consistency, and integration are necessary.

Goal Oriented.   Prescriptive style guides have specific results to achieve that are stated clearly. Desired, specific, and measurable results are defined. If the goals are not stated, then a UC product team does not start or continue developing a style guide.

Management Support.   Since there is significant cost in developing and applying a prescriptive style guide to an existing or new set of products, management support is required. There are changes to apply, debates with developers who do not want to make changes, schedules to be met, resources to be expended, and potential rework. Managers must be firm in support of objectives and making required changes. Otherwise, do not develop a prescriptive style guide.

Begin Early and Continue.   Style guide development begins during conceptual design and continues throughout development. Obvious style elements are discovered early, but subtle and nonobvious candidates are discovered and added over time.

Effective. Certainly, a prescriptive style guide must have the capability of delivering on the stated objectives in a cost-effective manner and within schedule constraints.

User Oriented. Desired product effects are expressed in user terms.

Developer Oriented. Desired user effects are stated in terms an implementation team understands. This is achieved by use of very specific guidance. Reference to the exact controls and style bits that a developer is to use is very effective.

Facilitated. The most effective style guide technique is example code (code snippets, algorithms, data structures, or page templates that serve as a pattern or example) for reuse by developers. This approach lightens the burden of implementation and testing.

Implementable. A prescriptive style guide always describes techniques that are implementable within schedule, resource, and skill constraints. Using techniques that are costly and detract from product and user value are not required.

Testable. Prescriptions are not written if they are not testable in an objective manner by an independent test team. Prescriptive test cases are written using a prescriptive style guide as a high-level specification of behavior, appearance, and user interaction. There is no subjectivity in how prescriptions are written and interpreted. There is no room for opinion— something is either right or wrong. In this regard, a guideline is measurable and easy to detect. If an application does not comply with a prescriptive style guide, defects are scheduled for correction.

Specific. Each prescription must be specific. Generality is avoided.

Meaningful. A prescription is written only if it is immediately useful relative to goals for the UI, usability, consistency, or integration. Otherwise, the prescription is not written or is deferred to a later time.

Relevant. A prescription solves specific and immediate problems or is not written.

Flexible. Prescriptive style guides are flexible and allow for meaningful variation among objects, commands, and interaction models. Diversity is sometimes meaningful across distinct end-user objects.

Comprehensive. The scope of a prescriptive style guide is the entire end-user experience. As such, installation, desktop behavior, appearance, documentation, performance, and other end-user perceived behavior and user interactions are valid content as needed by a project.

Size. Prescriptive style guides are as large as necessary to meet project goals. However, there are limits to what designers and implementers can comprehend, internalize, and apply within meaningful training and development schedules.

- Corollary 1. Don't write prescriptions just to write
- Corollary 2. Fifty printed pages is a good upper limit for an initial document

  Rule of Thumb: Just because a style guide is developed in electronic form does not mean that the volume of prescriptions can increase exponentially.

Usable. A prescriptive style guide provides sound guidance for all elements. Individual prescriptions are important when examined in isolation; however, the sum total must meet requirements.

Visual. Since a prescriptive style guide is focused on UI, liberal use of graphic examples is helpful. Interactive style guides are helpful.

Mappable to Products. Each prescription is mapped to one or more product screens and/or interactions. The resultant mappings are used for construction of product schedules that demonstrate when compliance to the prescriptive style guide is achieved.

Responsible/Accountable. One person is assigned technical responsibility for developing the prescriptive style guide and achieving desired results and another has similar responsibility from a management perspective. These two individuals are held accountable for delivery of the style guide and the desired product results. The management and technical team is made aware of the responsibility of these two individuals and the level of management commitment to achieving results.

Useful Techniques

Developing a product set with aggressive goals for UI, usability, consistency, and integration is a high-risk endeavor. During the course of developing prescriptive style guides, there are some risk-reducing techniques.

UCD. As with other project deliverables, a style guide is a significant candidate for application of UCD techniques. The users of a style guide are members of the project team. Early prototyping and evaluation of style guide components is appropriate. Iteration until user needs and requirements are met is important.

Before. Obtain screen captures of the products involved (these are the product images that demonstrate what the problems are). Construct collages of how the individual products look on a user's desktop together with sequences of user steps for common tasks across the products. If possible, ask users for their opinions.

Inconsistencies. Make a list of differences among the products. Categorize and prioritize the most significant ones for end users. Be sure to identify functional and UI differences across the entire product set. Again, ask users to help set priorities.

After. Building upon existing standards, revise the screen images until the desired effects are obtained (these are the images that remove the problems). Use a layered approach to achieve the after effects—suite level, object level, dialog, and control level. Construct collages of how the updated products look on a user's desktop with their common task sequences. Again, ask users what they think about the solution.

What it Takes. Construct the list of changes that lead to the desired effect. Work with the development teams to ensure implementability and cost for the effort to achieve the desired result. Secure commitments.

Show and Tell. Ask management if the results are good enough based on user feedback. If not, it is back to the drawing board. If the cost is too expensive, then negotiate for more resource, skill, schedule, or reduced effect. This process continues until the management and technical communities are in agreement on what can and will be done.

Prescribe.   Once the agreements are established, begin development of the prescriptive style guide. Manage product changes by use of measurable schedules and development plans. Ensure that test cases are written and assigned to evaluate compliance with the style guide. Continue maintaining the before and after images. Continue adjusting the prescriptive style guide and conducting show and tell until the product is developed.

Evaluate/Report Periodically.   Repeat the process of evaluating results and reporting to management until the product is completed. As user feedback is obtained, incorporate changes and keep management and developers informed.

A Management View

Prescriptive style guides provide a unique opportunity for managers of development teams whose products must be usable, consistent, and integrated. Because of the measurable nature of a prescriptive style guide, each product is tested for individual compliance. The collection of products of interest is evaluated for overall compliance and desired effect.

Obviously, if the collective desired effect is not good enough, more prescriptions are developed and implemented until desired results are achieved. If the overall desired effect is good enough but an individual product deviates from the effect, then corrective actions are applied to the product and/or its development team.

The major challenges for the management team are:

1. State goals clearly for UI, usability, consistency, and integration.
2. Require the developers of the prescriptive style guide to demonstrate that goals are being met.
3. Appoint the technical and management personnel responsible for developing the prescriptive style guide and tracking product implementation.
4. Require product developers to show compliance, even when schedules and resources undergo the strain of normal product development.

Principles and Guidelines for the Project_____

Because of the importance of the project, the senior managers are supplementing project staffing. Another team of developers has been assigned to the project. You do not know any of the people on the second team personally, but the general reputation of the team is of being argumentative and arrogant. Though experienced and having delivered some products very quickly, the additional team appears to have minimal skills in user-centered design and usability and moderate skills in UI design and development. This opinion is shared by many, including the project lead.

However, the second team of developers is very proud of its work and feels that its skills are very good in the area of UI and usability. This team believes that any failures of their products are due to senior management and poor marketing. The project lead mentions that perhaps people from the second team can help in such areas as printing, common dialogs, common widgets, and common features. You've noted that they can put up windows and pages very quickly with some interesting designs, but there are significant problems in the overall designs. In addition, their products have not done well in the field and user feedback is mixed.

Separate teams in the lab are working on other applications that could potentially extend the functionality and competitive aspects of the Conference Companion (e.g., expert systems and agents, email, telephony, video, fax, and other utility software). You've seen these applications and know that they have features of value but are very different in look and feel. Some of these teams could be diverted to implement components of the project.

Though these applications are not directly involved in conference scheduling tasks, the senior managers want the total collection of software developed by the lab to be perceived as a suite of applications with UI, usability, consistency, and integration rivaling industry-leading software suites. The project lead mentions that you are responsible and accountable for figuring out how to deal with the situation.

Senior management has asked the project lead for a briefing on how this is to be achieved by you and the UC product team for the Conference Companion. One of the senior managers expressed awareness of difficulties involved in achieving suite-level consistency in multiple applications. He was project manager for a project that developed a UI standards document which failed to achieve objectives, as did the project's UI and usability. He mentioned at the last meeting with senior management that he wants to be closely involved in this aspect of the project. You've heard that he will ask if "seeing what the customer sees" is a design principle, guideline, or design feature.

You know the drill: The project lead has committed to a briefing at 7:30 a.m. tomorrow. You have about two hours to prepare a briefing on the project's:

- Principles, standards, guidelines, and style guides
- How suite-level requirements for UI and consistency will be achieved
- How the various teams will become a smooth-working team of teams
- A schedule for when the style guide and other challenges will be resolved

The project lead mentions that three visual examples of style guide items would be helpful to show the senior managers what is needed to succeed. In particular, you should demonstrate the level of consistency achieved across the platforms being supported, namely, GUI, WUI, and HUI styles. The examples should suffice to show before and after results using the current products.

A complete set of principles, standards, and guidelines is not required for the briefing. However, something is definitely needed within two weeks for development teams involved in the project. Any style guide developed should be sufficient to support other teams involved on this and other projects/teams in remote locations.

Be sure to continue your research over the Internet. Be sure that you have access to the key standards for accessibility and ISO. Locate other guideline documents as references or to supplement what the UC product team will develop.

Any questions?

References

Grudin, J., "The Case Against User Interface Consistency," *Communications of the ACM*, Oct. 1989.

Human Interface Guidelines : The Apple Desktop Interface. Apple Computer, Inc. Addison-Wesley: Cupertino, CA, 1995.

Java Look and Feel Design Guidelines. Sun Microsystems. Addison-Wesley: New York, 1999.

OSF/Motif™ Style Guide, Revision 1.0. Open Software Foundation. Prentice-Hall: Englewood Cliffs, NJ, 1990.

Torres, R.J., "A User-Centered Design Based Approach to Style Guides," Eds. J. Vanderdonckt and C. Farenc, *Tools for Working with Guidelines*, Springer-Verlag, 2000.

Torres, R.J., et al., "Proofreading GUI-Based Applications," *Common Ground*, Ed. JoAnn Hackos, UPA Newsletter, V8.3, July 1998.

Vanderdonckt, J., "Development Milestones Towards a Tool for Working with Guidelines," *Interacting with Computers*, V12.2, Sep. 1999.

The Windows Interface Guidelines for Software Design: An Application Design Guide. Microsoft Corp. Microsoft Press: Redmond, WA, 1995.

Mockups, Simulations, and Prototypes

13

The early visualization of products is a best practice in many industries. It is a best practice for UI design and development. Users, business sponsors, a UC product team, and others on a product development team get an early peek at what is going to be delivered. The early peek gives the vested parties an opportunity to make mid-course corrections. For a UC product team, it is another technique and opportunity to be right before it's too late or too expensive to make changes.

Prototyping is a frequently abused, misused, and confused term. Regardless of the name or technical approach used, the goal of a UC product team is to visualize a design using one or more forms. Techniques include pencil and paper sketches, authoring tools, graphic programs, simulations, storyboards, and software prototypes. Adjectives to qualify prototyping approaches include rapid, fidelity, reusability, and accuracy.

Frequently, it is difficult to explain and understand what is and is not available when users, developers, or managers are reviewing an interactive software "prototype." Regardless of the approach being used, there are benefits to instantiating a design. Awareness of the limitations and value of any technical alternative are explored and resolved.

This chapter provides an overview of user interface prototyping. Techniques and methods are provided that, when applied in conjunction with other UCD-based techniques, improve the opportunity to generate great UI recipes. The topic is necessarily broad, but an overview of key elements is provided together with references for further exploration.

The following topics are discussed:

- Definitions
- Goals
- Design instantiation techniques
- Organizational considerations
- Throw-aways
- Misconceptions
- Back to the project

An Example. · A simple scenario helps illustrate how UI design instantiation and visualization is useful in high-speed environments. A high-speed environment is one where a product must be delivered primarily on a rela-

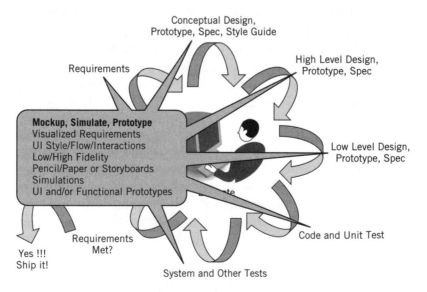

FIGURE 13.1
Prototyping within a UCD process.

tively short schedule. Secondary considerations include meeting requirements for cost, function, UI, usability, and performance. However, schedule is the dominant force behind a high-speed environment.

Right or wrong, web projects are believed to be high speed in nature. In a web-based development project, it is possible to move through various forms of prototyping very quickly.

- Hand-drawn sketches are used to capture task, screen flow, data, and UI needs during participatory sessions with users. The sketches are conceptual in nature and representative of function, data, behavior, and user interaction. The sketches are likely to be crude and not accurate representations of final appearance and behavior within a web browser.

- Quickly, the screen sketches and flow are transformed into a lightweight and interactive HTML prototype. Pages are built with graphics, labels, fields, and page-to-page navigation. Some user interaction is possible, but no data is saved and many UI representations are static and simulated.

- Once reviewed and approved by users, the HTML pages are moved into more serious development with addition of dynamic and real-time behavior and saving of data. These pages can remain in pure HTML, or have embedded scripting language, or become applets, Active Server Pages (ASP), or Java Server Pages (JSP), or have other types of support.

The planning, requirements, design, and development process from start to finish can be as short as a couple of days or as long as a couple of weeks depending upon page volume, functional and UI content and complexity, and access to users. The factors that influence such rapid turnaround are:

- Skills to extract requirements
- Design skills to instantiate requirements in an unambiguous but satisfying form
- Development skills to instantiate a design into a UI simulation or prototype
- Development skills to translate a UI prototype into industrial-strength software and its prerequisite artifacts
- Project management skills to keep the focus on delivery and effective iteration

Interestingly, the same process is applicable to other projects where speed is not necessarily the dominant project factor but where other factors, such as cost, functionality, usability, performance, and reliability, are.

Definitions

A good next step is to explore definitions to be used consistently. Not all design visualizations are created equal. Some are static, some are dynamic, and some are user-interactive. By looking at other industries, it is possible to derive a less confusing vocabulary. Any of these techniques are valuable at any point in a product development cycle as design issues arise, and it is likely that all techniques will be used during development.

Mockups and Storyboards.   A design instantiated as a set of static images is a mockup. Behavioral and dynamic states are represented by static images. A collection of static images that demonstrate system behavior during user interaction scenarios is a storyboard.

Mockups and storyboards can be implemented as pencil and paper sketches, graphic images, presentation graphics, and screen captures of simulations and prototypes. As with simulations and prototypes, some mockups can be very time consuming and labor intensive.

Simulations.   A simulation is an instantiation of a design that is built using implementation tools other than those intended for development of a product. There is no potential for any of the implementation to be reused in a product. Examples of tools used to create simulations include graphics software, authoring software, simulation software, and development tools other than those intended for product development.

Example.   A web UI design is simulated using a graphics software package. Screen images are created to mimic web pages and flow. None of the page instantiations are reusable. A product team must ensure that UI techniques and widgets demonstrated in the simulation exist in the intended environment.

    Rule of Thumb: Beware of designs that are built using tools other than the intended development tools.

Example.   A web UI design is simulated using a GUI-oriented programming language and tools. None of the code is reusable. A product team must ensure that UI techniques and widgets used in the simulation exist in the intended environment.

    Rule of Thumb: Beware of designs that must be ported across development environments. It's never as easy as you think it should be.

Simulations are useful within specific contexts for visualization of requirements and the early exploration of page layouts and flow. Some simulations are extremely realistic, others are conceptual representations. A UI design instantiated in a simulation may be reusable, but this is a suspect assumption in many environments. There are typically major translation steps between a simulation and an implementation for prototype or product. In addition, building a simulation is a task different than building a prototype or product.

> **Rule of Thumb**: Unless there is a wealth of time and talent on a project, don't pull developers off product work in order to build a simulation. Obtain different resources with appropriate skills.

Prototypes.   A prototype is an instantiation of a design that is built using the intended development tools for a product. The development tools include hardware, operating system, and programming languages. A prototype has the potential of having implementation components reused in a product, though not all components are guaranteed to be reusable.

A UI prototype focuses on UI and usability. Another type focuses on UI and non-UI features, and this is called a UI-NUI prototype. Another type focuses on non-UI features only, and this is alternatively called a technical prototype.

Example.   A web UI design is visualized using the tools intended for product development (e.g., HTML and JavaScript). Web pages, widgets, and navigation links are implemented, but data is not saved. Lists of database information is simulated. Page layouts and navigation are reusable, but all data loading and saving must be implemented.

Example.   A web UI design is visualized using the tools intended for product development—Hypertext Markup Language (HTML) and JavaScript. Web pages, widgets, and navigation links are implemented, and data is saved and lists of information are retrieved from a sample database. Page layouts, navigation, and some of the data methods are reusable, but final coding, error messages, and exception handling must be implemented.

Prototypes are useful within specific contexts for visualization of requirements and early exploration of UI and implementation design approaches. Some prototypes are realistic, some are conceptual.

Aspects of a UI design instantiated as a prototype are reusable, but this is always subject to validation as implementation design and methods evolve as a project proceeds. There are typically fewer translation steps between a prototype and an implementation for product. Building a prototype is a task closer to building a product, but there are still differences in the task.

> **Rule of Thumb**: Move from simulation to prototype as quickly as possible. Use actual implementation tools for all aspects of the user experience for the product.

Low-Fidelity Design Instantiations.

Mockups and storyboards are synonymous with low fidelity (low-fi) prototypes. However, care must be exercised in the use of terms. Even some simulations and prototypes can be considered low-fi design instantiations. These types of design instantiations are relatively low-cost and useful during participatory sessions and some forms of user testing to demonstrate system and user actions when a system is not available.

> **Rule of Thumb**: Use the term prototype very carefully in order to convey more precisely the type of tool being used for design instantiation and its reusability prospects.

Lightweight Prototypes.

Interactive prototypes do not need to be expensive to develop, and they can be developed quickly. There is the notion of a lightweight prototype, which is a construction of the software's conceptual flow, its major and typical screens, navigation between the screens, and simple but typical interaction. Functional and interaction depth is limited, and not all features are enabled.

The screens of a lightweight prototype provide intended appearance, aesthetics, features, data, and UI mechanisms with high fidelity for more realistic user evaluations. A lightweight prototype is sufficient for user interaction and input on a few very key scenarios. Again, heuristic and participatory methods are used to evaluate a design as depicted in the prototype.

> **Rule of Thumb**: Be able to use all forms of design visualization through all phases of a project.

Goals

Let's review the purpose of design visualization and how the technique applies to product development.

Product Visualization.

Visualizing a product is a journey of progressive refinement and elaboration as questions arise. During early phases, requirements and design concepts and alternatives are explored via low-cost and quick-turnaround approaches. Low-level design details are typically not explored in depth. Intended development tools are not necessarily used during these phases, but it does help clarify how a product will look and work within its intended environment. Use of intended tools helps assess training needs and development time.

Paper mockups or lightweight interactive simulations or prototypes of basic UI style and application UI layouts and user interaction are the way to go early in a product life cycle. Initially, hand-drawn conceptual versions of screens are used to instantiate and evaluate requirements within design options quickly. The operative word here is *quickly*.

> **Rule of Thumb**: Keep the focus on essential and representative elements of the product, UI, and usability.

Evaluating Design and Implementation.

Heuristic and participatory methods are used to evaluate a primitive and limited representation of a complex design. Team members and users are required to get past the conceptual limitations imposed by paper mockups, storyboards, simulations, and anticipated design problems or limitations using such tools.

As requirements are stabilized and design options are discarded, graphic tools are used to make visualizations appear more faithful to intended UI appearance, aesthetics, and flow. Paper or electronic storyboards begin to provide a sense of a user's interaction and system flow. Again, the operative word is *quickly*.

During middle phases of a project, intended development tools are definitely used to create UI and/or functional prototypes to visualize likely implementations. Issues of breadth, depth, risk, and sensitive or ambiguous area are addressed. High-level design components are represented in great detail. Lower level design details are not necessarily explored in depth.

> **Rule of Thumb**: Get to an interactive lightweight UI prototype using the intended development tools and components as quickly as possible. This helps make user interaction problems related to flow, steps, and tool limitations painfully clear.

The whole idea is to get a fairly realistic design instantiation in front of real users for hands-on feedback from the team and real users.

During later phases of a project, all forms of visualization are available to evaluate problems such as late changes in requirements, fixes to usability problems that escaped early detection, and exploration of alternatives for significant improvements prior to deployment.

Establishing Speed.   Speed is essential regardless of whether mockups, storyboards, simulations, or prototypes are employed. Some speed inducing techniques are:

- Establish a rapid schedule. Plan on at least one weekly build and review of new screens and techniques with the UC product team and participating users. Frequent reviews with sponsors and other critical vested interests are scheduled as needed to ensure buy-in.

- Move into prototyping quickly. Don't get bogged down in paperwork. Have a goal of moving into use of development tools within two weeks of conceptual design.

- Fix as you go. Sometimes a design looks good on paper but is really ugly from a UI, usability, or implementation perspective as prototyping takes place. Some of this effect is part of natural iteration of a design during prototyping. Implement and fix as you go.

- Hard coding is acceptable. During early visualizations, avoid spending too much time on developing actual data structures, algorithms, and build issues. Implementability must be ensured, but schedule visualization and functional prototyping tasks separately.

- Avoid getting bogged down in nonessential details. Focus on mainstream tasks and techniques. Avoid noncritical and nonsensitive paths and error handling. Avoid prototyping of UI techniques that are not significant to user interaction.

Challenges.   Goals to address using visualization methods include:

- Major components of satisfaction (e.g., features, UI, performance, reliability, and information)

- Little things that could become major barriers to satisfaction (e.g., appearance, feedback, and shortcuts)

- Relevance of issues for the project

Visualizations (see Figure 13.2) must have sufficient fidelity (accuracy) and completeness (breadth and depth) to address major goals. A UC product team matches the representational power of various techniques to the design components being addressed. For some issues, a mockup is sufficient, while a UI-functional prototype is required for others. As with other areas, tradeoffs must be made between the tools, skills, and schedule.

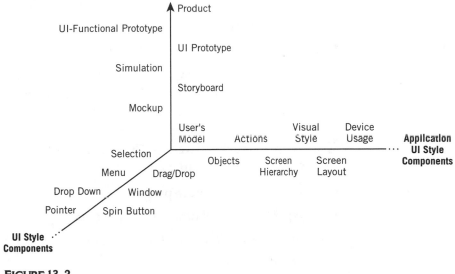

FIGURE 13.2
Visualization levels.

Design Instantiation Techniques

A critical decision facing a UC product team is what aspects of a design to instantiate for early evaluation with users and what techniques to utilize. For large products, there are many issues to address. There are features and usability dimensions associated with functionality and UI, and there are issues that need not be addressed. The dimensions of basic UI style and application UI style, critical design issues, and constraints are all balanced to select the appropriate levels and types of visualization to employ.

Things to Think About.   Regardless of the environment, a UC product team has many challenges to deal with. Technical fundamentals to address in any design instantiation include:

- High use, sensitive, and problematic tasks and scenarios to represent
- High use and sensitive functions, techniques, and data
- General use of the platform UI style
- Specifics of an application UI style, screens, and flow
- Problematic UI widgets
- Level of user interaction required
- Amount of environmental fidelity required

- Depth of actual implementation versus visualization needs
- Speed of representation
- Reuse objectives for any representations

Rule of Thumb: Remember that simulations and prototypes are just software—a UC product team deals with issues of goals, lines of code, quality, performance, design skills, development skills, and schedule.

Things Typically Avoided.   There are aspects of a software UI that are not instantiated prior to implementation:

- Infrequently used feature paths
- Infrequently used features of a UI interface
- Product information (help, tutorial, performance support)
- Exception conditions
- Messages
- Error handling
- Performance considerations

Rule of Thumb: Remember:
- Focus on the big hitters via the 80-20 rule
- A rapid and incremental growth/improvement approach is needed
- Visualization is a means to an end (not the end in itself)

Selecting a Visualization Technique.   Although there are many debates about the relative goodness of one method over another, selecting a visualization method for evaluating a design depends on many factors (see Table 13.1). Available time is a major consideration as are points within a development schedule, available skills, and issues to address.

TABLE 13.1
Visualization techniques for design evaluation.

Visualization techniques	Strengths	Limitations
Pencil and paper (including graphic tools and use of white boards)	• Use any time • Relatively quick unless platform and design fidelity is an issue • Relatively fast turnaround	• No reuse • Static representation of appearance and behavior • No user interaction • Design translation required

TABLE 13.1 *(continued)*
Visualization techniques for design evaluation.

Visualization techniques	Strengths	Limitations
Storyboard	• Use any time • Relatively quick unless platform and design fidelity is an issue • Simulate dynamic appearance and behavior • Good for demonstration • Relatively fast turnaround	• No reuse • Static representation of appearance and behavior • Design translation required • No user interaction
Simulation	• Use any time • Relatively quick unless design fidelity is an issue • User interaction possible	• No reuse • Appropriate skills needed • Design translation required • Possibly slower turnaround
Lightweight UI prototype	• Use any time • Relatively quick • Relatively high accuracy • Dynamic representation • User interaction possible • Some reuse	• Appropriate skills needed • Takes longer than simple sketches and board work
UI prototype	• Use any time • Relatively quick relative to development time • Dynamic representation • User interaction possible • Some reuse	• Appropriate skills needed • Takes longer than simple sketches and board work
UI-Functional prototype	• Use any time • Dynamic representation • User interaction possible • Some reuse	• Appropriate skills needed • Longer than other prototype methods
Implementation	• Use any time • Dynamic representation • User interaction possible • Reuse	• Appropriate skills needed • Longer than other prototype methods

Rule of Thumb: Before visualizing a design, consider available options and tradeoffs relative to the timing and design questions that need an answer.

Some techniques are not appropriate for some questions, while some techniques may be overkill. Some simple tradeoffs follow. For example, use of a UI-Functional prototype may not be appropriate for user evaluation of the text of a simple message. Likewise, use of pencil and paper may not be appropriate for user evaluation of complex behavior and very detailed user interaction.

Organizational Considerations

There are usually organizational considerations involved in any visualization effort.

- Management must support the expenditure of precious and costly resources for the effort and any perceived or actual delays in product deployment.

- In large organizations with competing and conflicting goals and groups, organizational behavior begins to play a role.

- Where there are people or groups with hidden agendas, barriers to success begin to appear.

- If a UC product team is separate from a development organization, technical commitment to a visualization effort is required.

Visualization and Implementation Team.   If a visualization team is different from the implementation team, excellent communication is required among the groups involved in product development. Otherwise, reverse engineering or guerilla warfare may occur.

> **Rule of Thumb**: It is better to use the same people for design, visualization, and implementation to minimize handoffs and transfer of knowledge, as well as to increase responsibility and accountability for results.

Supporting Infrastructure.   Visualization is extremely helpful for user evaluation of a design, as well as for communicating what a product is going to be, the infrastructure to support access to the visualization by users, a project team, and other vested interests. Along with access to the tool, the supporting infrastructure must support receiving feedback from users and vested interests.

What It Is and Isn't.   A UC product team must be sure to communicate what is required for visualization. Management support must be secured, organizational factors must be accounted for, and communication must take place with all stakeholders.

> **Rule of Thumb**: People and organizational considerations are probably harder than the technical issues. Communicate what the visualization is and is not, as well as provide the list of what is required to achieve product level status.

Throw-aways

Some complex projects require extensive evaluation that cannot be handled by low-cost methods. Thus, it is not unusual to select simulation and prototyping that requires developing thousands of lines of code in order to evaluate complex software suites with many screens, algorithms, integration, and consistency issues. As a result, management wants to ensure that minimal code is thrown away.

Begin with reuse as an objective. Identify what is most likely to be reused given skills, supporting infrastructure, and schedule, and do not promise that more is achievable. If more is desired or required, then the appropriate skills and infrastructure are required.

It is sometimes appropriate to throw away some of our hard work. When a design direction locks a product into results that don't meet requirements, it should be back to the drawing board! As with quality, usability and superior user interfaces cannot be tested into existence. Dedicated and hard work, good design starts, evaluation, and iteration are required.

No one wants to throw away anything that's useful, but if something is junk, or not helping a project meet objectives, it is not appropriate to hang on to it. Perhaps "parking" "not immediately useful" designs and code is the more appropriate action.

Misconceptions

There are many misconceptions associated with visualizations. Some of the more common and infamous quotes and last words heard on many projects using design visualization are:

- Prototyping can begin without a design
- A prototype is better than a simulation
- There's no throw-away code
- There's always something to ship
- It's easy to move from prototype to product
- Successive iterations become shorter
- Prototyping helps freeze the design early
- The prototype is the spec
- The prototype has all the answers
- The product will be better than the prototype
- Management support and protection is not necessary

Take care and listen for these and other last words. A visualization can be expensive. It is a means to an end but not the end in itself. Use of one or more visualization methods is usually required through the entire life of most complex products.

Back to the Project

Up to this point, you have probably used visualization techniques for preliminary design thoughts and show-and-tell purposes. Now it's time to apply visualization in a more formal manner.

Do the following before the project manager comes in:

- Consider how you would employ visualization techniques during the requirements and conceptual design phases of the project. What is necessary for demonstration to senior management, potential buyers of the product, and for evaluation by end users?
- For the project at a conceptual design level, develop at least three forms of visualization for appearance and navigation flow. For example, provide a home page and a follow-on page using a mockup, simulation, and prototype for a PC environment.
- For each environment in which the product is being deployed, develop one type of visualization, as you would expect it would be depicted during the project's life cycle. For example, provide a visualization of a home page and its navigation for each system during requirements, conceptual design, high-level design, low-level design, and implementation.

- Revisit the project plan to ensure that sufficient time and resources are allocated for visualization purposes.

The project lead has come in to discuss the next briefing with senior management. The management team is concerned about schedule, cost, and the implications of visualization upon schedule. There is a high probability of another headcount reduction, and any perceived nonessential tasks are targets for losing resource. Any person who is perceived as not contributing directly to building the product is a candidate for reassignment or layoff. The project lead wants to be very careful with anyone working on mockups or storyboards.

Senior management would also like an update on what the UI is looking like across the various deployment environments, especially cross-application and cross-platform usability and consistency. Management is also interested in seeing how comparable applications are approaching some of the tasks handled by the Conference Companion.

Be sure to continue your research over the Internet.

The next meeting with the management team is scheduled for 7:30 tomorrow morning, and you have about two hours to work on a 20-minute presentation. After the presentation, there is a briefing with a large potential buyer, and you are responsible for a 15-minute show-and-tell of the UI visualization. After the client presentation, there is a technical review of the UI direction with developers who are joining the team.

Any questions?

References

Brooks, F., *The Mythical Man Month*, Addison-Wesley: New York, 1995.

Isensee, S., et al., *The Art of Rapid Prototyping*, International Thomson Computer Press: Boston, MA, 1995.

McConnell, S., *Rapid Development*, Microsoft Press: Redmond, WA, 1996.

Nielsen, J., *Usability Engineering*, Academic Press: New York, 1993.

Torres, R., and Melkus, L., "Guidelines for Use of a Prototype in User Interface Design," Human Factors Society Conference Proceedings, Oct. 1988.

Usability Evaluation 14

A major element of product and UI development is testing with end users. If usability and other product criteria are met, the product is released to customers. If criteria are not met, product iteration and repair should occur in order to meet criteria.

During software design and implementation, customers typically gain insight into a product via presentations, specifications, demonstrations, and early install programs. Although presentations, specifications, and demonstrations give an idea of a product's general features and UI style, these methods are not sufficient to give a user good insight into the day-to-day operation of a product.

Early install programs give customers enough time to experience the look and feel of a product within a work environment. However, if there are major problems in terms of usage, it is probably too late to provide satisfactory resolution. A potential solution to this problem is early and ongoing usability testing using a variety of techniques.

Several usability evaluation techniques will be described that address how a UC product team for software products prepares, analyzes, and responds to product and information usability evaluations with real end users. As one developer said during a usability test at a customer facility, "What's so hard about this?" For a product team seriously interested in developing products with high user satisfaction, the answer is not too much if the right skills and techniques are applied.

Topics to be discussed are:

- Evaluation goals
- Types of evaluations
- Preparing for an evaluation
- Conducting an evaluation
- Data evaluation
- Developer participation
- A word about desk checking
- Back to the project

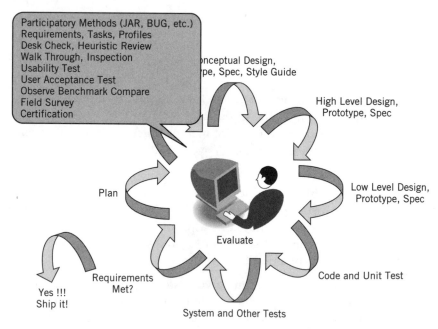

FIGURE 14.1
Iteration within a user-centered process.

Evaluation Goals _____

It is important to recall that usability, which is synonymous with overall user satisfaction, is influenced by many factors.

> **Rule of Thumb:** Relative to end user tasks and skills, software usability is a function of features, UI, performance, reliability, installation, and information.

The variables listed are basic factors that, if not provided adequately, lead to developing a system with high risk of being unusable, resulting in dissatisfied users and customers. Gathering user feedback on each of these factors is important for causal analysis of problems and an overall assessment of usability. Depending upon the product, there may be other factors important to overall usability.

Major goals for usability evaluation include:

- Predicting user satisfaction
- Understanding appearance, behavior, and user interaction approaches
- Problem determination and resolution
- Criteria validation
- Competitive assessment

Evaluations are designed to assess short- and long-term usability, or both. From a UC product team's view of software UIs, there are many design alternatives. Obtaining user-based answers to design questions and selection of design approaches is important and it is usually good to have users provide guidance and back up answers with their input. For iterative development efforts, validating product improvement over time is a major goal. Depending upon development and product goals, different evaluation techniques are available.

Types of Evaluations _____

Techniques of usability evaluation—reviews, walk-throughs, lab-based tests (with typical users), in your house tests (with real customers), and field tests—have been described in numerous texts. Evaluations are performed with evaluators, users, and other vested interests.

Ad Hoc Review. Performing an evaluation of a product without a structured technique or predetermined criteria, guidelines, and methods is an ad hoc review. The review is performed using documentation, prototype, or actual product. Each evaluator identifies perceived problems in an informal manner. An ad hoc review could be considered a seat-of-the-pants review.

>   **Rule of Thumb**: Avoid ad hoc reviews in favor of structured methods.

Heuristic Review.
In the literature, there are documented criteria, guidelines, and methods for evaluating a product's usability. The evaluation guidelines are called heuristics, or rules of thumb. Many tend to be design principles and subjective in nature. An example of a heuristic is minimizing a user's memory load.

Think about a heuristic review as a design or code review conducted by peers. However, there are many challenges associated with determining what is acceptable from a requirements, design, and implementation point of view.

>   **Rule of Thumb**: Establish objective heuristics based upon goals, principles, and guidelines for the project as well as common industry heuristics and evaluation procedures.

To be more effective, evaluation heuristics are translated into objective guidelines. A heuristic review evaluates a product via documentation, prototypes, or during actual end use. One or more individuals perform the evaluation using common heuristics and procedures.

Walk-Through.
Techniques that inspect a product by stepping through a UI with end-user scenarios are a walk-through. One or more evaluators perform a walk-through using documentation, prototypes, or products. Hands-on evaluation of a product is a good technique. A walk-through can also be conducted with end users who provide feedback.

Conventional Usability Test.
Conventional and formal evaluations of product usability are conducted in a laboratory environment with cameras, recorders, one-way mirrors, and the like. However, informal usability evaluations of an equally effective manner are conducted with a user and test conductor sitting side-by-side in an office or conference room.

Typical users are the intended test subjects in an evaluation based upon scenarios of intended use. Test duration can range from a few hours to a day in order to test initial learning and use. Extended testing during the latter part of a product cycle can last for days or weeks and is useful for evaluating long-term use. Users perform tasks with the product, and questionnaires are answered as part of the test. In general, the bottom-line question that users are asked is, "How do you like it?"

Comparative Usability Evaluation.

Many forms of usability evaluations are conducted in a stand-alone mode. These tests are good for understanding the basic usability of a product. However, this type of test does not always give insight into how a product compares to the usability of other products that a user may be using or have access to.

For this reason, comparative usability tests are exceedingly good. Users are given scenarios to execute on each of the products being evaluated. At the end of each scenario and at the end of a test, a user is asked to pick the product of preference. In general, the bottom-line question is, "Which do you prefer—Brand A or Brand B?"

Comparative evaluations are good for identifying features and techniques that give competitive edge and competitive advantage. For a UC product team intent on beating competition, comparison tests help identify what is most important to end users. This type of evaluation provides an acid test of how good a product is relative to competition and adds new meaning to egoless UI design.

In Your House Evaluation.

Because of the limitations of laboratory-based testing, it is advantageous to visit customer locations to conduct in your house usability evaluations. Real customers are used as hands-on test subjects for a product. As with formal and informal usability evaluations, users provide answers to questionnaires provided for the test.

An evaluation should be scheduled as early as possible within a product's development cycle. The goal is to evaluate a product with a broad and representative set of end users from a customer's population. The actual location of an evaluation is at a customer's work premises, in a private room. Potentially, it is better to conduct evaluations in the actual work area of customer end users.

In general, the bottom-line question is, "How does this compare to what you have?"

Field Tests.

Conducting an in-your-house evaluation is very similar to a field test, except that a simulation or prototype is used instead of a beta or final version of a product. Field tests are more formal but less structured in the sense that users are not required to perform scenarios. Users perform actual work using the product and answer more high-level questionnaires about the product.

Rule of Thumb: Use scenario-based evaluations with predefined criteria, methods, and user involvement throughout a product's development.

So Many Techniques, So Little Time!   The sooner that design evaluation takes place the better. Obviously, the sooner evaluations take place with users the better. Focus is kept on the areas that are frequently encountered problems. However, the factors that are most important in evaluations are:

- Predefined and objective criteria
- Structured and objective methods
- User involvement
- Techniques to determine what is right and what is wrong

Structured methods include test plans, procedures, scenarios, and known correct answers to steps and results. As with design, usability tests are not likely to yield the same results across evaluations—the process is nondeterministic. However, repeating a test should yield results that are in the same ballpark as prior results.

Using a relatively small number of test subjects, these types of evaluations are very good at identifying major usability problems associated with learning and initial use. Depending on the type of evaluation and duration, number of test subjects, and repetitions in scenarios, usability projections are possible for long-term use.

Preparing for an Evaluation _____

Since not all software groups have access to usability engineering professionals, an example of how a UC product team can prepare, conduct, and report a usability evaluation is discussed. Careful preparation, execution, and listening can provide a reasonable evaluation and feedback. Regardless of the evaluation method used, there are basic steps to follow for user involvement and credible results (see Figure 14.2).

Plan.   As with other major project activities, an evaluation requires careful planning. Setting objectives, schedule, dependencies, and selecting eval-

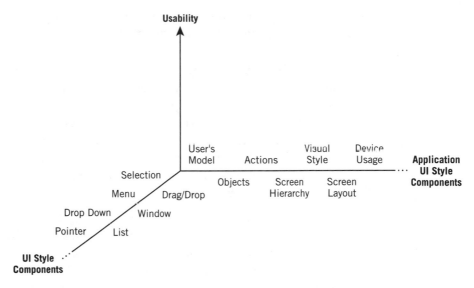

FIGURE 14.2

Usability axes to consider in test planning.

uation personnel are basic planning tasks. Other planning tasks are selecting an evaluation technique and determining the degree of user participation.

Design.   If available, usability evaluation personnel familiar with experimental design techniques can develop a plan for a usability evaluation. Complex evaluations or mission- or life-critical software require very careful design. Simple evaluations designed and conducted by a UC product team can yield very credible results. Areas of a product to explore are selected from the critical components of UI design.

Even a heuristic evaluation requires design preparation. At a minimum, heuristics are needed. Scenarios are useful to set context and evaluate common heuristics like a user's memory load and consistency. Criteria and right answers are also appropriate to set context (an evaluator does not want to test a product against unintended goals).

A simple but credible design for a usability test of most applications is achieved using a set of five to seven representative scenarios to be evaluated by six users from each audience population group. A more complex test has users perform similar tasks on competitive as well as project software. An experiment conducted in such a way alternates users between the software applications. One group uses the project software first, while the other group uses the competitor first. The groups switch products and perform the same tasks again. Results are compared.

Pre-Evaluation Briefing.

A briefing is highly recommended for participants in any aspect of an evaluation—mostly to set the right tone and context. Personnel who participate as an evaluator or as an observer are briefed on the goals, roles, and procedures of the evaluation. Whether a user is exercising a design via prototype or product, it is good to set context and tone in a positive manner. Before a test, each evaluator, observer, and user is reminded of one fundamental aspect of an evaluation—an evaluation is of a product and not a user.

This is done in order to obtain an informed consent about the purposes of the test and how the gathered information is being used. Each user is given access to a system with the product installed, a copy of any product documentation and artifacts, and instructions for tasks to be performed. A user is not necessarily required to read product documentation unless one of the purposes of the evaluation is determining the effectiveness of pretest training with the documentation.

> **Rule of Thumb**: Prepare briefings as carefully as other aspects of an evaluation.

Pre-Evaluation Questionnaire.

Before an evaluation, an assessment of evaluator and user skills is administered—it's good to know what people bring to the evaluation table. An appropriately designed questionnaire assesses how well a test subject matches the intended user audience. A person who does not fit the intended audience need not be evaluated.

There are some open-ended questions to ask related to how well a user matches an intended user profile. These questions are derived from the user profile for the product (refer to Chapter 10).

Examples of skill-related questions include:

- Rate your familiarity with the World Wide Web and web browsers
- Rate your familiarity with name of the task domain and its tasks
- Rate your familiarity with other software that supports these tasks

An example rating scale for skill questions is:

Unfamiliar			Limited use			Frequent use
1	2	3	4	5	6	7

In general, a pretest questionnaire takes no more than 10 minutes to answer.

Rule of Thumb: Have evaluators and test subjects answer skill-related questions.

Scenarios and Tasks. Most applications support a very large number of tasks. Regardless of the type of evaluation method, to attempt an evaluation of so many tasks is not cost effective or necessary. There are usually five to seven tasks that are the most significant to consider in each evaluation with users. Other tasks are added as necessary to explore potential problem areas that a UC product team has concerns about or those frequently encountered problems in UIs and systems.

For evaluators and test subjects, the selected tasks are described in very simple, step-by-step, easy-to-read, and concrete scenarios. Remember that the test is of the system and not of a user's ability to read and understand complex documents. Tasks are ordered in a likely initial usage manner. Then, less frequent tasks are introduced.

Rule of Thumb: For evaluations based upon prototypes or real systems, it may be appropriate to start and end with exploratory scenarios—one that allows a user to explore the options of a system without a specific task to perform.

Postscenario Questionnaires. Questionnaires are administered at the completion of each evaluation scenario. Questionnaires are designed to capture subjective user opinion in an objective manner. To obtain a comprehensive evaluation of a system, a question is needed for each of the foundation factors (i.e., function, user interface, performance, etc.). Other questions are added as appropriate, and user comments are gathered.

An approach is to formulate a questionnaire as a series of neutral questions or statements to be answered using a seven point scale, where 1 = worst and 7 = best. An alternative scale can be used where 0 = fail, 1 = neutral, 2 = pass. Space is left after each question for users to write comments. Examples of postscenario questions are:

Rate your satisfaction with the features in this application.

Very dissatisfied			Neutral			Very satisfied
1	2	3	4	5	6	7

Rate your satisfaction with the appearance of pages supporting this task.

Very dissatisfied			Neutral			Very satisfied
1	2	3	4	5	6	7

> **Rule of Thumb**: A postscenario questionnaire is about one page long.

Posttest Questionnaire.   A longer and more general questionnaire is administered at the end of an evaluation. The user gives overall impressions of the product as a whole, major product factors are evaluated, and other specific questions are added if needed. An example of a posttest question is:

Rate your overall satisfaction with this application.

Very dissatisfied			Neutral			Very satisfied
1	2	3	4	5	6	7

An example of an open-ended question to identify positive aspects of an application is:

What are the top three things you liked about this application?

> **Rule of Thumb**: A postscenario questionnaire is about two pages long.

Questions are provided to gather input on all foundation factors and negative aspects of the system.

Other Data to Collect.   Aside from questionnaire data, basic information to record while running through a scenario includes criteria-related measures, such as:

- Time to complete a scenario
- Number of times that help is requested
- User errors and problems
- User comments and questions
- Places where a user is not able to proceed or makes a serious error

Any other information that is specified for a product with measurable criteria is collected by these evaluations. If a test subject gets stuck, the test conductor asks the user to display Help or refer to other product documentation. If after reading Help or documentation, a user cannot solve the problem, then the test conductor coaches the user past the problem in a positive and neutral manner. The difficulty is recorded on the test problem list.

So Many Users, So Little Time.   Many people feel comfortable conducting evaluations with a large number of worldwide test subjects, however, current software development cycles make testing with large numbers of subjects impractical.

Conventional wisdom says that major usability problems are found in tests using as few as six subjects, but quantitative data is not statistically significant.

> **Rule of Thumb**: Small sample statistical methods are used with six or more subjects from the same user group, and sample sizes of 10 or 12 can give good analytical results.

A usability evaluation of most applications with up to 10 or 12 test subjects requires about one calendar week to execute. Analysis of statistical data and questionnaires begins with completion of the sixth test subject and continues until the last subject completes the test or the same results continue to be observed (no significant and new information is being gathered).

> **Rule of Thumb:** If results vary unpredictably, you may need to make design decisions based upon a snapshot of interim results, revisit the evaluation's design, and/or continue evaluation in a different manner.

Source of Subjects.

Usability evaluations require users who are representative of the intended audience for a product. The best source of test subjects is found by partnering with intended customers.

Test Platform.

Conduct evaluations with early documentation, mock-ups, simulations, prototypes, or the actual product. Since the goal is an assessment of the overall product, use early prototypes of product information, packaging, or other artifacts of a user's experience.

> **Rule of Thumb**: Interactive software used for evaluations should be well polished relative to basics prior to use by users or unintended negative results will occur.

The customer is coming from a very concrete environment and may not be in the mood to handle abstract concepts and explanations about why something isn't working or looking quite right. The test platform must match available scenarios.

Test Conductors.

Every UC team member, designer, and developer should have the opportunity to work with individual customers and end users. The major skill required of an evaluator is to be open and objective in receiving customer input and criticism.

> **Rule of Thumb**: There is nothing like directly experiencing a customer's reaction to products, especially the negative comments.

The intent is to establish a long-term relationship between a UC product team and customers. The long-term interaction is beneficial for follow-up on problem resolution and other product enhancements.

Conducting an Evaluation_____

Aside from planning and preparation, there are other basic steps to conducting an evaluation. Once materials and a test vehicle are ready, an evaluation team performs the tasks that follow. Let's assume an evaluation with end users is intended.

Set-up.   Required hardware and software configurations are put in place. The location for executing the evaluation is set up with the product and supporting information. Questionnaires, scenarios, and briefing information are available for each subject participating in the test.

Pilot Test.   A preliminary evaluation is conducted to validate test materials and procedures. A pilot test is a dry run for an evaluation. The subjects of a pilot test are actual users. Depending upon how the test proceeds, pilot test results are kept or discarded. If appropriate, test materials and procedures are adjusted to ensure a valid evaluation approach.

Pretest Questionnaire.   Conduct a user briefing. Administer a pretest questionnaire to gain insight into a user's background, skills, job, and tasks. If a user does not fit the desired skills and background, then decide whether or not to proceed.

Executing Scenarios.   Ask test subjects to perform the designed tasks on the test vehicle. Anticipate that the test will last up to two hours.

> **Rule of Thumb:** Design a test that takes one to two hours. Allow time for users to ask questions and provide unsolicited comments and requirements.

In general, each user should perform a test without prompting or interruption by a test conductor. When a user cannot proceed further, a test conductor objectively prompts a user to explore the system or look at Help for a solution. If Help is not sufficient, the test conductor intervenes and offers guidance.

> **Rule of Thumb:** Remember that a test is designed to evaluate a product and not a user.

Evaluation Notes.   Write down all user comments and note what needs to be explained to an end user. Keep track of how much time is spent on each UI artifact and step of a task. Be sure to write down where users get stuck or make mistakes. Be sure to take note of whether product information helps users overcome problems. Write down user comments about product information.

> **Rule of Thumb**: Sometimes, it takes two people—a facilitator and an observer—to monitor a user during an evaluation.

Comparisons.   If possible, have test subjects perform the same tasks on current systems. If this is not possible, have test subjects describe how their current or other systems work in accomplishing the task.

Postscenario Questionnaire.   Administer evaluation questionnaires after each scenario and at the end of the test. The bottom line question to ask is, "How do you like this product (compared to what you are using today)?"

When All is Said.   The questionnaires and comments are evaluated by a UC product team in conjunction with a debriefing of test conductors. Statistical analyses and summarization of information are performed at this time.

Follow-up.   If possible, follow up with customers as soon as possible after test results are analyzed. Provide feedback about what changes are being considered based upon their comments and test results. This could give insight into whether changes are headed in the right direction.

> **Rule of Thumb**: Fix problems ASAP!

Over Time.   Mockups, simulations, and prototypes are replaced by real product software as it becomes sufficiently robust to handle customer scenarios and testing. Again, scenarios and questionnaires are administered to gain ongoing assessments of customer satisfaction.

> **Rule of Thumb:** User satisfaction and performance should increase over time as full UI and functional features are available. Otherwise, the project may be heading in the wrong direction relative to goals.

A Word About Comprehensive Evaluations.   For evaluations of a heuristic nature, it is possible to evaluate an entire system in a cost-effective manner. Evaluators use a system so that each feature and UI component is exercised. Each component is evaluated relative to product heuristics and criteria. Results are summarized and reported as product deviations from the heuristics.

Data Evaluation

When an evaluation with end users is complete, a test conductor has a set of data that is depicted in tabular form for task and final questionnaires. There is also a set of user comments. The question now is what to do with the user self evaluation and product evaluations. Where possible, measurable results are depicted.

Typical Results.   For software with good usability, a typical graph reveals that time on task decreases rapidly to a best time as the system is learned and usage patterns (work habits) are established. Similar curves are constructed for other usability metrics (e.g., calls for help, user satisfaction, and user preference). As with time on task, a more usable system tends to demonstrate fewer calls for help, higher user satisfaction, and higher user preference.

> **Rule of Thumb:** In comparative evaluations, the software with better usability should demonstrate better time on task, user satisfaction, and user preference. However, it is not unusual to observe trade-offs in these factors.

Along with quantitative data, qualitative information is available in the form of comments by test subjects and conductors. Users state what is liked or disliked. Test conductors describe what and how users do tasks, and describe problems.

Statistics and Interpretation.   Descriptive statistics, confidence intervals, and tests of hypotheses are several statistical techniques available for analyzing data. The methods discussed are applicable to both small and large sample tests. Descriptive statistics (mean, variance, minimum, and maximum) are important. Confidence intervals, hypothesis testing, and analysis of variance are important analytical tools as well.

Causal Analysis.   Given typical learning and usage behavior, analysis of test results should focus on detecting trends among multiple users. Software changes are not based on one-subject comments and observations unless a nonobvious but real problem is pointed out.

> **Rule of Thumb**: Review all questionnaires for each user participating in a test.

An evaluator gains a better sense of how individual users are evaluating the software and the comments that are being made, as opposed to evaluating only summarized comments.

Reporting Results. Unless required to be extensive, simple reports are sufficient. At a minimum, the following is provided:

- An analysis of test subjects
- An analysis of user performance and variation (descriptive statistics)
- An evaluation of overall satisfaction as a function of the foundation factors of capability, UI, performance, and so forth
- An evaluation of overall satisfaction by user and task
- Solicited and unsolicited user comments
- An assessment of whether the software passed relative to criteria
- If the software did not pass the test, a set of suggestions for what might overcome problems and achieve criteria
- Prioritized problem lists (with a count of how many users encountered specific problems)

Sufficient data is provided so that a UC product team can reproduce a problem from an end user's perspective.

Developer Participation _____

For most evaluations, test conductors develop and document an evaluation approach, sample tasks and scenarios, questionnaires, metrics, and criteria. Evaluations can be designed to collect data for short- and long-term usability of software.

> **Rule of Thumb:** Review test subject screening materials, review scenarios, walk through the test, review questionnaires, begin usability testing when the product is sufficiently ready given test objectives, and help conduct the test.

Participating in the test provides first hand understanding of what a user is trying to do and how. In addition, it's good to see the unexpected and surprising problems that are encountered; for example, defects that are easy to overlook or become insensitive to during implementation. Observing a user (customer) having problems initiates the problem-solving process, where many times fixes are designed and implemented quickly (versus waiting for a report after a test). This is another form of iteration.

Once evaluation results are received, a UC product team determines what to do next. What must be changed? What can be left alone? Guidelines for how to approach evaluation of test results and iterating the product to correct problems and improve usability are discussed in Chapter 15.

A Word About Desk Checking

Evaluation of software usability and other aspects of a user's experience has been relegated to usability testing of one form or another, many times without participation by the project team. A method that requires further exporation is the notion of usability desk checking. Given that: $U = f\,(C, U, P, R, I, D)$, a developer evaluates software for sufficiency relative to usability variables.

Simple desk checks take the form of questions based upon product principles, guidelines, and heuristics. These questions are asked relative to the software's intended requirements, audience, and the tasks that a product is intended to support:

- Is sufficient capability provided in the software (are there sufficient functional features to accomplish tasks well)?
- Are UI features and techniques sufficient to accomplish the tasks well?
  - Does the interface satisfy key principles of simple, aesthetic, productive, customizable, and other?
  - Are common UI problems avoided (high knowledge load, obscurity, too many screens, too many mouse-keyboard transitions, too many steps)?
- Is response time fast enough?
- Is installation easy?
- Is the software sufficiently reliable?
- Is documentation and performance support minimalist in nature? Does Help answer the right questions?

    Rule of Thumb: It doesn't take a test with users to ask these fundamental questions.

Back to the Project

Up to this point, there has been relatively little feedback except through the UC product team, senior management, and demonstrations to visiting customers. All the feedback based upon the prototyping to date has been very positive and appears to indicate that the product design is heading in the right direction. However, there are conceptual design alternatives and various mockups, simulations, and prototypes. Prior to closure of conceptual design, there had been intent to conduct a usability evaluation with end users.

The product manager came in late today and said that senior management was wondering how usability testing is going. They would like a briefing in the morning. Also, the senior manager who wanted to work with you on the style guide has not had time to participate. However, he told the product manager that he wants to perform a detailed review of the UI prototype. You need to respond to this request in the morning.

Since no real evaluations have been performed to date with users, all you can do is formulate a plan for how usability evaluation of the product is to be performed. In addition, you can perform a quick personal review and a heuristic review and walkthrough of the design to date with members of the UC product team.

Provide a presentation that discusses evaluation methods planned for the project. Formulate a schedule for when the evaluations are to be performed. In addition, provide:

- The top heuristics used in your review of the product
- The areas where you have usability concerns on each platform supported
- Areas where you have usability concerns with the application software
- Typical problems faced by applications similar to the project
- Rational for why you recommend certain methods
- Typical questionnaires to be used in evaluations
- Number of people to use in evaluations
- Anticipated problems and solutions if known
- Anticipated compliance to UI and usability requirements
- An assessment of how well the design performs relative to heuristics and common UI and usability problems

Continue your research by exploring usability evaluation topics on the Internet.

You have about three hours to work on the request.

Any questions?

References

Devore, J.L., *Probability and Statistics for Engineering and the Sciences*, Duxbury Press: Belmont, CA, 1991.

Nielsen, J., *Usability Engineering*, Academic Press: New York, 1993.

Nielsen, J., and Mack., R., *Usability Inspection Methods*, John Wiley and Sons: New York, 1994.

Rubin, J., *Handbook of Usability Testing*, John Wiley and Sons: New York, 1994.

Shneiderman, B., *Designing the User Interface*, Addison-Wesley: Reading, MA, 1987.

Torres, R.J., "Graphical User Interfaces: Usability Evaluation," Share 84 Conference Proceedings, Aug. 1995.

Iteration 15

Iterative development approaches demonstrate that it is possible to improve the UI, usability, consistency, integration, and satisfaction with almost any product. Iteration refers to a process of design refinement based upon user evaluation of mockups, simulations, prototypes, and an actual product. Based upon evaluation results, potential improvements or problems are identified, improvements designed, assessed relative to benefit-cost-schedule trade-offs, implemented, and re-evaluated. The cycle of iterations repeats until criteria are met and/or a product is implemented and shipped to customers for the acid test of satisfactory use.

The underlying goal of iteration is to meet real product requirements, correct real problems, and implement necessary improvements (see Figure 15.1). The basic assumption is that some form of valid evaluation input from a usability test or actual customer use of a product, is available. With increasing pressure to reduce development time, it is tempting to implement a design and then iterate the product in the field. However, a product team is fortunate if such a product is successful.

Topics to be discussed include:

241

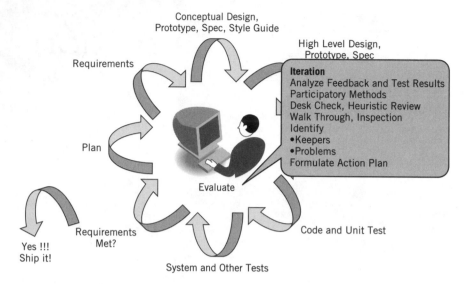

FIGURE 15.1
Iteration within a user-centered process.

- Prerequisites
- Finding the big hitters
- Defects, keepers, and trade-offs—techniques and diagnostics
- Short term and long term effects on rapid turnaround and optimization
- Follow-up analysis
- Organizational and technical considerations
- Back to the project

Prerequisites

There are several criteria to satisfy before entering into iterative development. Some requirements are technical and some are organizational and management related.

Motivation.   A commercial software product is fortunate to be able to ship copies to one million users. However, if 5 percent of those buying a million-user product are dissatisfied, then there are 50,000 dissatisfied users. This is a large number of unhappy people, many of whom complain and require special handling. For a web-based Internet site (in a sea of millions), dissatisfaction may result in a loss of future visits to that site. A user-centered product team wants to avoid these situations.

Iterative techniques are applied to product development in order to detect and resolve major problems and significant improvements early in a product development cycle. Certainly, a major goal of iteration is to avoid product rejection and expensive rework in the repair of avoidable customer problems or implementation of major enhancements. Along with good design practices, product iteration is a development technique similar to accident prevention, namely, dissatisfaction avoidance.

Delaying marketing of a product means higher development costs, higher purchase costs, and potentially more competition. Iteration just for the sake of iteration is not appropriate for serious product development efforts. Significant product improvement is not automatically guaranteed between consecutive iterations. Iterative improvement actually becomes harder to achieve as simpler aspects of product change are implemented in early iterations. The potential gain of additional development iterations must outweigh the cost to both development and customers.

> **Rule of Thumb**: Remember to keep using all prior techniques during iteration (e.g., participatory methods, heuristic reviews, etc.). These methods are useful while sorting out problem solutions and potential improvements.

Ability to Change.   Hopefully, a product is designed and implemented in anticipation of iteration. Without an ability to change rapidly and frequently, product iteration may be ineffective and fruitless.

> **Rule of Thumb**: Design a product with ease of change in mind.

Comprehensiveness.   Recall the components of user satisfaction. Assessment of overall satisfaction and usability must account for user performance and attitudes toward the foundation factors of:

- Features (domain and user interface)
- UI (appearance, behavior, user interaction)
- Performance (response time)
- Reliability (overall quality)
- Installation
- User assistance (performance support, help, training, and hardcopy)

Input from usability tests or directly from users yields a conscious or uncconscious evaluation of all these parameters. An accurate evaluation of a system is dependent upon an accurate assessment of foundation factors.

>   **Rule of Thumb**: A major goal of iteration is to:
>   - Assure an accurate causal analysis of actual or potential problems
>   - Find actual or potential solutions to key problems
>   - Identify other areas of potentially significant improvement
>   - Leave satisfactory features alone

Listen.   A willingness to listen to usability evaluation personnel and users discuss and explain problems and results is important. Sometimes, it is hard for a developer to accept criticism of a product designed and implemented over a long period of time. However, willingness to change a product in order to improve its usefulness to customers is necessary to achieve meaningful results during iteration.

Trade-offs.   Understand the trade-offs and competing factors involved in making change to a product. Figure 15.2 depicts competing factors and trade-offs that affect user attitudes or performance. For example, detailed design factors that influence ease of learning may compete with ease of long-term use by expert users. Other factors impose constraints on what is achievable, such as a short schedule or insufficient experience with the development tools.

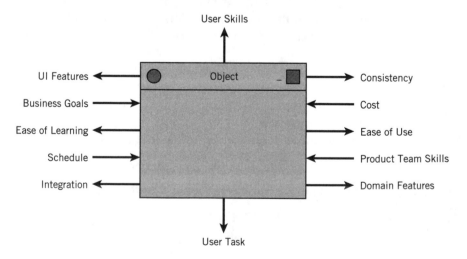

FIGURE 15.2
Competing factors and trade-offs in user-centered development.

Even when focusing only on change to the UI of a product, there are many elements that interact. Many times, iteration of a product is similar to playing a game, where changing one feature of a product has expected and unexpected effects on other areas. A UC product team balances the trade-offs and conflicts to the overall benefit of a user.

Finding the Big Hitters

A good designer needs insight into how to evaluate the results of a usability test or other forms of end-user evaluation of a product. A second pass of analysis follows a first round to be sure that short-term and long-term usability has been carefully evaluated.

Assume.   At this point, let's assume:

- The usability evaluation is understood by a UC product team
- Users who evaluated a product are typical of the intended audience
- The scenarios used are typical for the product and are adequately supported by the test vehicle in terms of the major satisfaction factors

To Fix or Not to Fix!   A UC product team must continually ask what must be fixed or changed and what must be kept intact as quantitative and qualitative information is analyzed. The most important question is what change is most likely to improve

- User satisfaction
- User productivity
- User frustration (meaning reduce)
- Competitiveness
- Meeting other goals and criteria

Given a collection of test results, a UC product team determines what to fix and what to leave alone. Tests tend to focus on problem detection, so care is taken to determine what's wrong and what's right with a product.

Defects, Keepers, and Trade-offs—
Techniques and Diagnostics

Early during development or during very focused evaluations, it is possible to obtain sufficiently detailed diagnostic information at a low level of detail. A low level of detail includes usability evaluation at a screen level during conceptual design, which is harder to achieve during high-level or detailed design. The key practice to learn is change only what needs to be changed to meet criteria and a user's needs.

At First Blush.   Some diagnostic rules of thumb include items listed in Table 15.1. A UC product team looks for a pattern of results based upon multiple users. However, even input from a single user is useful to confirm the intuition of a team about a potential problem area or a potential improvement. Care must be taken not to jump the gun to solve a problem or improve a satisfactory product feature based upon a single data point.

TABLE 15.1
Test diagnostics

Result	Action
Positive comments	Keep
High subjective rating	Keep
High objective rating	Keep
Negative comment	Evaluate cause
Low subjective rating	Evaluate and Fix
Competitor better	Evaluate and Fix
Criteria not met	Evaluate and Fix
Suggestion from a single user	Consider
Multiuser suggestion	Evaluate and Fix
Too much time on task	Evaluate how spent by step
User error	Evaluate cause
Request help (many)	Evaluate cause

Keepers.   Features meeting criteria are definitely kept in a design. However, if users express dislike of a particular feature or preference for another, it's time to listen and respond with a solution. If users respond positively to a particular feature, you know that you have a keeper.

"If it ain't broke, . . ."   Positive comments and high objective/subjective ratings indicate areas where a product should be left alone. Obviously, negative comments, error-prone areas, help-prone areas, and low subjective ratings indicate areas that require change. Areas where a competitor or predecessor is better indicate where improvement is needed. Clearly, if firm usability criteria are not satisfied, then product changes are required.

Rules of Thumb:

1. Remember that usability is a function of features, UI, performance, documentation, and other factors.

2. Understand the real cause of a problem before fixing something that may not be broken. You may fix a symptom, potentially introduce other problems, and still have a problem to fix.

Be sure to define a category for must-fix items due to low end-user ratings, criteria failure, or noncompetitiveness. Be sure to define a leave-well-enough-alone category.

On the other hand, if a particular approach is getting in the way of a superior result, it may be appropriate to break it and do better.

Severity and Frequency.   Early on, there is typically a wealth of problems to work on, later there is likely to be a perceived overabundance of problems. There is a definite need to assess the risks associated with individual and collective problems.

Assess problems for likely frequency of occurrence, as well as likely impact to a user, sponsoring business, and the customers ultimately supported. In some cases, a judgment call may need to be made. For example:

- A problem with severe penalty to a user but which may not happen often can be assessed as needing correction.
- A low-impact problem with high nuisance value that occurs very often is likely to be on the list of problems to fix.

User Suggestions.   A customer may not always be right, but remember who pays the bills! Suggestions are considered, especially if a product is not meeting major task needs for a user. A UC product team interacts with users in order to understand:

- What system and domain skills are applied (naive, casual, expert)
- What a user is trying to accomplish in the real world using the product
- How a user is trying to do the work using the software

This provides a better context for why comments are made by a user and whether to accept and act upon them.

Short-Term and Long-Term Effects

A UC product team grapples with whether potentially real problems are related to the effects of short-term learning and use, whether they are long-term usage problems beyond initial learning, or both. Usability evaluations are designed to establish the nature of some of these tough problems.

The Short and Long of It. In the context of short-term and long-term use, requests for help or long task times are not necessarily indicators of problems. Typical user performance on a new system or application depicts short-term and long-term results. On well-designed software, learning occurs quickly during the first few tasks, speed and accuracy improves quickly, and knowledge is extended over time. In general, time on task and calls for help decrease over time.

Break each task down into subtasks where a user interacts with individual screens or dialogs. There is a potential problem if there is a pattern where:

- Users spend too much time trying to use a particular screen or control
- Errors happen or users consistently request help on a particular screen or control

If users are stuck at this point, there is a problem with both the product UI and supporting information. Follow-on analysis of user ratings and comments are in order.

Initial Learning and Use. Problems need to be classified as short term and long term. Problems of initial learning are disregarded in many cases. For example, a UC product team cannot do very much to help a novice user become more comfortable with using a pointing device. Similarly, a UC product team cannot do very much to help a novice user become comfortable with the basic elements of GUI, WUI, or HUI style. However, a UC product team for an application does have control over getting a user comfortable with an application's content.

Another example of initial learning is finding the location of menu choices, where a novice GUI user must learn the location of *all* menu choices and a more experienced user must learn the location of application specific (nonstandard) menu choices only. This is like learning where the drinking glasses are stored in someone else's kitchen.

Memorizing shortcut keys, mouse buttons, and mouse-keyboard augmentations is attributable to initial learning and is not necessarily a real problem.

Initial learning of this type of information cannot be solved by conventional means.

Long-Term Usage.   Unless thrown out quickly by an end user, a UI-based application is used over a long period of time. With luck, the software has an extended lifetime over a period of years and use across multiple versions. This is where long-term usage problems are discovered and become noticeable.

Severe, long-term problems *must* be fixed if a product is to achieve acceptance. There may be long term *nuisance factors* that won't go away (e.g., the infamous but very common too-many-windows-and-too-many-steps problem). Inconsistency with respect to highly used and standard UI features, such as incorrect shortcut keys or incorrect placement of Edit Menu choices like Cut, Copy, and Paste, is a long-term problem.

There may be steps that do not get easier over time (e.g., a sequence of required steps that, if not performed exactly, will result in the loss of user information or work). There may be places where users consistently get stuck trying to accomplish work.

FUPRID Factors.   Satisfaction and usability are a function of features (F), user interface (U), performance (P), reliability (R), installability (I), and documentation including all forms of user assistance and performance support (D). Combining the first letter of these factors leads to the FUPRID acronym. Along with classification as short-term or long-term, problems are classified into the FUPRID categories.

Studies of FUPRID factors indicate that features, UI, and performance are the most important to overall application satisfaction and usability. However, if basic reliability, installability, and information are not provided, then these become dissatisfaction issues. Test questionnaires are designed to obtain user feedback on the major contributing factors of usability and overall user satisfaction. Look at user ratings and comments for these and other factors deemed important to the product.

Features refer to having sufficient domain and UI functionality to meet task needs. Sufficiency of function does not necessarily imply that a product initially has all the elements normally carried in extensive domain feature checklists. However, there is a critical mass of features required, below which an application starts to become unusable.

The line between UI and function blurs very easily, so care must be taken to separate what can be done from how it is done. UI refers to sufficiency of visual (look), behavior, and user interaction elements (feel) for a user's tasks.

Clearly, the usability of a UI is extremely important but not the only factor considered. The base UI style of a system determines a portion of the rating. However, UI-based application elements influence a significant aspect of a user's satisfaction. Both must be separated carefully. Both must be easy to learn and use.

Performance is most easily related to the interactive response time of an application, (e.g., from the start to finish of an operation). In some cases, performance includes evaluation of batch or background task throughput. If interactive response time is not fast, users do complain.

Reliability is interpreted as the basic quality of the product in terms of defect-free behavior. A user's basic confidence in the system's integrity and secure behavior is captured here. Will data be destroyed by the system? Will work be lost during navigation? This is an issue of trust in a product.

Installability refers to the ease of setup and installation that leads to the initial use of a product. Documentation captures satisfaction with the information supporting use of the product, whether in the form of hardcopy documents or online help.

Follow-Up Analysis

Usually, it's a good idea to have the product running as usability test results are evaluated. The basic question is, "What change in the product achieves improvement in result?"

Desired Result.   Aside from resolving major problems, the goal of an iteration cycle is to achieve measurable improvement in key usability metrics, such as:

- Reduced time on task
- Increased user satisfaction
- Reduced calls for help
- Fewer reported problems
- Reduced severity in problems
- Increased number of positive comments
- Decreased number of negative comments
- Higher preference over competition

An example of a desired result for time on task is depicted in Figure 15.3 (time on task improved between Iteration 1 and Iteration 2 for a product). Other results can be graphed in a similar fashion.

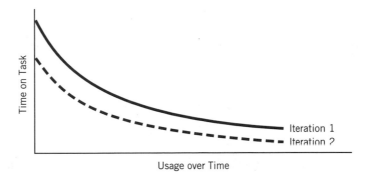

FIGURE 15.3
Improvement with iteration.

Engineering Change. Features not meeting criteria or unpopular with users require repair. Make change in small increments. Change occurs quickly for daily distribution and follow-up evaluation. Change requiring a large development cost needs to go through a replanning phase.

Compare to Competitors/Predecessors. A good technique for evaluation of design effectiveness is comparison to competitive or predecessor systems, especially those considered state of the art. Use of quantitative techniques is very good here (e.g., information loads, work step counts, time on task, user errors, and user attitudes for the same or comparable user tasks).

This approach keeps focus on design areas that can be improved. Obviously, the goal is to beat the system being compared with. This is especially helpful if the evaluation information is diagnostic (capturing actual user time spent on each screen used while performing the assigned task).

Work a Mile in a User's Shoes. As with functional problems, usability defects should be *recreated* by a UC product team. Test scenarios are exercised to get a feel for where an end user encounters difficulty with either product or information windows and procedures.

Bang for the Buck. Certainly, changes that are likely to make a real difference are taken care of first. These are the most likely to take longer to design and implement so as to achieve an improvement.

> **Rule of Thumb**: Focus on fixing the long-term problems first. If short-term learning problems are easy to overcome with change, fix those as well.

This includes making things easier to learn and understand.

SAPCO Factors.   While considering FUPRID factors, revisit the problem list using SAPCO design principles. At this time, begin to ask solution-oriented questions.

How can the product be made more *simple*?

- What does a user *need to know* and *need to do* in order to use a product effectively?
- How can the UI be more intuitive and become its own documentation?
- How can feedback on what's going on be made clearer?
- How can high-use tasks be made easier using the product?
- How can a product become easier to explore without penalty to a user?

How can a product be made more *aesthetic*?

- How can screen and dialog graphics, layout, and sounds be made clear and pleasing to the eye and/or ear?
- How can alignment, spacing, colors, and fonts be used effectively?
- How can information be visualized to a user's benefit?

How can the product be made more *productive*?

- How does using the product compare to previous methods?
- Are there any screens or worksteps that can be combined or eliminated?
- How can techniques of using defaults and remembering prior user input be used?
- Are sufficient domain and UI features implemented?
- Is the product fast enough and reliable enough?

How can the product be made more *customizable*?

- How can the product support the needs of novice and expert users?
- Has sufficient flexibility been built in to accommodate variance in end-user preferences for layout and interaction styles?
- How can window-sizing behavior be improved for different end user needs?

How can the product meet *other* desirable features of UI-based applications?

- Is the application sufficiently forgiving of end-user errors?
- How can direct manipulation and direct entry techniques be applied to the product?
- Is supporting documentation accurate and clear?

Problems in UI Components.   Many times, there are problems inherent in the components of a UI style being used or there are problems with how the component is used by the application. A UC product team asks a basic question—"Is the right UI component being used for what a user needs to do at this point?" A slightly different spin is, "Is the right UI component being used correctly?"

An example of a problematic component is the spin button. Studies have shown that about half of novice users click the "up arrow" to increase the displayed value, and the other half use the "down arrow" to perform the same task. Users behave this way probably because of user models for how the button should behave in the context of integrated use with other UI components (e.g., scroll bars on fields and windows). Some users believe the up button should increase the value while other users believe the down button should. Given this user tendency, a UC product team should consider whether it is appropriate to use this component heavily in an application and in what situations.

Problems in Application Components.   The lion's share of problems attributable to a product's UI is in the UI-based application components. As previously discussed, good use of a UI style is the first thing that must be established. This includes avoiding the too-many-screens-and-too-many-steps type problems. Interaction flows help determine typical paths that a user traverses in accomplishing tasks. Look at test results to see if problems are attributable to how a UI style is used. After that, consideration is given to:

- Intended user's model
- Terminology, icons, and bitmaps
- Objects and actions
- Dialogs and interaction steps
- Device usage

Screen captures help determine clarity and consistency of individual screens, dialogs, icons and bitmaps, feedback, and messages. Work step flows help determine exactly what a user must do to achieve a given result on a given screen or dialog.

> **Rule of Thumb:** If SAPCO elements don't jump out at you, fixes may be in order.

Determine and Weigh Options.   As major problems are identified, look for design alternatives. There are usually multiple alternatives available for fixes, and a lack of alternatives may lead to a poor decision. Each option is evaluated for how well it integrates into an existing product framework. Options are weighed against the product cycle elements (i.e., plans, requirements, conceptual design, design (interface and noninterface), implementation, and testing).

Then, Just Do It!   Options with the best overall tradeoffs are selected and applied to a product. The cycle is repeated until requirements are met.

Rapid Turnaround and Optimization _____

Implementation, whether via prototyping or product, is an expensive activity that is a means to an end and is not the end in itself. Some tips and techniques that enhance effectiveness follow.

Watch Testing.   One approach to evaluating a product is relatively passive. The passive approach basically tosses the product over the wall to usability test personnel. This approach waits for test results to come back before determining how to improve the product. Depending upon execution, a calendar month may pass between the two tosses. Usually, the subsequent iteration results are not impressive.

A better approach is more proactive in nature. In spite of schedule pressures, UC product personnel are actively involved in evaluation of a product. Team members can conduct and monitor usability tests. Watching users struggle with a product sometimes leads to designing better alternatives earlier and more effectively. The lead-time from problem detection to solution availability is reduced to as little as same day turnaround.

> **Rule of Thumb**: Don't worry about not being objective when analyzing test results. It's hard to argue when you achieve qualitative and quantitative improvement. Besides, there is no benefit to you or anyone else if problems are swept under the rug.

Asking Permission?   Even when committed to user satisfaction, development managers and leads don't like to hear about iteration of a product. So, don't tell them when small and easily containable improvements are being made. There is truth to the expression that asking forgiveness is easier than asking permission.

When change is costly, likely to impact the work of others, or likely to impact the overall schedule, it is appropriate to put the proper project plans and controls in place. For example, if severe criteria failure takes a month to design, implement, and retest a potential solution—and will definitely hold up the work of the rest of a project team—there should be management and sponsor agreement and support for the planned work. Otherwise, what is important is commitment to results and achieving rapid turnaround.

Optimization Criteria.

A UC product team needs measurable objectives and criteria for a UI. In addition, criteria are established for when change should take place as solutions to design problems or design optimizations are discovered. Changes that produce insignificant quantitative or qualitative effects are delayed, while those producing significant user value are evaluated more seriously.

The overall criteria for climbing a mountain of complex product development is clearly specified and understood. Once understood, management and developers must accept the criteria. The agreement goes beyond superficial acceptance to true personal commitment by the entire development team.

When the Rubber Meets the Road.

Some problems cannot be fixed. An example is where there are user expectations about how something should work that are not logical, realistic, or feasible.

> **Rule of Thumb**: Face the music on expectation-related issues earlier rather than later.

Participatory Methods.

It continues to be a good practice to keep user participation high and active during the process of sorting out results and potential solutions.

Know When to Start Over (Redesign).

Dead ends are often encountered in design. If a locally optimized design does not achieve desired results, the design is discarded. Otherwise, a bad design is refined and polished—an effort which doesn't lead to a great design. Each design component is evaluated against a criterion of delightful enough to keep. If the current approach does not lead to a great design, throw it back. There are many other fish in the sea of design alternatives.

Beware of Local Optimizations.   When the goal is to climb a mountain, don't spend too much effort optimizing the climb of a foothill! A nonoptimal approach is used when climbing the foothills of a product's design (e.g., iteration of product features that are unimportant to overall product results). The important part of a climb is knowing the difference between a foothill and a mountain and then spending maximum and effective effort on the mountain climb.

Know When to Stop.   Before starting, know when to stop. Iteration is a means to an end, and it is hard to predict how much iteration or how long it takes to meet objectives. The majority of products yield user satisfaction ratings somewhat above neutral. The climb to the mountaintop of very satisfied customers is significant. Achieving this result is achieved only by concerted, focused, and dedicated hard work by management and technical personnel. Because major competitors are conducting iterative design based upon prototyping, the number of needed iterations continues to increase.

Organizational and Technical Considerations_____

There must be real commitment to iteration as a methodology. Perhaps more importantly, there must be real commitment to achieve results relative to product goals.

Management and Technical Commitment.   Product management and technical personnel must understand what is being developed and why. There must be real commitment to iterate the software design until customer requirements (function, UI, noninterface, performance, etc.) are met. Once employed as a development technique, iteration will likely continue through the implementation phase of the product.

Product and Prototyping Personnel.   Unless the prototyping team is the same as the implementation team, product development personnel must be totally integrated and participating in the design iteration. Otherwise, a development team must reverse engineer the desired interface and noninterface design into the product implementation. This does not work well. An alternative is to commit the prototyping team through product ship in order to avoid loss of knowledge and to maintain accountability.

Supporting Infrastructure.   Many competitors say that hundreds of iterations are performed with functional software prototypes. The prototype instantiates the UI and noninterface software design. Furthermore, functional prototypes are:

- Distributed to a large audience daily
- Critiqued daily
- Fixed daily
- Repeated as prototype evolves to product
- Not shipped until requirements are met

Appropriate infrastructures must be in place as the prototyping efforts begin.

Think Ahead.   Remember, a prototype is just another form of software, but one that is guaranteed to change. Formal development processes may not be necessary, but random hacking may not be appropriate either. Consider the items that follow during prototype and product development and iteration.

Design and Develop with Iteration in Mind.   Anticipate iteration while designing and developing, think about how to make changes to the design and code easier and efficient. A common approach is to separate (segment) interface from noninterface design and code.

Design and Develop with Alternatives in Mind.   It is likely that many design alternatives will be evaluated. Make it easy to add design alternatives. One technique is to add feature switches that are easy to surface via the user interface.

Evolutionary and Incremental (vs. Big Bang).   Start small and grow the software, implementing the most significant and most sensitive feature first. Since there is less invested in early implementations, incremental change works better than approaches attempting to develop all features at once. Also, evolutionary change to improve the design must be driven by measurable and objective evaluations with end users.

Questions.   How would you design and develop software if you were told that 100-plus iterations of the design and code were likely? How would you design and develop software if you believed that 25-plus major design alternatives would be considered for UI and noninterface features?

Iteration Effectiveness Is Up to the Developer.   Iteration can work!

- For one product that went to market, initial lab based usability results were quite average, i.e., about 4.5 on a scale of 7 = best. After several minor iterations, usability improved from 5.2 to 6 in one iteration.
- A product that was not released went from 5.5 to 6.3 in one iteration.

The lesson is that usability and satisfaction can improve significantly with hard and focused work, dedication to results, and making the changes that make a difference. If meaningful changes are made early, usability and satisfaction results can be quite dramatic and impressive.

Back to the Project

User feedback is available from the initial usability evaluation of the conceptual design for the project. An independent test was arranged and conducted, and feedback is available from heuristic reviews and walkthroughs. The project manager is anxious to review the results at the same time you do. He mentions that senior management wants a briefing day after tomorrow. You have about four hours to analyze the results, assess compliance to requirements and criteria, and assess problems and potential solutions.

In addition, you must determine:

- Changes required for the product to meet requirements and solve any problems
- Changes to the design that would result in significant improvement over competition
- Aspects of the UI that should be left alone and aspects that should be corrected or improved
- Project schedule impacts if any

Be sure to justify your answers.

Be sure to continue your research over the web.

Any questions?

References_____

Schneiderman, B., *Designing the User Interface*, Addison-Wesley: Reading, MA, 1987.

Melkus, L.A., and Torres, R.J., "Guidelines for the Use of a Prototype in User Interface Design," Human Factors Society Symposium, 1988.

Torres, R.J., "Graphical User Interfaces: Iteration," Share 85, Feb. 1995.

Part 3

Getting Serious

Once conceptual design is complete, a road map is available to guide the next steps of the journey of UI and usability design and development. The volume of work, its complexity, and the level of detail increase as time goes on. People and organizational issues increase as well. At this point, management has made major commitments of resource, funds, and personal capital to the project. A UC Product Team is committed to

- Requirements
- A design approach
- Schedule

The tasks include

Chapter 16. High Level Design (semantics and structure)

Chapter 17. Specification Techniques

Chapter 18. Low Level Design

Chapter 19. Product Construction and Deployment

High Level Design 16

There are many approaches to design a UI: waterfall, inside-out, outside-in, iterative, and so forth. There are also multiple techniques within each approach. Regardless of the high-level approach used, very specific techniques are required to design low-level and high-level interactions. Figure 16.1 illustrates a user-centered high-level design approach.

What is discussed in this chapter is an approach appropriate for iterative design and implementation of applications utilizing various UI styles. An OO approach is described in this chapter, although conventional development techniques can be substituted for many design steps. Design outputs generated from this technique are useful for documenting, simulating, prototyping, evaluating, and implementing UI based-applications.

The following topics are discussed for high-level design, which defines the semantics and structure of a user interface and potentially the supporting underlying software:

- Setting context within a development cycle
- Definitions and design input

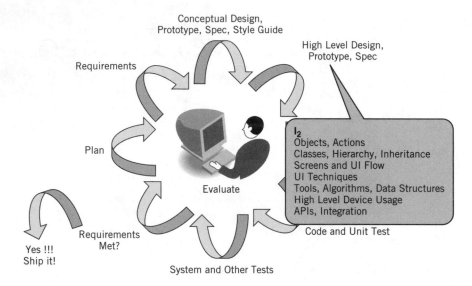

FIGURE 16.1
User-centered high-level design.

- OO components
- Desktop behavior
- A UI flow
- Major screens—features, content, menus
- Major dialogs
- Identify supporting windows
- Installation, print, and other system features
- Back to the project

During the process of design, a UC product team analyzes, validates, and iterates a design. I_2 is a major iteration that can have many smaller steps within it. A goal is to identify major reusable components not previously identified.

Designing UI-based applications is a challenge. There are many approaches and techniques that suffice for the various tasks. There are many details that must be accounted for and designed well in order to ensure ease of learning, use by end users, and other UI/usability goals. However, the surest way to develop a UI-based application with usability meeting requirements is an iterative approach with user involvement.

Setting Context within a Development Cycle_____

Up to this point, our activities have been focused on the first major design iteration for the project, conceptual design. On a short-cycle for small- to medium-size software projects, the closure of conceptual design takes place in as little as three to four weeks. On medium to large projects with a longer schedule, the conceptual design takes place in four to six weeks.

During this time, a UC project team has been involved in:

- Project planning, sizing the effort, staffing, and training
- Formulating and understanding requirements
- Acquiring and setting up tools and environments
- Designing and prototyping alternatives for a conceptual direction
- Working with users and vested interests to select and confirm a design direction
- Integrating the UI design with the infrastructure design

    Rule of Thumb: Conceptual design sets a project's direction in a relatively short period of time and must be reasonably accurate and flexible. High-level design fleshes out more details, and low-level design completes the definition.

We'll now explore the next major phase of the project—high-level design.

Definitions and Design Input _____

Design is an underlying scheme or arrangement of elements that makes up an application, screen, command, widget, or underlying components. A UI design is a collection of end-user perceptible features of a software program that includes user input, interaction, and system response. Implementation design for a UI is the scheme of using programming language and system features to achieve a UI result. A clear distinction is made between a UI and the underlying software that makes it work. We'll continue to focus on UI design.

End user perceptible features of a software program include those for UI and application domain. An example of a UI feature is a menu bar for a GUI, while an example of an application domain feature is a field supporting a search on a web page. End user perceptible features of a UI-based software program include application usage of screens, windows, icons, menus, pointers, and other UI components. In addition, UI application layer features perceived by end users are an intended user's model, object and command semantics and syntax, physical device usage, and interactions that go beyond the basic features of a UI style being used.

Recall that a product UI design is instantiated in specifications, mockups, storyboards, simulations, prototypes, and ultimately product software delivered to users. A design does not necessarily deal with how a UI is implemented.

Motivation.   Developing a UI-based application is a challenging endeavor from a design, implementation, and test perspective. This is where the hard work begins.

There are at least two layers of a design (see Figure 16.2). The UI of an application is the topmost layer (i.e., system and application provided screens, icons, menus, pointers, controls, structures, and interaction style). Some of a design is implemented using facilities provided by an OS (e.g., visible components and behavior of the Maximize button on a window).

The next software layer is UI support, which provides data structures and algorithms required by UI or application domain features and not explicitly supported by an OS or its tools. Examples of UI support are direct manipulation or search actions. If an application requires a data base or other software infrastructure, then more underlying non-UI or Application Programming Interface (API) software is designed and implemented in a manner that complements the desired behavior of an application's UI.

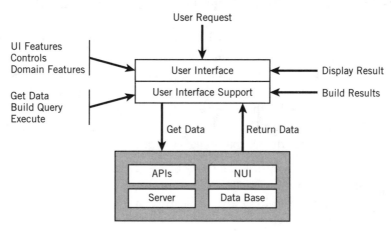

FIGURE 16. 2
Structure of a UI-based application.

Rule of Thumb: With respect to schedule and resources, be aware that design can outpace implementation capabilities by at least 3 to 1.

High-Level Design.   As with designs for other software, there are at least two other levels of detail for a UI. The first level beyond conceptual design is high-level and an opportunity for another major design iteration. Part of the challenge of high-level design is dealing with UI and product detail beyond the conceptual level. This is the first time that all major components are dealt with in detail concurrently and in an integrated manner.

Components of a high-level design for a UI are:

- Approach to use of the platform UI
- Intended user's model
- Object, property, and action features
- Structure and flow of windows or screens
- Major windows, screens, views, and dialogs
- Standard and optional views
- Graphics, audio, and visual style
- Menu style and command choices
- Installation, drag/drop, clipboard, print, and desktop behavior

Low-Level Design.   The level of design after high-level design is a low-level design phase, which includes all details not necessarily considered in depth during high-level design. As implied by the name, low-level design

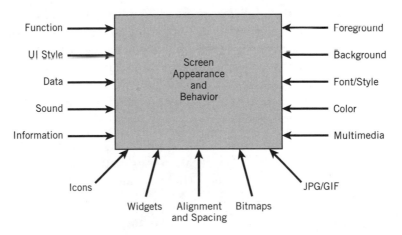

FIGURE 16.3
UI design complexity.

work includes defining all the myriad details for screen layouts, pointer-related behavior, command choice graying, access key characters, access keys, shortcut keys, keyboard and pointer mappings, display color and graphics, messages, user feedback, and nonstandard device usage. In addition, low-level design is the start of implementation design, which provides details of how a UI and software features are translated into programming instructions and data algorithms.

> **Rule of Thumb**: As with other aspects of design, all these features are dealt with in a planned and proactive manner.

Because of the volume of work and detail, there is high appeal for iterative or evolutionary approaches to design, evaluation, and implementation of UI-based applications. Pragmatically, such approaches provide time for a UC product team to work through the high-level details early without getting overwhelmed by the myriad low-level UI and implementation details.

An Example.   To illustrate the elements of a UI design, an Address Book application is used. The Address Book is an application designed to support a user of the Conference Companion who is attending a conference or symposium. In summary, it is intended to integrate with the Companion, allow viewing a list of conference attendees, provide detailed information for each attendee, and create records for people and organizations. Features such as email and paging can be integrated if supported by a user's hardware and software platform.

Design Input.   Before proceeding into the task of high-level design for a UI, recall the set of inputs developed up to this point. Information available to a UC product team at this time includes requirements, style guide, platform standards, conceptual design, early prototypes, usability feedback, a development plan, and a notion of how to iterate the design. A high-level UI style and structure (screen flow) of the software is determined by an intended user's model.

Selection and refinement of an application's UI style is a design input. For example, a WUI-based application uses platform features such as windows, icons, menus, and pointers. There are also low-level controls such as lists, spin buttons, and so forth.

A UC product team must design how system UI elements are used, together with application-unique elements not supported by the system UI. Use of the many available UI interaction techniques must be considered explicitly. UI approaches related to consistency of style within the application must be designed.

For example, a platform standard may describe a particular control, a toolbar for example, and how it should be used. A given application may use this control in a way that is standard within the platform and even more standardized within the application by use of common terms, graphics, and arrangement of buttons in a common manner. Special use of UI features like pushbuttons, terminology, and windows must be considered.

Any specialized or unique UI controls (widgets) implemented by a UI-based application are designed. Typically, UI controls are complex, and implementation considerations must be weighed carefully because the application must handle all the low-level interaction and behavior with the keyboard, pointer, and display.

Rule of Thumb: Use standard platform controls as much as possible.

Corollary: Avoid construction of custom controls as much as possible.

OO Components

Some amount of time is spent discussing OO design as it applies to a UI. From a user standpoint, users live in an OO world but think in terms of object orientation in a very high-level manner. From a practical design standpoint, it is easier to perform many design tasks based upon OO notions, regardless of the approach to structuring the software application and the choice of programming language for implementation. This may become more obvious when menus are designed for a screen.

A High-Level Definition.   To be truly Object-Oriented (OO) requires that a system have:

- Classes of objects
- Class hierarchy
- Inheritance via the class hierarchy

Any system meeting the first condition only is object-based. If a system meets the first two conditions, it is class-based.

In an OO sense, an object is a collection of data and the actions are performed on it. Objects are organized into classes, where objects in a class have similar actions or properties. A collection of classes is organized into a hierarchy with levels of subclasses. Classes of objects inherit (reuse) actions or properties from classes higher in the hierarchy, where refinement of actions or properties may occur to suit specific class needs.

> **Rule of Thumb**: From a UI point of view, users are most aware of objects and behavior of similar objects. Classes, class hierarchy, and inheritance do not need to be made explicit for an end user, but these notions are very useful for any implementation design where reuse is a major goal.

As an example, a user normally thinks of a pet dog as simply a dog. A user does not necessarily think of the animal as an instance of the dachshund class, which is in the canine class hierarchy and inherits certain properties from the hierarchy. Most users think of software objects in a similar manner. An Address Book is an address book and not an instance of a container class within the implementation tool's class hierarchy.

Methodologies.

Effective development of an OO system potentially requires three major activities.

- Object Oriented Analysis (OOA) evaluates a user's needs and problems to be solved. Outputs provide a conceptual design for the static, dynamic, and functional aspects of a user's problem.

- Object Oriented Design (OOD) translates the results of OOA into system and object designs more closely related to implementation needs.

- Object Oriented Programming (OOP) translates the OOA and OOD outputs into product software using implementation tools.

There are several methodologies suitable for OOA, OOD, and OOP. It is not necessary to become obsessed with any of them because detailed discussion is beyond the scope of this book. What is important is for a UC product team to find an OO development process that is suitable for the skills and tools of the team and the user problem to be solved.

> **Rule of Thumb**: There are many ways to solve a problem in an OO manner.

Object-Based Considerations.

All application functions and features are expressible in terms of objects, actions, and the attributes of objects and actions.

> **Rule of Thumb**: Regardless of how a UI or underlying software is implemented, OO techniques are extremely useful in design.

The objective of the technique is to define from a user's view objects and actions that a user works with. As a part of the analysis, objects and actions are defined in terms of primitive elements and relationships to other objects and actions. Attributes of objects and actions are extracted and defined in order to further clarify definitions. Analyze design input to extract objects, actions, and their attributes. Requirement documents are analyzed to identify implicit or explicit objects and actions. A useful technique is to highlight all nouns in one color and verbs in another.

Typical requirements for an Address Book would state:

- Provide a system that allows users to *display* and interact with a *list of names*
- Allow users to *create* their own *personal entries*
- Provide *maps* and *directions* to access resources such as conference rooms and offices
- Provide *find*, *search*, and *print* capabilities
- The product must be accessed via GUI, WUI, and HUI

Identify Objects.   Objects are entities named with a noun. Object usage is separated from the characterization of the object in order to develop a correct definition. To properly characterize an object, a UC product team must:

- Define what it is (its nature)
- Describe its usage
- Define characteristics, properties, and property values
- Describe object relationships to other objects
- Define the set of actions valid on the object

Examples of end-user objects from an analysis of Address Book requirements are Address Book, Person, Group, Resource, and Distribution List. An example of an object with variation in properties is Address Book, where an organizational Address Book is not editable by a nonadministrative user but a Personal Address Book is editable by all users. Another example of a similar object is a group or distribution list, which has To: and cc: information.

Identify Actions.   Actions are entities named with verb words. Ultimately, actions become commands in a UI. To properly characterize an action, a UC product team must:

- Define what the action is (its nature)
- Specify how the action is used, separate from its nature

- Define action characteristics, properties, and property values
- Define action relationship to other actions
- Define the objects to which the action applies

Actions are likely to be context sensitive in that different behavior is observed depending upon the object. Each object-action pair is examined carefully to determine the exact result of the action.

Example actions for an Address Book include Find, Search, and Print. An example of an action with variations in properties is Sort, which can be performed by Name or City Address. Actions that are required based upon analysis of requirements are Drag, Cut, and Properties.

Establish the Primitives.   A primitive is a basic or fundamental entity not derived from another and which is a building block for other entities. Primitives are abstracted during reviews of objects and actions, especially as redundancy in the collection of objects, actions, and properties is exhausted. The designer analyzes the set of objects, actions, and properties for primitives. The primitives form the basic building blocks for construction of other entities.

An example primitive action is a locate action, which can be used to build the Find and Search actions. An example of a primitive object is group, which is used to build a Group and a Distribution List.

Build Object-Action-Property Matrices.   To facilitate analysis, a UC product team constructs matrices for objects and actions, objects and properties, and actions and properties. The team determines the potential collection of valid actions for each object, including system features like drag/drop and clipboard operations. Similarly, the team analyzes which properties are relevant to each individual object and action.

A likely result of building these matrices includes discovery that they are potentially filled in almost completely (i.e., there is potentially very dense feature coverage across objects, actions, and properties). For example:

- Many actions historically limited to certain types of objects are found to be valid for many objects in general
- Many properties of specialized objects also apply to other more common objects
- Many properties of certain actions also apply to other actions

This is usually a counterintuitive and surprising result for many designers. In reality, dense matrices are a desirable result because new or added capabilities are discovered. An additional and excellent result for end users is that very consistent and even functional coverage is provided across the objects and actions of a software product. If follow-on planning and analyses are performed correctly, all the features described in the matrices are developed and provided to users over time.

Classes, Hierarchies, Inheritance.

Just having objects and actions leads to an object-based system. As mentioned earlier, an OO system requires classes, a class hierarchy, and inheritance via the class hierarchy. Classes, class hierarchy, and inheritance are abstracted from the end-user object, action, and property definitions. The major benefit for an end user is similarity in behavior for similar types of objects. However, users don't spend lots of time and effort categorizing visible software objects into various classes or hierarchies.

> **Rule of Thumb**: Keep the notions of OO transparent. A developer maps end-use objects and features to templates, algorithms, and data structures in a reuse library.

Class Abstraction.

A good technique is to begin establishing potential groupings of objects based upon the objects-actions analysis. Some objects naturally fall into similar groupings while some types of objects are naturally distinct. For example, Address Book objects are different from printers and map objects are different from containers. However, an entry for a Person is somewhat similar to an entry for a Resource that is added to a Personal Address Book. Some distinctions between objects are very subtle and require additional considerations. An intended user's model helps clarify the distinctions.

Types of Relations.

A good test for determining whether an object belongs to a class is referred to as the "is-a" relation. For example, every frog is a reptile and every trashcan is a container clearly define the class to which an object belongs. If "every event is a container" is a false statement, then an event belongs to another class.

> **Rule of Thumb**: It is rare to find an object without class.

Another good technique to contrast whether an object is a component of a class or a part of another object is the "is-a-part-of" relation. For example, "a leg is a part of a dog." Similarly, "a page is a part of a note." However, a map may or may not be part of an event.

As the classes are abstracted from the collection of objects, review the property and action sets of the objects to ensure that class properties also belong to the instance or subclass entities.

Other OO Considerations.   For the purposes of implementation design, a UC product team deals with construction of class hierarchies and inheritance. When finished, a UC product team will have constructed one or more trees (class hierarchies) depicting the relationships among the various classes of an application. It is extremely important to have a good user's model and object definitions to ensure sensible end-user definitions.

Following formulation of the class hierarchies, inheritance features are evaluated. Single and multiple inheritance features are considered. As part of the analysis, a UC product team may find examples of actions that are meaningful from both a user's and a designer's point of view but which impose difficulties upon the system and/or the user.

Design for Desktop Behavior

With more design preliminaries out of the way, let's get back on track. Major operating systems and platforms have desktops that are used to represent and allow access to software applications. The predominant UI styles are:

- GUIs for workstations and some handheld personal computers
- WUIs for software accessed via intranet, extranet, or Internet
- HUIs for handheld computing platforms

A web-based application is accessed from within a GUI or HUI browser window. Access is not provided from an operating system desktop per se (at this time).

Desktop Access.   GUI-, WUI-, and HUI-based software is accessed using multiple techniques. Common techniques for accessing software from a desktop include an icon on a desktop, a choice on a startup menu, and a button on a taskbar on a status area. Desktop access techniques respond to pointer and keyboard behaviors. Menus and menu choices are provided for many of the access techniques.

Design choices that a UC product team works through include:

- Objects represented or accessed via desktop icon or menu choice, including main and minimized objects

- Subobjects represented or accessed via desktop icons
- Menu choices for valid commands on a desktop icon including pop-up menu and menu bar
- Valid drag/drop operations and valid behavior of source and target objects, including other icons that represent objects in closed, open, and minimized states

Desktop Icons.   Along with commands to associate with desktop icons, a UC product team decides what type of icon to display. A desktop icon is either static or dynamic.

Design a UI Flow

The structure of a UI-based application consists of the flow, content, and layout of screens, menus, operations, and end-user interactions with a UI. In many respects, a structure of an application UI reflects the UI's syntax. A UI flow starts with how software is accessed initially and depicts:

- All the screen-level components of a UI
- Commands performed immediately or using dialogs
- Access to help, message, tutorials, and performance support
- Links to other software

The UI flow depicts how the application is accessed from other areas of the system.

> **Rule of Thumb**: UI software applications have a common structure.

Software applications have a very similar UI structure regardless of whether a GUI, WUI, or HUI style is used. Once the objects and actions of an application are known, the features are mapped to a structure implicit for the target OS or the application style of a UI. If a menu bar is supported, an OO style leads to certain menus, menu content, windows, and window flow. Following OSF/Motif, Mac, and Windows yield somewhat different models for the content of a set of menus.

Object UI Flow/Structure.   Figure 16.4 shows the basic navigation among screens associated with a UI-based application. A flow chart is used to give a bird's eye view of how the application's UI is structured. Such a depiction is called a site map in a web-based application.

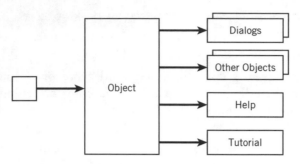

FIGURE 16.4
General UI flow.

A UI flow shows the movement of information and control from an object's initial access point to all screens with which a user interacts. A flow contains all user-selectable actions and depicts whether other screens are displayed as a result of end-user actions.

> **Rule of Thumb**: Build a UI flow starting with the initial access point and the object screen that is displayed as a result. Keep the UI flow shallow and avoid building a hierarchical menu system using windows, intrawindow screens, or web pages.

A more specific UI flow for an Address Book application is depicted in Figure 16.5 and shows access from a desktop, calendar, and mail applications. In addition, the Address Book UI flow accesses screens for specific dialogs, help, tutorial, and entries for people, groups, resources, and distribution lists, which in turn access dialogs, the calendar, and mail.

In general, a major benefit for end users of UI-based applications based on a GUI style is that a flat screen hierarchy with reduced user interactions is possible. Another major benefit is that a user maintains a point of reference during interaction with an object. The menu system allows a user to control the flow of operations with an object while working directly with the object. Comparable benefits are possible with web-based software with appropriate navigation aids.

There are some natural shortcuts to implement that facilitate and automate interaction. A major example of these natural shortcuts is when a primary object and related objects are open on a desktop. A single command on the primary object is applied to all related objects (e.g., a close on an Address Book automatically closes all open objects related to the Address Book).

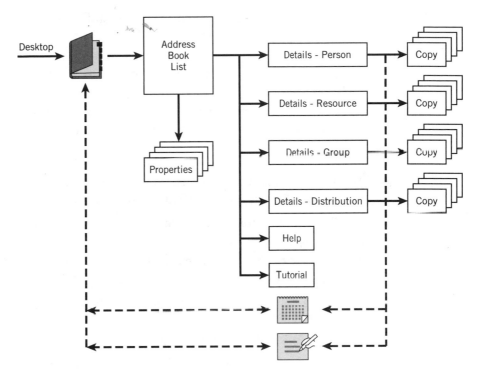

FIGURE 16.5
Address Book UI structure.

Design Questions.   There are always high-level design questions with which to deal. For example,

- When dealing with a system that allows multiple objects to be open and visible at the same time, should an application support the feature, or should it allow only one of its objects to be open at a time?
- Is there a limit to how many instances of the same type of object can be open at one time?

The answer can be:

- It all depends
- Yes, no, or maybe
- Overlap, overlay, or surface an existing object

    Rules of Thumb:

    - When there are multiple screens to be displayed at the same time, pick a central point to display the primary screen

- Overlap subsequent screens down and to the right of the primary screen
- If the edge of the display device is encountered, follow the same diagonal line for opening subsequent screens starting at the top of the display
- If a user changes the position of a screen or its size (in windowing systems), remember what was done for the next time the screen is used

Hierarchy Flattening Techniques.   If window depth tends to become too large, step-saving techniques to explore include:

- Peeking at information within a flow without opening lower level screens
- Trackers to identify where a user is within a flow
- Maps of the hierarchy
- Direct entry of visible information (thus avoiding dialog screens for entry and edit)
- Explorers (with multilevel object views)
- Hybrid views (2-level objects)

Design the Major Screens—Features, Data, Content, and Commands

Each object in an object-action table has the potential of being represented as one or more screens. Actions from the object-action table are associated with each screen via menus or other command access techniques. Depending upon project requirements and constraints of a project, multiple views or presentations are designed for an object, together with supported customization for the objects, screens, and views.

Screens.   A screen is a presentation of an object, dialog, message, help, or tutorial to a user. In a GUI-based application, a screen is typically displayed within a window. In a WUI-based application, a screen is displayed within a web browser. On a HUI-based system without windowing support, a screen is displayed on the display device with or without window-like features depending upon whether a dialog or message is displayed.

Each object from the object-action matrix is mapped to an object screen and is mapped to a command on the UI, which is either a command performed immediately or mapped to a screen for a command dialog. Messages, Help, and tutorial information screens are associated with objects and commands.

Views.   A view is the specific manner in which an object, command, or information is presented to a user. For example, optional views for an Address Book are

- An indexed book with tabs
- A telephone directory list
- A search-results based entity

Each object has at least one view. For example, different models are possible for displaying the details of a person in an address book (see Figure 16.6). Depending upon project constraints and user requirements, optional views are designed for objects, commands, and information. The vast majority of objects, commands, Help, messages, and tutorials have only one view available.

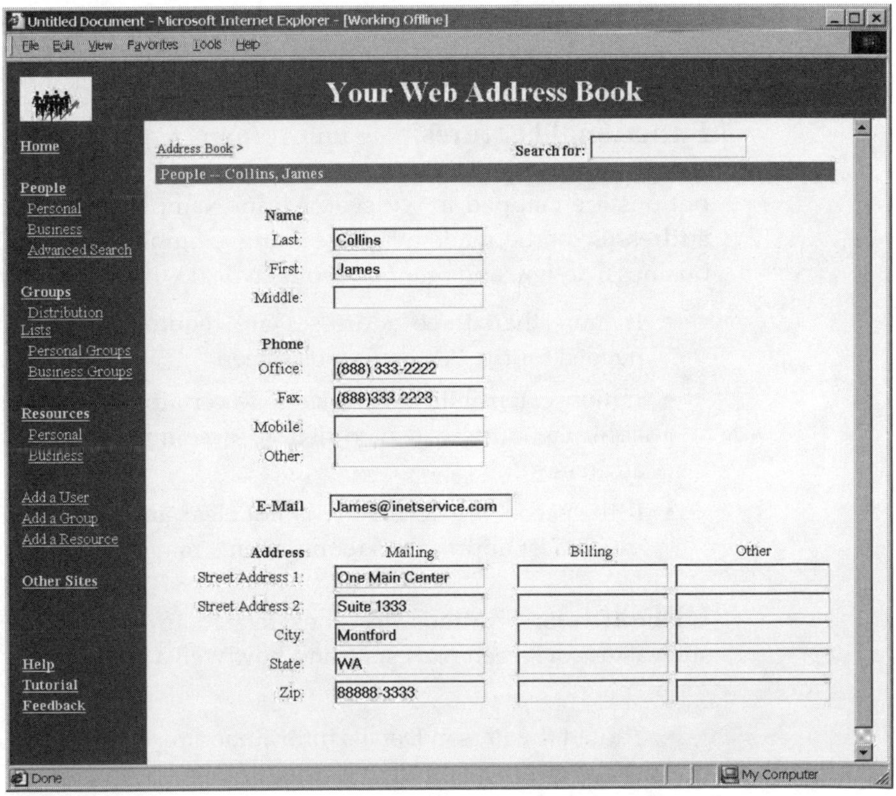

FIGURE 16.6

Example of details about a person.

To design a view for an object, start with its intended user's model. For example:

- If a real-world equivalent exists, sketch it as a visual object and then as an electronic object
- If no real-world equivalent exists, make up a visual equivalent (as if it did exist in the real world or if it was printed). Then sketch an electronic version.
- Consider an advanced view that is a hybrid or that has automations or augmentations to the visual or electronic views
- Add any appropriate window dressing elements like window titles, menu bars, graphics, and so forth.

  Rules of Thumb:
  - Try to provide two or three meaningful views
  - Design views using the default font, colors, and graphics for the system and anticipate that a user will increase font size
  - Follow design guidelines for layout, color, and graphics

Functional Features.   Features from requirements and conceptual design are mapped to a high-level design screen. Features include how options are mapped to widgets. As an example, the number and types of addresses can be made available using a number of techniques. There are business, design, and other tradeoffs to deal with:

- If more than three addresses are required, a different technique is needed for the Person Details screen
- If more extensibility is needed for a certain future and resource is available, the design is modified to accommodate a larger number of addresses
- If the need for extensibility is not clear and constraints are limiting, a minimalist approach to requirements may suffice

UI Features.   Various decisions related to UI features must be made, such as use of screen real estate and how well a screen ports to another environment.

- Should the Person Details information replace the address book screen or display in a pop-up window?
- Is a bread crumb trail needed for navigation?
- Is Search required when drilling down into details?

- How will information be displayed if a user is not authorized to edit information?

Data.   Information and data is grouped and ordered on a screen in a manner appropriate to the priorities of users. For example, some tasks may lead a UC product team to place phone number immediately after name, while others might lead to a design with addresses immediately after name. Other data related issues include data types, data lengths, formats, ranges, and default values. Selection of an appropriate widget for the data is very important.

Graphics.   Some of the simpler issues associated with layout include alignment of labels and fields, field widths, interfield spacing, and use of fonts and font emphasis. More complicated issues arise with use of color, graphic images, and other media.

Commands.   Once object screens are designed, it is time to design menus and other command access mechanisms for the objects. A good place to start is with the object-action matrix, which contains all possible commands for an object. The actions for an object are assessed for possible feature details, whether they are implementable within constraints, and detailed behavior.

Commands are named and mapped to UI access mechanisms like menus, toolbars, links, and command buttons. Depending upon command complexity and data requirements, decisions are made about whether the command is performed immediately or whether a dialog screen is required. An immediate command does not require a dialog screen but performs its operation once selected.

Rules of Thumb:
- Use simple, end-user terms for command names
- Place ellipses after a command's name when a dialog is required to collect needed command input data
- Update the object-action matrix with changed command names and ellipses if any

Pop-up Menus.   Once object screens are designed, it is time to design menus for objects. A good place to start is with the object-action matrix. The actions for a given object form the commands used in menus or other means of access, such as command buttons, toolbars, or links in navigation structures.

Default pop-up menus are provided for objects and controls in many environments. Provide a custom pop-up menu for an object if there are a sufficient number of commands to place in the menu. If there are too few actions, use alternative command access mechanisms.

Rules of Thumb:

- A pop-up menu is designed when it provides more than two commands for an object. Otherwise, use command buttons or other methods of access

- Follow platform standards for ordering commands in a pop-up menu

- Follow platform standards for assigning access key characters to command names

- If submenus are required for ordering and grouping a large number of commands, design the menus so that only one sublevel is required

- Place destructive actions last in a menu

Menu Bar and Pulldown Menus.   Each OS UI style has a design structure for mapping of commands to a menuing structure of some form. A menu bar is the primary mechanism for access of commands on GUI-based systems. Even for a screen that displays different kinds of objects within it, menu bar content should remain constant. Menus are not added or removed to produce a dynamically changing menu structure. However, the content of a menu may change to reflect commands appropriate for a selected object within a screen.

Commands placed in pop-up menus for objects are mapped to a menu bar and its drop-down menus. Platform standards are followed for placing commands in menus.

Rules of Thumb:

- A menu bar is used if there are a sufficient number of commands to warrant it. Otherwise, a toolbar, command buttons, or links suffice for user access to commands.

- A menu should contain more than one command. Otherwise, place a single command into another menu.

- Follow platform standards for ordering commands in a pop-up menu.

- Follow platform standards for assigning access key characters to command name.

- Follow platform standards for assigning shortcut keys to command names.
- If submenus are required for ordering and grouping a large number of commands, design the menus so that only one sublevel is required.

Toolbars.   A very visible and quick mechanism for accessing commands on GUI-based software is a toolbar, which is essentially a menu or a set of command buttons. A row of graphic and/or textual information is displayed below a menu bar by default. High use commands are placed in a toolbar, and software with a large number of commands may even have multiple toolbars that are displayed concurrently. Comparable techniques exist for WUI and HUI styles.

Rules of Thumb:
- Place high use commands on a toolbar
- Use platform graphics and terms to represent commands on the toolbar buttons
- Use ToolTips for the toolbar buttons

For aesthetic purposes, there should be a sufficient number of buttons on a toolbar to span the entire width or height of a screen that uses a toolbar. Otherwise, use of command buttons may suffice.

Command Buttons.   If there are only a small number of commands, use of command buttons is sufficient for access of commands. Command buttons display textual, graphic, or textual and graphic representations for commands.

Rules of Thumb:
- Use platform graphics and terms to represent commands on command buttons
- Use ToolTips for command buttons

Links.   On web pages, use of hyperlinks is similar to use of commands buttons. Links are used to display other web pages, launch other browsers or browser dialogs, and launch other applications.

Rules of Thumb:
- Use platform colors and styles to represent links
- Use ToolTips on links
- Map command features to links and/or menus
- Terminology associated with a link describes the result of its use

Design the Major Dialogs

The commands from an object-action matrix form the basis for all dialogs. From the perspective of a high-level design, the UI to major commands and dialogs include those used with high frequency, potentially error-prone, difficult, highly sensitive, or high-risk operations.

Dialogs.   A dialog is displayed for commands that require explicit user input before a command proceeds. Find (a text string) is a dialog (see Figure 16.7) and is an example of a command that requires explicit user input before proceeding in a meaningful manner. At a minimum, a Find dialog for a GUI-based application requires:

- A title bar with a Close (x) icon
- A window title for the name of the command
- An entry field for a user to type text that is to be located within an object
- A label for the field
- Command buttons to begin (OK) or cancel (Cancel) the Find command

Depending upon the OS platform, other design decisions include whether to have a system menu icon, a What's This icon, and access keys for input fields and command buttons. Within a web environment, design choices include whether to display Find as a unique page within the browser, or launch a separate dialog, as in a GUI, or use a common find area across pages.

Appropriate widgets are selected for obtaining required explicit user input. A text entry field is appropriate for collecting random text input from a user, while a list box is appropriate for collecting input from a fixed set of choices.

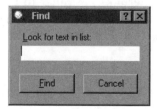

FIGURE 16.7
Dialog window for a simple find command.

Rules of Thumb:

- Construct a dialog for a command following platform standards
- Input items are placed in the dialog ordered by simple and high-use items first
- More complex and low-use items are added to the dialog after the higher priority items
- Labels are assigned to each input item
- Widgets are selected for each input item
- Command buttons are added as needed

As appropriate for the OS platform and depending upon UC product team decisions, access keys are assigned to input widgets and command buttons. Graphic design guidelines are followed for proper layout of items within the dialog.

Rule of Thumb: Once the basic widget set is identified, attempt to visualize the inputs so as to employ direct manipulation techniques.

An example of a widget for a more complex Find dialog is one to select the scope of the command (e.g., from the cursor position to the end of a document, from the cursor position to the beginning of a document, or the entire document). Three textual choices in a simple drop-down widget or a set of radio buttons are options for how to present the choices. However, a more visual alternative is to use a graphic attribute depicting the direction of the search and its scope.

Complex screens are required for dialogs with many fields that collect user input. Design alternatives for such complex dialogs include the following in order of preference

- A dialog with buttons with more and less choices
- A notebook-based dialog
- Buttons to display additional dialog screens

Rule of Thumb: When possible, avoid multiple dialog screens to complete a command. Recall problems related to too many screens and too many steps.

Properties Dialog.   If there are features for customization of an object, it is appropriate to support a Properties command for grouping options. Alternatively, it is possible to design a set of commands to customize features of the software. Typical command names for customization of specific features include Options and Customize.

There are other commands to customize features that are standard to applications or suites on the OS platform. There are also features to customize UI features like toolbar on/off, views, fonts, colors, menu bar on/off, and window dressing on/off.

Rules of Thumb:

- Employ customization for end user benefit and not to avoid design decisions
- Follow platform standards and common examples

Direct Manipulation.

Commands not typically represented in an object-actions matrix include direct manipulation operations. Intraobject and interobject operations require design and support.

- An example of an intraobject operation is dragging an icon representing a Person from an Address Book to an icon representing a Group within the Address Book.
- An example of an interobject operation is dragging a Person icon from an Address Book to a Calendar icon, which represents scheduling a meeting with a person.

Another major example of interobject direct manipulation is dragging objects to a desktop. Such operations lead to interesting design questions like whether Address Book objects are dragged to the desktop and allowed to maintain an existence separate and independent of the Address Book.

Move and Copy are two major operations performed via drag and drop. If there are special operations that an application needs to support, these are handled by pointer-keyboard combinations not already used by the native UI.

Rules of Thumb:

- Direct manipulation operations should be natural and consistent
- Design the basic commands first (e.g., Move and Copy)
- Don't conjure up operations just to do so

A useful design technique to employ is to create a separate drag-drop table (see Table 16.1) to identify the object being dragged (source), the object being dragged to (target), and the valid operations, e.g., move or copy. Then, the specific semantics of the operations are defined, together with specific object data exchange information and formats. The example table follows for the address book example, with intraapplication and interapplication actions.

TABLE 16.1
Examples of intraapplication and interapplication actions.

Object	Target	Move	Copy	Other (via Move or Copy action)
Address Book Person	Address Book Group		Add person to a Group	
Address Book Person in a Group	Address Book Group	Move Person to another Group		
Address Book Person	Calendar			Schedule a meeting
Address Book Group	Email letter to field			Add to addressing list

Direct Manipulation within Dialogs.   Often overlooked is use of direct manipulation techniques within action dialog windows.

> **Rule of Thumb**: Ask how can a pointer be used to avoid keyboard interactions?

Options include use of selection lists, visual data representations, sliders, and buttons. Selection and auto-fill-in techniques are useful. For example, instead of only data entry fields in a Search dialog, drop-down lists of valid search inputs are provided. Typing into the fields is allowed in order to generate hybrid searches.

> **Rule of Thumb**: Avoid more than one pointer-keyboard transition per screen.

Clipboard Operations.   Once the direct manipulation work is completed, clipboard and other data transfer operations are designed. Potentially, the same data structures are usable by direct manipulation and clipboard operations, especially for Move and Copy commands. A good technique to employ is construction of a clipboard table as an addendum to the direct manipulation table.

Planning, design, implementation, and test work is required for both source and target objects. Design questions include:

- If object data is on a server, what data is picked up initially?
- When a drag operation completes, when is data dropped and control given back to a user?

Rule of Thumb:

- It is better to give than to receive
- There is plenty of room for design interpretation; define clipboard semantics sensibly

User Feedback. User feedback to provide awareness of what is going on is very important but sometimes hard to anticipate. Critical feedback to users includes response time, confirmation of completion of commands, and messages associated with errors.

A UC product team has some hints of where response time feedback is likely to be needed by looking at the UI Structure for the software. Typically, it takes longer than expected at a few key points, such as loading software initially, opening another screen within the same application, and computational or disk intensive commands.

In general, anticipate that some form of response time feedback is required for each command or screen level navigation. Table 16.2 provides a summary of typical response time goals for a UI and the feedback mechanisms that support such response times.

- Keystroke or pointer level operations include cursor motion and pointer selection. These operations are expected to be instantaneous, i.e., no perceived delay.
- Displaying an hourglass pointer suffices for high-use and simple actions that include displaying a dialog for a command, simple and short immediate commands, and completion of drag-drop operations.
- Complex and longer duration commands should display an hourglass pointer or a dynamic message like a flying icon or other animated message.

TABLE 16.2
Typical response time and feedback.

Feature	Time (seconds)	Feedback
Keystroke or pointer operation	0.1	Not needed
High-use and simple command	< 2.0	Hourglass
Complex command	2–5.0	Hourglass or dynamic message
Startup and long complex commands	> 5.0	Progress indicator or dynamic message

The next class of feedback is where a user needs confirmation that an operation has completed successfully. A proactive approach to provide consistent, unobtrusive, onscreen, and prompt-like messaging feedback is usually beneficial.

Rules of Thumb:

- Initially, provide an hourglass pointer at each delay point
- Provide feedback mechanisms that do not require user intervention to remove when no longer needed.
- Regardless of speed, provide feedback where users need confirmation of success

User Assistance.   Providing effective content for ToolTips, Help, messages, status area, tutorial, training, performance support, and hardcopy materials is very hard to do. Typically, the work is started late and materials are not truly evaluated for effectiveness. The result is delivery of helpless help, encumbered performance support, confusing and mixed messages, or dumb training.

A UC product team has a real challenge in doing early work in this area. As with a UI, a high-level view is provided during high-level design. Not all user assistance is designed during high-level design. However, some very typical examples are delivered for each type of user assistance intended.

Rules of Thumb:

- Design a UI for intuitiveness, which is defined here as a user only has to be told once
- Provide user assistance design for early evaluation with users
- Depending upon product requirements, a UC product team should think of user assistance as a last resort to overcome design problems in a UI
- When implemented, user assistance is tested with users as strenuously as a product UI

Platform Standards.   Throughout design, you'll be using standards and guidelines developed for the application. Remember to design to follow platform standards not encompassed by the style for the application.

Installation, Print, and Other System Features _____

A designer's work is never done. There is always more to do during the high-level design that affects users.

Installation.   As with other software features, the design of a software installation approach is very important. An installation process loads and configures software and data structures required to run a software application. Software is installable from diskette, CD, LAN, or Intranet/Internet.

Installation, the first thing that a user experiences for many software products, sets the tone for user attitudes. Installation of software updates is experienced infrequently but multiple times over a long period of time. At some point, a user uninstalls the software application. An end user's requirement is that the process be extremely easy. Requirements that seem to persist across products include:

- Check for prerequisites (hardware and software) at the beginning of an installation process
- Ask only essential questions at the start of the process
- Have the software set up and configured to run when the installation is completed

If an installation is complex because of the nature of an application, use installation software tools with an installation wizard. Complex software may require the design of specialized installation screens. As with other UI components, installation software requires design in a modular and iterative fashion. Usability evaluation techniques are important to apply to installation software.

      Rule of Thumb: Start with installation very early.

Print.   The amount of work involved in generating effective and usable printed outputs is typically underestimated and started relatively late. Effective print layouts are at least as complex as effective display layouts because of the large number of printers and print drivers available. System facilities help some, but a great deal of learning and iteration is required to achieve proper results. The work also tends to be somewhat tedious.

Some key decisions that are identified in requirements and design relate to the level of display to print fidelity desired (WYSIWYP [what you see is what you print]). A UC product team works to determine display-print fidelity, number of print views to provide, and print preview features if any.

Rules of Thumb:
- Start design of print layouts as soon as screen design begins.
- Plan on dedicating a developer to the task
- Exploit platform features as much as possible

Use of Sound.　Defer this work to low-level design if possible. Begin thinking about it and exploring how it can be used and controlled by a user.

Other System Features.　Depending upon the desktop and environment, there are Recycle Bins, Trashcans, email, synchronization utilities, and other things to consider. Users are accustomed to using features that are not similar or familiar across platforms. The challenges are strenuous. It is better to start sooner rather than later.

Identify Other Required Design Work.　Not all screens need to be designed during high-level design. However, all screens and commands must at least be identified. A UC product team must ensure that the UI structure is correct and all required widgets identified. With the major screens and commands identified, it is possible to construct a catalog that classifies the design work remaining. The work includes design for screens, graphics, and information. With a little luck and solid design, there is a significant similarity and reuse between design completed during high-level design and design to perform during low-level design.

Closure of High-Level Design.　Prior to completion of high-level design, there are some good things to do. As at the end of conceptual design:
- Conduct design reviews with the entire team and vested interests.
- Demonstrate how requirements are being met.
- Ensure the design is under change control and changes identified.
- Update the overall plan relative to schedule, skills, and resources needed. Continue to explore risk areas.

Deliverables for the project are saved and copies made for subsequent elaboration.

Back to the Project

Part I.　The project manager has run into your office in a very agitated state. Senior management and marketing have just told him that new handheld and tablet devices with a dominant GUI-based operating system must be supported. They need a briefing on the impacts of such a move to the project schedule and resources, as well as the UI impact. The project manager needs a briefing in 30 minutes. Senior management wants a briefing this week, perhaps at the regularly scheduled project review.

Part II.   The project lead has asked you to update the schedule for detailed activities through closure of high-level design, together with a high-level assessment for low-level design. You must provide an updated inventory of screens that must be designed and developed. This must be reviewed with senior management in two days.

This is what you must do:

- After the schedule update, begin and complete the work on high-level design for the project. Be sure to apply the results of the usability evaluation and iteration design thoughts.

- Be sure to map the screens/features to the requirements for the project to ensure that nothing is left out and that nothing extra is being done.

- Update the structure of the Conference Companion and the key object and action screens for each environment supported.

- Remember to consider integration of other software (e.g., the Address Book and office software applications likely to exist on supported platforms).

- Provide examples of all interaction techniques (e.g., keyboard, pointer, drag/drop, clipboard, shortcuts, user feedback, user assistance).

- Consider what form of prototyping to employ at this stage, and begin applying the techniques to the appropriate screens of each implementation environment.

- Identify the key usability issues to address and plan for usability evaluations.

- Anticipate the types of changes likely to be required in the next iteration.

- Continue desk checks, heuristic reviews, walk-throughs, and other participatory methods.

There is a preliminary project review of high-level design within three weeks. Reviews with users and senior management are scheduled during the week following the preliminary review. Be sure to provide a high-level design indicative of how the product behaves on GUI, WUI, and HUI environments.

Continue your research on the Internet.

Any questions?

References

Galitz, W., *User Interface Screen Design*, John Wiley & Sons: New York, 1993.

Gery, G., *Electronic Performance Support Systems*, Weingarten Publications: Boston, MA, 1991.

Horton, W., *Designing and Writing Online Documentation*, John Wiley & Sons: New York, 1994.

Lynch, P., and Horton, S., *Web Style Guide*, Yale University Press: New Haven, CT, 1999.

Mayhew, D.J., *Software User Interface Design*, Prentice Hall PTR: Englewood Cliffs, NJ, 1992.

Mullet, K., and Sano, D., *Designing Visual Interfaces*, SunSoft Press, A Prentice Hall Title: Englewood Cliffs, NJ, 1995.

Norman, D., "Design Rules Based on Analyses of Human Error," *Communications of the ACM*, Apr. 1983.

Torres, R.J., "Graphical User Interfaces: Design and Development Overview," Share 81 Conference, Aug. 1993.

Wegner, P., "Dimensions of Object-Based Language Design," ACM/OOPSLA Conference, 1987.

Specification Techniques 17

There are several approaches to specify a user interface (e.g., behavioral, constructional, and functional). There are multiple techniques within each approach. Many of these approaches and techniques are appropriate for specification of low-level and detailed appearance, behavior, and user interactions. However, specification of large software applications developed by relatively large teams on relatively rapid schedules requires a somewhat different approach.

What is discussed is a functional approach appropriate for specifications produced during iterative design and implementation processes for applications with a UI. Minimalist specifications generated from this technique are useful for simulating, prototyping, evaluating, and implementing UI-based applications.

The following topics are discussed:

- Needs and challenges
- Specification approaches
- Minimalist specifications

- Levels of specification—conceptual, high level, detailed, implementation
- Outline—in the beginning, middle, and end
- An approach for projects
- Specifications for the project

Developing specifications for UI-based applications (see Figure 17.1) is challenging, especially on short cycle projects. At a minimum, not having a specification for UI-based applications results in many low-level design decisions being made during implementation and consistency defects within the application and across applications. Developing minimalist specifications for UI-based applications may be a partial solution to the difficulties.

Needs and Challenges

Developing a GUI-based application is a challenging endeavor from a design, implementation, and test perspective. Web-based and PDA-based applications are no less challenging, especially if industrial-strength and complex tasks are performed. Conventional approaches to specification of

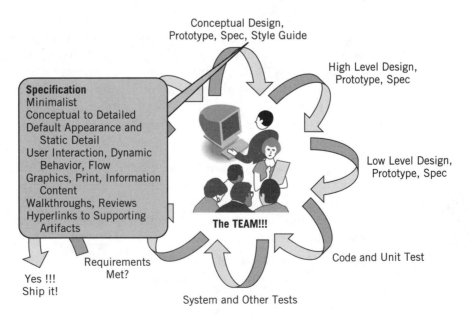

FIGURE 17.1
Specification within a user-centered product process.

UI-based applications do not make the task easier, especially if the development cycle is short and users of the specification include personnel who come into the product cycle relatively late (e.g., a conventional approach to use of an independent test team).

Details! Details!! Details!!! The reason for specification difficulty is inherent in the nature of the interface styles and techniques used: GUIs, WUIs, and HUIs. Many interaction techniques must peacefully coexist within even the simplest UI-based application. In addition, the number of design decisions and possible end-user interactions with system presentation is extremely large—on the order of thousands of behavioral, appearance, and interaction items for relatively small applications. Describing these clearly, comprehensively, and precisely for independent implementation and testing personnel brought in late onto a project is a daunting task. We often know what we want, but putting it down on paper for others is extremely difficult.

An Example. A single text entry field is a small part of a UI. However, the number of related user interface design decisions is large. The following are required for a GUI:

- Field definition
- Label for the field in sentence- or book-style capitalization
- Label punctuation
- Internal widget name for the label
- Internal widget name for the field
- Access key character for the field
- Placement of the label and field on the screen
- Space between label and field
- Space between label, field, and other controls on the screen
- Text baseline alignment of label and field text
- Required field indicator if appropriate
- Data type, format, range, default data value
- Field width
- Input masks if any
- Data alignment within the field
- Tabbing order
- Special input device behavior in the field (e.g., keyboard or mouse)
- Appearance (font, style, size, color, effects, graphics)

- Behavior (enabling and disabling, view only or edit, use of sound, etc.)
- Validation rules for the field by itself and in interaction with other data on a screen
- Business rules governing handling of data
- When to perform any validation
- Menus and menu choices associated with the field
- Messages, field, performance support, help, and tutorial information for the field

Web and PDA-based UIs deal with a large subset of the items listed; the detail is quite large even for simple widgets. The detail is larger for more complex widgets, and the list is long and incomplete. The list becomes even longer when integration with other widgets on a screen is considered.

A Definition.   A UI specification is a document that describes end-user perceptible features and interactions of a software program. A specification is a representation (instantiation) of a design for a software UI. However, even with many graphics and hyperlink techniques, a specification tends to be a prose-based description of complex appearance, behavior, and user interaction elements. A conventional specification describes what a UI does in response to user or other system interactions. A specification does not discuss how a UI is implemented.

End-user perceptible features of a UI-based software program include application usage of screens, windows, icons, menus, pointers, keyboards, displays, printers, and other devices. In addition, UI application layer features perceived by end users include an intended user's model, object semantics and syntax, physical device usage, and interactions that go beyond the basic features of the UI style being used.

Motivation.   In well-designed software, the majority of UI appearance, behavior, and user interaction is simple or standard, but there are cases where specifications make an implementation task easier in certain situations. For example, defining specific, detailed, complex, and/or confusing behavior and business rules, specifications help clarify what a user or UC product team must do. There are situations where specifications facilitate the low-level design or implementation task. Examples where specifications help gather details in a common location are access keys, keyboard mappings, data formats and layouts, consistency checking, and a preproduct walk through. Perhaps the best thing that a specification can do is list out all the things supported by the software in order to properly estimate development activities in product plans.

Specification Approaches

Behavioral specification approaches require a level of detail too low and involved for even small UI-based applications. Constructional techniques using transition diagrams, state charts, and interface representation graphs generate too much information that is not usable except in very low-level implementation design and program debugging.

Functional approaches to specification include use of tools like simulations, prototypes, and storyboards to supplement written documents. However, these techniques require design specification (implicitly or explicitly) prior to development of the tool. An additional problem with functional approaches is that the tools generated from these approaches may be available too late in the development cycle to allow for evaluation and iteration of the interface with users.

Minimalist Specifications

One common problem with specifications is that they tend to be large, prose-oriented, difficult to develop, and difficult to use. The writing skills of specification authors are sometimes questionable relative to the task, and the reading skill of specification users is also suspect. Even with the best of intentions and skills, specification documents leave a lot of room for discussion, debate, imagination, ambiguity, and error. Many times, a specification does not address the needs of its users in an adequate manner.

A Middle Ground.   Conventional UI specifications are quite large; all user interactions and screen appearance/behavior variations are stated explicitly. An explicit form of specification for small GUI-based applications yields documents that are easily at least 100 pages in length. A method is needed that gives a sufficient UI description and easily communicates to product developers and other users of the specification.

Necessary and Sufficient.   An alternative method is a UI specification employing minimalist concepts. Minimalism has been applied primarily to hardcopy and online documentation for end users. The goal of a minimalist document is to focus on the information required for immediate application to productive work. In many cases, this is a sufficient catalyst for getting implementation work started and productive quickly. Once the minimalist work is done, productivity has a chance to increase so that moving on is easier.

End-user documents following a minimalist approach employ three major principles:

- Brevity
- Task related
- Support for error recognition and recovery

Brevity.   Documentation is brief, straightforward, and to the point. A large, prose-oriented specification is not created just for the sake of writing. An author documents only what is needed by a UC product team and other required users—no more and no less.

Task Related.   The task supported by a specification is that of design, implementation, and test of a UI. A specification addresses:

- Default and dynamic appearance
- Independent behavior
- User interaction requirements
- Interaction with other system and program features
- UI results

System results are represented as well.

Support for Error Recognition/Recovery.   UI design and development is an error-prone and labor-intensive effort. Error avoidance during design is extremely important, as the cost of error repair increases exponentially as project calendar time goes by. A specification is written in a way that facilitates error avoidance, early error recognition, and easy error recovery.

A very common example of a conceptual error is use of mixed metaphors within a complex application or software suite. Errors at the conceptual level cause difficulty of learning and remembering. A very common example of a low-level error is use of incorrect access keys. Use of a nonstandard access key character in a menu is common, though an insignificant aspect of a UI. These errors are costly to repair if not detected until late in a product development cycle.

Rules of Thumb:

- Focus specification efforts on avoiding common errors in UI details
- Take note on what the common errors are for your team
- Two to three pages should suffice for most screen needs (including a graphic of the screen)

A way to approach the task of error recognition/recovery is in the use of extremely visual style guides and specifications. If descriptive content is required, techniques for ease of reading, understanding, and use are applied. Bulleted or numbered lists for detail-oriented writing enhanced by graphics are useful. Annotated pictures supplemented by simulations or prototypes are very good as well. As with other endeavors, the documentation technique used requires testing with the ultimate users.

Benefit of a Minimalist Specification.

For an end user, a minimalist approach helps define the elements needed for basic operation. For a developer of UI-based software, more detail is required. However, not every detail requires explicit description, especially for short-cycle development projects.

Rule of Thumb: Write a UI specification under the assumption that you are present and available to answer questions during implementation, and are accountable for product accuracy and results.

Minimum Content.

Minimalist specifications are not the same as minimal specifications. Given the tendency of specifications to get big, a UC product team is sensitive to document what is really needed for the intended users of the specification. Many organizations have elaborate and lavish formats that drive the content of specifications. Certainly, some documentation is always going to be needed. However, as with other areas, precious people resources must keep the focus on users and delivery of the product under design and development.

Rule of Thumb: Specify what the UC product teams need—no more and no less.

Technology Support.

The most difficult aspects of a UI to describe are those that are dynamic. As an example, consider describing the appearance and behavior of the animated feedback messages used during file deletion or file transfer. Factors to describe include:

- Background color, size, and features of the message window
- Size of graphics involved

- Distance between graphics
- Starting, intermediate, and ending positions of a flying icon
- Intermediate icons to use
- Amount of time between start to finish of the flying icon
- Repetitions of the cycle if needed
- Behavior when the action is complete

How long would it take to describe this very simple window and its complex dynamic behavior with only a written specification? How many errors are likely during implementation and testing? Prototypes are typically constructed to demonstrate or test usability. However, it is difficult to rely on a prototype as a substitute for a specification.

Perhaps prototypes and storyboards used in conjunction with a minimalist and prose story line would help. Further, communication is improved by using other technologies, such as hyperlinks navigating from the specification to:

- A running prototype or example
- Example design or source code that generates the desired effect
- A presentation video to supplement the specification, prototype, and documentation

The issues associated with such an approach are for people resources to build the examples efficiently relative to the cost of less effective specification methods. Once again, the running picture must be right in order to save thousands of words.

Levels of Specification—Conceptual, High Level, Detailed, Implementation

Regardless of UI styles required by a project, certain elements seem needed on a consistent basis. For UI-based software, the elements identified next constitute items to specify if supported by a UI. If these items are not explicitly documented, they are accounted for in design and construction.

As with design, there are levels of detail in specifications. The content of higher-level specifications is refined and expanded at the next level. The content is complete when:

- The construction team has enough detail to perform implementation design and coding

- The information development team has enough detail to describe behavior in help and training

- The system test team has enough detail to write, execute, and validate test cases

- Other users of the specification have sufficient detail to perform their jobs

Rule of Thumb: Early in the project, know who the specification users are, and what their information needs are in order to properly plan the specification effort.

Conceptual Specification. A conceptual design specification is an architectural view of an application's UI style and its interaction techniques. It is a big picture view of a product and how it all meshes. Typically, 10–12 pages of prose and graphics serves as an executive summary. A conceptual design specification is the verbiage stated during an overview presentation for a product and is maintained as a standalone document or as an introductory chapter of a high-level design specification.

High-Level Design Specification. A high-level design specification adds more flesh and bone to a UI description. The UI structure, major screens, screen behavior, and detailed behaviors and features are identified and described. A reader of a high-level design specification walks away with a very good idea of what a product does, looks like, and feels like.

Detailed Design Specification. A detailed design specification provides even more detail. Features and techniques not needed during previous design phases are added. For example, infrequently used screens, access key characters for dialogs, detailed field definitions, specific user assistance, and specific messages are provided. The specification outline started during HLD is filled in sufficiently well to begin construction, as best a UC product team knows.

Implementation Design Specification. There is still more design detail required to implement a specified design. During this very low-level design activity, a UC product team uncovers other aspects of a UI that may require specification prior to implementation. Implementation design describes how a UI is to be implemented. Some complex implementation requires specification prior to programming. A UC product team decides what is needed.

Rule of Thumb: Some form of specification is needed on each project, usually to describe appearance and behaviors not included in early prototypes but which are needed in a product.

An Outline—In the Beginning, Middle, and End _____

In the event that a specification is needed for a project, any UI component designed is a candidate for instantiation in a specification. We'll briefly identify a potential outline for a specification.

In the Beginning—An Introduction

An introductory portion of a UI specification gives a high-level view of a product, its goals, its users and tasks. In some regards, a specification is a restatement of other work already performed. A starting point for a UI specification is providing an understanding of the ending. Knowing the objectives and success criteria for a product and its major function and UI features is required and is documented. Knowing the users of a product and what a product is used for has a great influence on what a product is.

UI Objectives.   The goals and criteria that a UI-based application is attempting to meet are included in a specification. The major factors of usability are addressed in a measurable manner. The objectives and criteria are the most critical factors that determine the degree of difficulty expected during design, implementation, and iteration. For example, developing a GUI-based application requiring user satisfaction better than 80 percent is less difficult than one requiring user satisfaction better than 95 percent.

User Description.   Provide a high-level description of an intended user of the software. The most important design point resulting from user descriptions is the amount of UI and domain knowledge an end user is bringing to use an application. If end users already know UI basics, the design and information task is simpler than if computer and UI-naive users are the primary intended audience.

Common Tasks.   A description of end-user tasks that a software UI supports is provided. Task descriptions focus on the 80/20 activities of end users, that is, common tasks performed frequently. The most important design point resulting from identifying common tasks is what the most frequent or important user activities are. A UI-based application is optimized for these tasks, or a UC product team consciously chooses to provide an interface that is task neutral.

In the Middle—A UI Overview

A UI-based application must use the basic UI style of a system within which it operates. For example, a UI-based application uses screens, icons, menus, and pointers. A specification either declares standard use of UI features or describes any nonstandard behavior.

Basic UI Features.   Use of available UI interaction techniques is explicitly stated. However, characteristics of basic UI features need no description. A specification states whether platform UI style is followed, refers to appropriate documentation, and lists any deviations. For example, if direct manipulation techniques are being utilized by the application, this is stated. If access key navigation within command dialog windows is not implemented, this is stated.

Application UI Style.   Document any UI decisions related to consistency of style within the application. For example, platform standards may describe a particular control, such as an icon. An application may use this control in a way that is standardized within an application, and this is documented. Special use of UI features like command buttons, terminology, and windowing decisions are documented. For example, if action dialogs are modal to the application, this is documented as a matter of style.

Unique Controls.   Any specialized or unique UI controls (widgets) implemented by a UI-based application are specified. Typically, UI controls for UIs are complex, and their specifications are large due to a description of keyboard, pointer, and display behavior.

Toward the End—Application-Specific UI Components

The major focus of a specification for a UI-based application is a description of the application layer of the interface. The following items are described in a minimalist fashion in order to show considerations for an application.

Intended User's Model.   Briefly describes how an end-user is intended to perceive the software object's user interface and functions. An intended user's model basically sets the tone for a design and implementation of an application.

Functional Overview.   A high-level description of the functional features of an object is included in a specification of a UI-based application. In general, a one-page description is sufficient as an overview for most UI-based applications. A functional overview maps to the objects and actions accessed through the user interface.

Installation and Set Up.   Before describing end-use aspects of a UI-based application, a description of what an end user must do to get software operational on a workstation is provided. The task includes a description of any interactions with windows, commands, diskettes, or LAN-based techniques. Knowledge that a user must have to install and set up is explicitly stated.

A Scenario of Use.   Many times, depicting a flow through user-system interactions is helpful to convey what an application is all about. A high-use task provides an overview of user interaction with a product. A user-system interaction flow describes user input and system output.

Behavior on the Desktop.   Behavior of application icons and other features associated with access, behavior, and appearance of a software object on the desktop is described. Behavioral descriptions include keyboard and mouse interactions, direct manipulation behavior, and menus available when an object is not visible or in iconic form. Interaction of an object with other desktop objects is provided.

UI Flow/Structure.   A UI flow or site map depicts basic navigation among screens associated with an application. A graphic depiction of a UI flow in a tree structure illustrates the overall structure of an application. A site map for a web-based application is an example of a UI flow. A UI flow shows the flow of information and control from a desktop icon to all screens with which a user interacts. The flow contains all user-selectable actions and depicts whether other screens are displayed as a result of an end user's actions.

Icons.   Graphics for each icon, together with the icon's name and a textual description of each icon, are provided. Icons associated with software objects include desktop icons, icons depicted in lists, and icons contained in toolbars and buttons.

Object Screens.   Each object of a UI-based application is depicted in graphics or screen capture of its views. The basic features of a screen, the major UI components, and the information contained within are depicted. If multiple views are provided for an object, a graphic for each view is provided. Unless believed to be standard behavior, considerations like cursor position on display, display position and size, and screen memory are defined. View and field validation rules are provided. Behavior on open and close is provided.

Pop-up Menus.   The action set of a UI-based application is reflected in pop-up menus available for a software object. In cases where there is variability in menu content, each menu and the conditions under which it changes are discussed.

Toolbar.   Icons and behavior on toolbars is provided. The features that each toolbar button represents are described.

Menu Bar and Pull Downs.   The action set of a UI-based application is depicted in menu bar and pull-down choices. Actions are depicted using the correct order and terminology for the platform where the application executes.

Graying Behavior.   Conditions under which choices in fields, menus, or buttons are disabled is described. There are platform standards for this behavior.

Menu Access Keys.   The access key characters for menu choices, pull-down menus, and pop-up menus are specified. Follow platform standards where appropriate.

Shortcut Keys.   The shortcut or access keys for menu choices are specified. Follow platform standards.

Status Area.   If used, the behavior of status areas on screens is described. Examples of the information contained within the status area are helpful.

Direct Manipulation.   A description of direct manipulation features for a software object is typically needed to clarify supported actions and action semantics. The scope of direct manipulation applies to intraobject and interobject behavior. A table depicting the interactions is an easy way to convey the information. Follow platform standards.

Clipboard Behavior.   A description of clipboard operations valid for a software object is provided. This applies to intraobject and interobject behavior and formats. A table depicting interactions is an easy way to convey the information. Follow platform standards.

Keyboard Mappings.   A description of all valid keyboard operations for the software object is provided. Follow platform standards. Tables work best for capturing platform and application use of the keyboard.

Pointer Mappings.   A description of all valid pointer operations for an application is provided. Follow platform standards. Tables work best for capturing platform and application use of pointers.

Pointer-Keyboard Augmentations.   A description of all valid pointer-keyboard augmentation operations for the software object is provided. Follow platform standards.

Object, Action, and Class Definitions.   All objects, commands, and classes supported by the software object are described. Some actions are platform standard. These are not specified unless the software object implements some form of special behavior. Class hierarchies are described if appropriate.

Command Dialogs.   As with object screens, a graphic and description of each command dialog for the software object is provided. The basic behavior and modality of dialogs is provided, together with a description of each component. All fields, field lengths, and data types are described. Describe behavior of all command buttons.

Print Formats.   A description of formatted print outputs for a software object is provided. This is done as soon as display layouts are available.

> **Rule of Thumb**: Don't wait too long to begin print layouts.

Help.   The structure of Online Help is provided.

User Feedback.   Techniques employed for keeping a user informed of system status are described:

- The use of the hourglass for short response times
- A progress indicator, status area, or other methods for longer response times

The use of confirmation messages is sometimes required to give a user confidence that an operation completed successfully. These are described.

Exception Handling and Error Messages.   Descriptions of error and problem handling are needed. There are errors in the software and usage errors by users. The approach to use of messages and prompts that respond to problems is described.

Performance Support.   Use of performance support methods is described just like any other aspects of a system that a user experiences. Any scripting, ToolTips, interventions, or other techniques are specified.

Other Appearance and Behavior.   Document any specialized appearance and behavior. Initial, interim, and dynamic states are described. This includes use of sound.

In the End—Issues

Document all known problems associated with the application. Problems include organizational, technical, and integration. Action plans are included where possible.

References.   A list of related documentation is provided. Key documentation include requirements, prototypes, other specification, implementation, test plans/reports, and so forth.

An Approach for Projects

As with other areas of usability engineering, there are few absolutes and lots of room for maneuvering when specifications are involved. In high-speed environments with small teams that have a track record of working well together to generate results, there are some rules of thumb to guide specification activities.

Specify if You Need to.   A specification is not developed just to follow a process. Specifications are expensive to develop, maintain, and use. A specification is a communication tool that is used for the right reasons and only if really needed.

> **Rule of Thumb**: A specification is not a substitute for good communication within a development team.

Write Down What a Team Needs.   Document what needs to be written down to support a design and an implementation team. Do not write more or less. Complexity is usually a hint of something that needs to be written down simply or clarified in a UI.

Write Down What a User Needs.   Describe what a user needs to know to operate a UI. This allows a development team to assess what information needs to be taught or explained in product tutorials, help, or other forms of performance support.

> **Rule of Thumb**: If the amount of required knowledge is too much, some rework is required.

Explain Twice, Then Write.   If a feature of a product is explained more than once to a development team or to a user group, it needs to be clarified and/or written down clearly.

Design and Document.   The design task must be performed. A specification documents a design and is an instantiation of a design. Good design practices must be followed.

Specify in Layers.   A UI design can be specified in stages. A first stage is a conceptual design that gives the big picture of an application. A high-level design is next and describes the objects, screen flow, object screens, actions, basic interactions, and nonobvious features. A third stage is a low-level design that identifies all the required details.

Synchronize with Implementation.   As a UI is specified, verification that underlying non-UI design and implementation is feasible takes place. Underlying support includes the non-UI data structures and algorithms.

> **Rule of Thumb**: Conduct periodic design walk-throughs that includes UI and non-UI components using the key scenarios.

Refer to Platform and Style Documents.   Do not describe information that is written down elsewhere. For a UI-based application, refer users to platform documentation for a description of basic UI techniques. For common elements described in a style guide, refer to the style documentation for details.

> **Rule of Thumb**: Follow platform standards.

Refer to Software Models.   There are many examples of UI behavior on the system that an application will coexist with. Refer development personnel to appropriate examples as a learning aid.

Refer to a Prototype and Other Materials.   If there is a simulation or prototype of a UI-based application, refer to it as part of the UI specification. However, a simulation or prototype supplements a specification and is not a substitute for it.

Managing Change.   It is very common for software projects to undergo change throughout a development cycle. Requirements change and evolve, feature expectations are clarified, and surprises happen. Change management is practiced effectively to control the project, specifications, code, user information, test cases, and prototypes.

Back to the Project

The project manager has asked for a product overview document—as a handout for briefings with executives and clients. In addition, he would like to see an outline of what the project specification contains and an example specification for a single screen. There is a *big* executive briefing tomorrow afternoon. The project leader needs the product overview by 8 a.m. for review. You have about two hours to work on this.

The outline and sample specification for one screen can wait until the following day, but you only have about four hours to work on this task.

- Of course, the screen example must be one that exists on all platforms and must be described for each
- The outline must address all interaction styles and identify when certain elements are completed (e.g., during high-level or detailed design)

You've reviewed what the development lab requires in a specification, and the requirements are quite extensive. The specification process for the organization identifies several groups as reviewers of the documentation, and these are groups that you are not familiar with and who have not been involved in the project to date.

As an exercise, estimate how large a complete specification is going to be. Also, estimate how long it will take to create the document and review it with all the appropriate people and organizations. Does the project schedule and resource allow for such an effort?

As an exercise, identify what you think really needs to be documented. How large is such a document? How long will it take to create it? Are there any shortcuts to a review process with organizations not previously involved? Does the schedule allow for such an effort?

The project manager pops in to advise you that the project must support some new blue architecture item for pervasive technologies. He'll try to get details for tomorrow. He asks you to do some research as well. You'll probably be asked about it at the senior management meeting tomorrow, and you will need to wing it.

Remember to continue your research over the Internet.

Any questions?

References

Etlinger, H.A., "Teaching Programming: the Minimalist View," IEEE Software, Mar. 1991.

Gong, R., and Elkerton, J., "Designing Minimal Documentation Using a GOMS Model," *ACM/SIGCHI '90 Proceedings*, Apr. 1990.

Myers, B.A., "State of the Art in User Interface Software Tools," CMU-CS-92-114.

Rettig, M., "Nobody Reads Documentation," *Communications of the ACM*, July 1991.

Torres, R.J., "Graphical User Interfaces: Minimalist Specifications," Share 81, Aug. 1993.

Torres, R.J., et al., "Proofreading GUI-based Applications," *Common Ground*, UPA Newsletter, Summer 1999.

Torres, R.J., et al., "The Rule Book: A Guided Expert System," IBM Technical Report TR 71.0039, 1995.

Low-Level Design

18

We'll now follow up on more detailed design of components required for UI-based applications. We'll take an approach appropriate for iterative design and subsequent implementation of applications utilizing derivatives of GUI styles. Techniques and rules of thumb are provided for the detailed design and I_3 iteration of application windows, screens, icons, menus, pointers, and other elements of a UI-based application that were not necessarily completed during high-level design.

Detailed design is like the final lap of a long-distance run. The goal is to fill in the gaps, close the loops, cover all the bases in a UI design prior to implementation. Following an old rule of thumb, sufficient design information is provided in order to complete implementation design and begin coding. In the best case, sufficient information is available to complete coding. However, because of the complexity of UIs and the aggressiveness of schedules, completing designs using conventional methods may not be feasible or practical. As a result, design elaboration continues through implementation design and coding.

The approach is generally applicable to any implementation architectures and conventional development techniques. Design output generated from this technique is directly useful for documenting, simulating, prototyping, evaluating, and implementing UI based-applications.

The topics covered include:

- Details! DETAILS!! DETAILS!!!
- Designing the detail
- Things hard to predict
- Low-level design for the project

Details! DETAILS!! DETAILS!!!

A UI is rampant with detail. Design decisions for even simple applications easily number in the tens of thousands. Complexity is increased when multiple applications are being handled concurrently by a UC product team and industry level consistency and integration is required. Complexity goes exponential as multiple platforms are considered—there is more code to design and more testing to perform. During low-level design, appearance

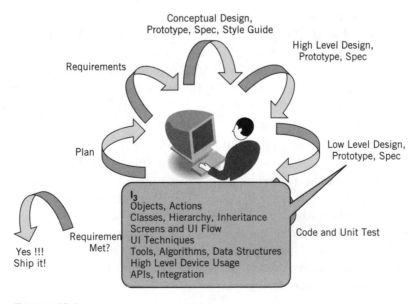

FIGURE 18.1
Detailed design.

and behavior for all known windows, screens, pages, and help is designed for all supported platforms together with all user interactions.

Detailed Features, Appearance, Behavior.

High-level design focused upon broad design decisions at the screen, flow, and interaction level. There are always more details to work out, especially as implementation gets closer. Rapid schedules require taking risk on knowing all the details with absolute certainty.

> **Rule of Thumb**: Risk taking should be calculated and not foolhardy during low-level design. All ambiguity is going to get worked out.

It is sometimes difficult to draw a clean boundary between high-level and low-level design. Some schedules allow or require going from conceptual through detailed design for specific components in a relatively short period. Regardless of approach, the goal is to peel the onion of design to obtain details required for implementation and to be sure that nothing is left to chance.

The usual design elements are revisited for all features being provided with a product:

- Use of the platform UI and standards
- Intended user's model
- Object, property, and action features
- Structure and flow of windows or screens
- Major windows, screens, views, and dialogs
- Standard and optional views
- Special UI features
- Graphics, layouts, audio, and visual style
- Menu style and command choices
- Installation, drag/drop, clipboard, print, and desktop behavior
- Use of display, keyboard, and pointer features
- Use of feedback approaches for confirmations, in progress, and errors

In addition, some work not specifically mentioned as part of high-level design is definitely performed, revisited, and completed. Examples of such work include:

- Mapping of data elements visible in the UI to the data structures of the database
- Designing interaction and functional algorithms to support validation and business rules

- Tuning of the UI to optimize worksteps, reduce screens, and clarify intent
- Obtaining required approvals from management and stake holders
- Moving the design into change control

Nonstandard Behavior.

High-level design may have focused upon achieving standard behavior in the UI and in user interactions. However, as more detail is added, it may become more difficult to achieve standard behavior across components in a consistent manner. Compromises and surprises are usually lurking in the details.

> **Rule of Thumb**: Document nonstandard behavior as it occurs by accident or by design.

Updated Graphics.

Initial graphics and visual themes were developed in earlier phases of the project. Refinement of graphics is likely required. Identifying other uses of graphics beyond original design thoughts is very likely. Final layout details for screens and messages are required.

Response Time.

With careful analysis or simulation, obtain estimates of response times for critical and high-use areas of the software. Based upon the likely response time of each end-user function, the appropriate feedback mechanism is designed into the software.

Ticklers and Grabbers.

As a design is finalized and likely schedule, skill, and resource constraints are known, a user-centered design team has a last chance to identify features and techniques that provide competitive advantage or significant value add to users with minimal impact. Natural shortcuts are identified, and natural integration points are found. Cutting screens and work steps are evaluated.

> **Rule of Thumb**: Detailed design is the last opportunity for design iteration of components or features that really need it.

User Participation.

Keeping users involved during detailed design is as important as ever. Lower level design questions continue to surface. End users are very good at validating potential decisions. Design walk-throughs that use real-life scenarios and tasks continue with users and the product team. Keeping a prototype executable continues to be a good technique.

Prototype and Evaluate.   As in earlier phases of a product's development, use of prototypes and participatory methods continues. UI prototyping is used to evaluate areas not explored during high-level design. A UC product team must consider whether to expand the scope and nature of UI prototypes. At a minimum, potential solutions to earlier problems are validated with users to be sure that the right problem is corrected.

A key decision is whether to expand the prototype in breadth and depth in order to evaluate other tasks and screens with users. Evaluation with users continues to verify that the software is still on track relative to goals and criteria.

> **Rule of Thumb**: Conduct usability evaluations of as many distinct scenarios as possible.

Another key decision is whether to begin the migration of the prototype to product code. More technical prototyping explores the implementation environment and approach. The intended design approach and techniques are verified, potential problems areas uncovered, and challenge areas identified. More technical UI prototyping validates implementation feasibility of a design.

With migration to a more technical approach, such things as programming standards and naming conventions must be followed. When possible, existing software and UI models are discovered for potential reuse and its consequent speed and reliability improvements.

> **Rule of Thumb**: With hard work and attention, the major problems are determined early and avoided or work-around techniques are formulated.

Another area where prototyping is a major tool is evaluation of cross-platform tools and environments. The evaluation by a UC team includes UI and technical feasibility across platforms in order to ensure that requirements are met and an acceptable product is delivered.

By the time low-level design is complete, cross-platform issues and risky implementation areas and techniques are eliminated in order to avoid implementation surprises. Risky UI features and approaches are eliminated as well.

Specification Level Detail.   Assume you have to hand off, but the receiver of a specification doesn't have time or interest in reading all the details. The most important design details must be communicated in an effective manner. Minimalist specifications are still the best to employ.

Rule of Thumb: Don't overspecify during low-level design.

Implementation Design and Implementation. Up to this point, UI design has focused on the "what" of a system (i.e., what a system can do, what a user sees, what a user must do, etc.). Implementation design focuses on the "how." For example, a UI design formulates screens with behavior, and an implementation design formulates the algorithms, flow, and data structures to support the UI results.

Implementation is making it happen via programming instructions, memory, database, and other infrastructure. Among other things, implementation design also determines what components are usable in multiple contexts. For example, some screens are reusable for more than one set of information display without a user knowing the underlying details and believing that each is a unique screen.

Designing the Details—Sizing, Focus, Cursor Placement, Graying, and More

Completing the details is a process of refinement. Low-level design is another phase of refinement that a UC product team performs with user participation. The high-use and well-known features have been designed, refined, and polished. The lesser known or previously unrefined features are considered in more depth.

Design of Infrequently Used Features. The high-level design phase handled the basics and high-use tasks, features, and UI. However, there is the remainder of a system's functionality and UI (perhaps up to 80 percent) that now requires the level of attention and refinement that other system features have received. Obscure, infrequently used, and painful tasks, features, and UI components require smoothing and usability engineering.

In general, tasks to which these features and UI apply may be difficult in the real world. The goal of a product is to make these tasks easier (or at least no worse) than before software automation and augmentation is applied. Surprises, and less than desired results, occur but should not detract or compromise the high use or highly usable aspects of a system.

Rule of Thumb: Keep the focus on optimization of the key design points to achieve a highly usable system or run the risk of a system compromised to average or less.

UI Flow.   The flow of screens, information, and controls is reviewed again relative to known tasks and requirements. The UI flow is updated to include needed messages and user feedback. If task flows look too long (too many steps), optimization is required.

Layouts.   Screen content, groupings, ordering, and layout of information is refined. Alignment of labels and fields, placement of information on layout grids, and compliance with UI standards is reviewed again.

Audio and Visual Resources.   Graphics and the use of sound are refined. Usually, new uses of graphics and sound are discovered as the design task proceeds. The initial wave of graphics is created for basic actions, objects, and other purposes. New uses are established for changing attributes, representing states of objects, messages, and aesthetics.

Focus.   Setting keyboard focus on a key field when a screen or dialog is displayed is finalized in order to facilitate keyboard users. Of course, revisiting tabbing order is appropriate. Highlighting and initial selection of items in lists is a design detail to finalize.

Graying.   If any controls or buttons are not valid in any screen state, they are identified. The initial state of a screen is the easiest to consider. If a screen has any dynamic behavior and appearance, a behavior table is a good way to represent variation in enabled and disabled controls.

Size.   An update to screen sizes and widget details is in order. By the time low-level design is complete, a very good approximation on the height and width of screens and each widget is available in order to accommodate supported display devices and resolutions.

> **Rule of Thumb**: For windowing software, design to be desktop friendly. A user is likely to use more than one window and application to accomplish work. Window management activities increase with use of full-screen applications.

Placement.   The design for a product is reviewed again in the context of the system desktop on which it will coexist with other applications. For example, the location where screens and windows are displayed by default is revisited for the entire system desktop. Placement of secondary screens and dialogs is important to review.

Rule of Thumb: Remember user actions that control the size and placement of windows and screens. Extra work is required to achieve this kind of memory.

Keyboard Mappings.

Initial assignments of shortcut keys are typically oriented to standards. During low-level design, a UC product team discovers other candidates for shortcuts, and assignments are made together with mnemonic characters.

Pointer Mappings.

As with the keyboard, initial usage of pointing devices is oriented to standard usage. Initial use of pointing devices is typically extended during low-level design. More assignments and augmentations and interactions with other devices are discovered and designed.

Pointer Appearance.

Most software applications need only standard pointer appearance and behavior. However, there are instances where specialized pointers are useful and where specialized pointer behavior is appropriate. An example is changing a standard pointer to one with an attached hourglass.

Display Device Usage.

A very common feature of display devices is use of color. Display resolution, animation features, sound, and other characteristics are available to a UC product team to use in order to communicate with users.

Rule of Thumb: As with other complex features of a UI, construct a table to list details of possible and actual display device usage.

Designing use of the features of the display device is finalized and applied.

Print Layouts.

Print layouts are refined. As skills improve, the number of printed views and print previews may increase and require additional scrutiny. With printer technology increasing as rapidly as display devices, many printers and print features are refined.

Rule of Thumb: Update print design concurrently with screens.

Training, Help, and Performance Support.

On typical projects, the components of user assistance and support are started late and delivered with very little iteration or validation of effectiveness. However, user-centered projects deliver components of user assistance earlier and subject to validation. By low-level design, major elements of training, help, and performance support are designed and included in UI prototypes. Usability evaluation of the components of user assistance validates effectiveness and usability of such materials relative to criteria. These materials are iterated and refined as required.

User Feedback—Messages and Progress Feedback.   During low-level design, a UC product team begins to understand the many areas where users require feedback, such as confirmation about the completion status of a command, information about input or software errors, and duration of completion of user requests. As mentioned during discussions about high-level design, user feedback can take the form of dynamic messages, confirmation of success, and minimal user intervention to remove.

> **Rule of Thumb**: Provide feedback where users need it.

Error Avoidance and Handling.   In the heat of daily work, users sometimes make mistakes. Use of an Undo feature has long been advocated. However, even simple Undo approaches may be costly and out of reach of small projects with rapid schedules. An alternative approach is to seek error-proofing approaches and error handling approaches:

- Use of recognition-based widgets (a drop down) to replace entry fields
- Specific feedback on an error
- Use of confirmation messages prior to performing commands with drastic results

> **Rule of Thumb**: Review screen designs for error prevention, avoidance, proofing, and handling during detailed design.

Things Hard to Predict

In spite of all of the best intentions of a well-formulated design, there are many challenges, surprises, and stress points along the journey of product development. Design and prototyping by the few and skilled tends to become detailed design and implementation by the many with different types of skills. Careful attention and perseverance is required of a UC product team, management, and new technical personnel who may join a project in anticipation of product development. A very good product design stands the risk of becoming quite average due to poor decision making, compromises, and trade-offs dealing with design details.

Rule of Thumb: The devil is in the details.

Use of technologies and tools new to the product team poses quite severe risks, especially on constrained schedules with constrained resources.

The typical UI problems are related to setting cursor focus, initial selections on widgets, and getting and receiving data from underlying data structures. Many common widgets have uncommon behavior across platforms, especially using new development tools. There are also many unexpected results due to sequencing of code and system-level behavior that require repainting or refreshing the visible UI image. Even with typical prototyping, many of these effects do not surface until integration later in product development.

> **Rule of Thumb**: Continue to prototype in depth and breadth to understand system and software interactions and odd behaviors.

Compromises and Trade-offs.   There are invariably surprises to anticipate, manage, or otherwise deal with during all phases of product development. There are increasingly more surprises the further into development that one progresses.

> **Rule of Thumb**: Design a really good product and don't compromise the essentials.

Take time to anticipate likely problems and risk areas. With long development cycles, there may be surprises due to the need for increased or different functional or UI features. With short development cycles, there may be surprises in misunderstanding users, business needs, and development tools.

> **Rule of Thumb:** Avoid errors and handle them carefully when they occur.

A Final Check Before Moving On _____

There are many things to do to deliver a software product that is usable, liked, productive, and meets requirements and constraints. For even simple applications, simple counting yields thousands of potentially critical UI decisions. However, there are salient focus items to do and/or avoid in a UI design. Although oriented toward GUI-based applications, the guidelines can be extrapolated to other styles.

Top 10 To Do Items

Let's start with the Top 10 things to do.

1. **Simple**. Keep it simple. Many user tasks are complex and confounded by business rules, mounds of data, time constraints, and critical measures. Software UIs do not need to add more and needless complexity. Applications must facilitate and augment the task that users are performing. Simple tasks should be enabled simply and difficult tasks should be easier to perform. Employing natural models of work and intended user views form the basis for achieving software simplicity. Comparisons of the effect of "before and after" designs help to ascertain relative simplicity. One measure of simplicity in learning how to use software is that a user has to be told only once.

2. **Aesthetic**. Make it look good. Appearance is important. The impact of appearance on usability should not be minimized or trivialized, but heavy use of graphics does not necessarily yield an interface that performs well. Basic size, placement, organization, alignment, and layout of screens and information is extremely important. Comparisons of the effect of "before and after" designs help to ascertain relative aesthetics.

   Effective organization, layout, and use of fonts form the base about which additional graphic symbols, color, and added graphic effects are employed. A best practice is to employ the skills of a professional computer graphics designer to formulate visuals (at a minimum). Creation of a single graphic of 32 x 32 resolution requires manipulation of up to 1,024 pixels in multiple colors. Special skills are required to achieve effective results.

3. **Customizable**. Make it customizable. As much as designers intend to deliver the best interface possible, users like to have it their way. There is no single UI mold that suits the needs of all users. Features that allow users to shape the software to meet personal needs are required. Customization includes available function, UI, and information styles.

   There is also the need for a system to remember what a user has done. Use of techniques such as progressive disclosure allows users to select and modify features of importance.

4. **Productive**. Keep it short and sweet. A common complaint about UI-based applications is too many screens and too many steps! Usable and effective products provide an effective balance of features, UI, performance (response time), and reliability. The software must have the right features (function, data, UI), the right UI style and detail, and fast response time and throughput, and it must stay up and provide correct results.

While providing simple learning and usage paths for beginning users, the software provides shortcuts and fast paths for expert users. The system is optimized for the most frequent and high probability tasks while being effective on less frequent tasks. Measurable goals should be set all the way down to screen-level interactions for critical functions. The best types of metrics are those that require comparison to other known solutions, especially competitive or comparative situations. Once goals are established, mechanisms are established to determine performance to goals.

5. **Flat UI Hierarchy.** Provide a flat UI flow. Many UI-based applications provide conventional screen hierarchies using windows or browsers. The goal is to achieve a minimal number of steps and to avoid tortuous routes to achieve results.

6. **Standard UI**. Provide standard screen framing, layout, and structures. Commands are mapped to common menus or link layouts. Information is displayed in familiar and common UI controls/widgets when possible. Users are not surprised with the unfamiliar. Application level layouts and organization of information strive for standardization within an across application data types.

7. **Familiar Domain Features**. Provide objects and actions related to a user's task. Once beyond the basics of a UI style, software terminology, graphic symbols, data, window data layouts, and print layouts are comfortably familiar to a user. If a user is interfacing with external customers, user views match what the customer sees.

8. **Friendly Feedback**. Provide feedback for every user action. Acknowledgments are an important form of politeness during verbal communication. Acknowledgments take various forms. Simple use of an hourglass icon to replace a pointer during processing for relatively quick actions is effective. Progress indicators are effective during processing of long actions. Animated dialogs are effective. If dialogs are used to provide feedback, do not require a user to click a button to clear the dialog prior to continuing the conversation. Remember that communication from the software UI to a user should be friendly, relaxed, and yield no surprises.

9. **Keyboard Optimized**. Provide keyboard-optimized interaction. There are still many users learning how to use the mouse or other pointing devices comfortably, and it takes time to learn how to use these devices effectively. For every mouse action there is an equal and smoothly flowing keyboard action. The keyboard may not directly enable a direct manipulation action like a drag-copy, but an equivalent copy action must

be enabled via the keyboard. A key design factor is to have no more than one required mouse-keyboard transition during the completion of any given user task. Use of mnemonic navigation in lists is very popular.

10. **Other**. Regardless of their experience and knowledge, a designer must approach each UI design task with humility. Iterative design is a professed best practice of all software development methodologies with good reason—no one person has *all* the knowledge required to deliver effective designs efficiently. With this in mind, effective guidelines and techniques include:

- Follow common design principles like "Keep the user in control," "Keep the interface transparent," "Be consistent (internally and externally)."
- Follow industry standards and diverge only when significant gains are possible and only with user agreement
- Map to existing and popular UI models where possible
- Keep users involved throughout the software development effort. Designers must respect users. Understand the real needs of users, listen to and act upon what they say.
- Understand the real needs of developers (short schedules, tool limitations, skills, etc.). Separate these needs from personal needs
- Explore many design options, then narrow to two or three, and then pick one
- Design, prototype, evaluate, and iterate until requirements are met

10 Things to Avoid

Just as there are things to do, there are things to avoid.

10. **Full Screen Windows**. Design a desktop friendly application. Avoid designing screens and windows that require the entire display area. Remember that other software is displayed concurrently with the screens being designed. Large screens introduce unnecessary and unproductive window management work steps. A good design technique is to consciously consider the software being designed as only one of many applications that a user interacts with on any given task and budget screen usage accordingly.

The initial (default) size of a screen should be appropriate to the task it supports. For example, a utility type window intended to support the primary task is designed to use one-fourth of the possible screen space. On the other hand, a major domain object that is the primary means of performing a task is designed to use one-half to two-thirds of the possible screen space. In addition, these windows employ golden proportions for client area height-to-width ratios (e.g., 1-1 (2x2 sticky pad), 1-1.62 (3x5 index card), 1-1.41 (5x7 sheet of paper), etc.). Using these techniques make object windows look better and reduce work steps.

9. **Many large and dependent windows**. Worse than one large screen is many large screens for the same software application. Providing many large screens that are dependent upon one another is worse yet.

8. **Multiarea Screens**. Keep screen designs simple. Avoid creating multiple areas that require odd tabbing orders.

7. **Gray Screens**. Avoid gray as a dominant background color for screens. Readability is one issue and a somber look is another. Refer to the dominant color scheme of platform objects, which is typically black text on a white background. Use of gray is restricted to dialogs.

6. **Many Clicks and Key Presses**. Avoid as many mouse clicks or key presses as possible. These are unnecessary and unproductive. Utilize techniques that eliminate needless screen and window management. Compress screen hierarchies. Utilize techniques that provide choice selection via defaults and/or intelligent look-ahead. Utilize techniques to automate such actions as saving interim data and worksteps.

5. **Nuisance Messages**. Avoid confirmation and feedback messages that require user intervention to remove. These messages introduce unnecessary and unproductive work steps. Use of dynamic messages, status areas, or window title bars may suffice for most user feedback.

4. **Unfamiliar Surroundings**. Follow platform standards for screen framing, menus, and keyboard mappings. Avoid terminology that is unfamiliar to users. Objects, commands, and property names should be recognizable. Data, data values and ranges, and data formats should be familiar to users. Visualizations and graphics should be familiar as well.

3. **Helpless Help**. Implement meaningful and useful help. Design, prototype, evaluate, and iterate until helpful help is provided.

2. **Initial Complexity**. The entry into an application should be simple. A complex entry point can begin a cycle of confusion.

1. **Design in Isolation**. Just as a UI must communicate with a user, a UI designer must communicate with what sometimes appears to be everyone. Designers must communicate effectively with business users, developers of the software, and management. A designer who is isolated from user feedback and usability test results is likely to iterate ineffectively and is heading for a failed product. A designer who is iso-

lated from developer feedback about implementation tool and software implementation challenges is likely heading for a failed product.

Closure of Low-Level Design. Prior to completion of low-level design, there are the usual good things to do. As at the end of conceptual and high-level design:

- Conduct design reviews with the entire team and vested interests.
- Demonstrate how requirements are met.
- Ensure the design continues under change control and changes are identified.
- Update the overall project plan relative to schedule, skills, and resources needed. Continue to explore risk areas.

Deliverables for the project are saved and copies are made for subsequent elaboration during implementation.

> **Rule of Thumb:** The overall design is pretty much in place. However, there's lots of work yet to do.

Back to the Project

Times Are Hard. The development organization has been hit with a surprising and significant layoff. Many associates are gone, including a small number from your project, mostly from additions to the project team who were to handle tasks later in the project. Many projects have been cancelled, and some experienced developers have been transferred to the project's team. However, no one on the current team has worked with any of these people before.

Some of the senior managers have resigned or transferred, including one of the key sponsors of the project. Several cost-management practices have been put in place. Rumors are rampant and people on the team are fairly pessimistic about the future.

Your project has survived the cuts. The project manager has survived and is more determined than ever to drive the project to completion as quickly as possible. The surviving senior management team is turning up the heat to get an earlier delivery. You feel optimistic about the project and its viability.

Project Status. High-level design has successfully exited technical, usability, and other project evaluations. As usual, there are problems to address but no show stoppers. Usability testing and customer feedback have pointed out some missing (desirable) features, and a couple of key screens are confusing. However, the UI design is holding up generally well.

The project lead has asked you to update the project plan for activities through closure of low-level design, together with a very detailed assessment of:

- All work for implementation, unit test, system test, and activities leading to deployment
- Assignments/schedules for project personnel defined all the way through deployment
- The date when each person has completed assignments and is able to move on to other assignments.

The updated plan will be reviewed with senior management tomorrow morning. Be prepared to defend the need for anything that is related to iteration and rework. Senior managers are focused on getting the product to market faster and are looking for shortcuts and accelerating techniques.

Low-Level Design.   After the schedule update, begin the work on low-level design.

- Update the UI flow for the software.
- Design/prototype all the appearance and behavior details for each of the following types of screens in each environment to support three common tasks for the Conference Companion:
  - Object screen
  - Command screen
  - Help screen
  - Message screen
  - Feedback technique
  - Performance Support screen
- Complete the design of all screens
- Update the UI prototype and specification as required
- Verify implementation techniques and tools are workable
- Document everything that requires communication

There is a project review of low-level design information within two weeks. Reviews with prospective customers and senior management are scheduled during the week following the project review. Be sure to provide a low-level design indicative of how the product behaves in a GUI, WUI, and HUI environment. When complete, implementation design is expected to begin with only a minor overview to the programming team.

Task Assumptions. The duration of a conference is three days, and each day has three presentation sessions performed in parallel. There are some after-hours activities each evening. Common conference tasks to consider include:

1. Create your personal agenda for the conference
2. Prepare for one presentation of interest by prereading a published paper, reading the background information about the presenter, annotating the paper, and prereading and annotating presentation charts
3. Check the conference agenda for last minute changes and directions to the next presentation

An example of an infrequently performed task is locating a near-by pharmacy that is open at night so you can purchase aspirin.

Continue your research on the Web to get information about low-level design, techniques, templates, examples, and tools for each of the operating system platforms supported. If you have not yet located such sites, begin to find sources of reusable code for various algorithms and techniques that are being used on the project.

Any questions?

References

Rettig, M., "Nobody Reads Documentation," *Communications of the ACM*, July, 1991.

Soloway, E., "How the Nintendo Generation Learns," *Communications of the ACM*, Sept. 1991.

Torres, R.J., "Graphical User Interfaces: Designing Object-Oriented Components," Share 83, Aug. 1994.

Product Construction, Test, and Deployment

19

There are many forms of instantiation of a design but the one that counts is the final form of design instantiation that is deployed to users. All ambiguity is removed when software is put together for functionality, appearance, behavior, required user actions, help, training, response time, reliability, usability, and other software features.

The implementation phase is given many names—build, code, construction, and development, among others. The term used here is construction. The scope of the construction phase is implementation design, implementation, unit test, system and other tests, user acceptance test, and the final assessment of whether requirements are met.

During construction, the major goal is completing the transition from design and prototype to a final product that still meets criteria and expectations set during earlier phases. Final iterations and tweaking of UI components is possible. However, major iteration of design is not expected if a UC product team has worked with diligence. Major usability problems may exist, but there should be no show stoppers that seriously affect schedule, constraints, and requirements.

The topics covered include:

- Ensuring a smooth transition from design
- Implementation design, code, and unit test
- System and other tests
- Challenges, solutions, and lessons
- Trade-offs, compromises, and surprises
- Deployment
- Construction for the project

By the time construction is completed, a working product that meets requirements and criteria is available.

Ensuring a Smooth Transition from Design

Requirements are instantiated in documentation and a specific design. A specific design is instantiated in specifications, mockups, storyboards, prototypes, and the information not yet extracted from the brains of members of a UC product team. The volume of work for a UI can vary between 30 percent and 50 percent of total product software, depending upon the type of

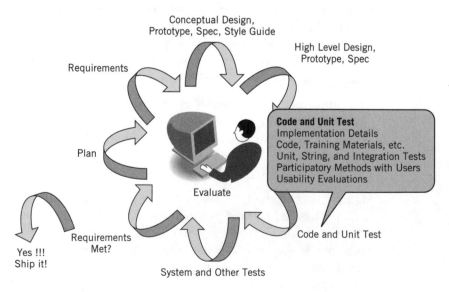

FIGURE 19.1
User-centered construction.

product and its hardware and software architecture and infrastructure. Software products typically encounter a large amount of UI code bulk, stringent UI requirements, schedule constraints, or limited skills that influence the productivity of UI construction.

Rule of Thumb: It's never as easy as you think it should be.

Experts say that the actual calendar time for coding is as little as 15 percent of a development schedule. This may be true for some small projects. However, the number doesn't fare well with medium- to large-size projects.

Good Design Shortens Construction.

There are many complicating factors that turn a small estimate into a significantly larger number—an order of magnitude increase in logic, detail, and complexity should not be surprising. In addition to having to work with obtuse and picky programming languages and implementation tools, there is usually some surprising behavior in the languages and tools that requires time and tricks for determining such things as setting initial focus on certain controls or repainting a screen after certain events. Hopefully, oddities in languages and tools are worked out in earlier phases or have known experience-based solutions.

A UC product team takes into account what skills are needed and available on the overall team for the project's language and development tools. The team must also be aware and sensitive to schedule pressures, stability of requirements, and completeness and quality of input design.

Rule of Thumb: UI software is like other software—only worse!

Transition from UI Specifications.

Construction of a UI strictly from a specification document is a challenge. Typically, there is quite a bit left to the imagination. Even when very detailed and well written, reading and understanding a specification is also difficult because of the volume of information that is required to explain static appearance, dynamic appearance and behavior, user inputs, and the interaction techniques available to access software features.

Once a desired result is understood, a UC product team must perform a major leap to translate the desired result into specific actions to perform using available construction languages and tools. Many times, the leap is over a very wide chasm of tools and constraints that may not support the desired result easily.

Transition from UI Prototypes.

An easier transition is from existing prototypes. However, even with the development of interactive prototypes using the intended product development tools, there may be techniques that are:

- Designed but not yet implemented in any manner
- Implemented in a simulated manner for UI purposes but not even close to an implementation approach
- Implemented in a prototypical manner (i.e., underlying algorithms and/or data structures work but are not deemed acceptable for implementation in a product for one reason or another)

Rules of Thumb:

- Ensure that the tough algorithms and data structures are functionally prototyped, understood, and sized by those who must implement them.
- Since languages and tools are usually not all they're cracked up to be, ensure that limitations and constraints are understood and adequately planned for.
- Estimate how much of a prototype's software is reusable for a product and set expectations accordingly.

The Head Cases.   The hardest information to transition is that which remains in the heads of designers. Given the volume and complexity of UI design detail, there is always some information that is not represented in a specification or prototype. The situation is even worse when designers have moved on to other projects as some of the knowledge and design intent typically goes with them. Unless another person holds the information, it is difficult to make up for the lost knowledge.

Rule of Thumb: Keep the designers around for the duration of the construction phase.

The Best Case.   In the best case, a specification, prototype, and the original designers are part of an actual implementation team and available. This should be planned and managed. This helps with transfer of knowledge and project accountability.

Details, Details, and More Details.   All the issues that are relevant to other types of software apply to UI software. The amount of work, quality, performance, skills, and schedule are all relevant. All software paths are dealt with, including exception conditions, combinations of inputs and outputs, error handling, and messages. Prototyping issues of depth and breadth are no longer relevant. Interface to non-UI features and support is handled as well.

Rules of Thumb:

- Beware of compromises due to surprises and schedule pressure.
- Avoid compromises of design integrity and requirements.

Implementation Design, Code, and Unit Test _____

Under an assumption that necessary and sufficient design information is available for a UI, there is still a long way to go in order to finish product construction and deploy it to users. There is still implementation design, coding/writing, unit test, and other forms of testing that demonstrate whether a product meets requirements and is deemed ready to deploy.

There are many products that approach scheduled dates for test completion with many outstanding problems. Problems can be functional, UI, usability, performance, or other types of defects. Many times, some requirements are partially satisfied. Regardless—or as a result—there is usually a formal and final go/no-go judgment of whether to deploy and under what conditions.

Implementation Design. Given a UI that provides access to software features using various techniques, implementation design deals with the issue of how to do it using programming and development toolkit algorithms, techniques, data structures, and data sources. Ultimately, an implementation design uses one or more programming languages, language instructions, development toolkit components, and database and OS commands and resources.

Issues addressed include internal structure, modularity, flow of control, intermodule interfaces, and the logic for specific software functional, information, and UI features. Selection of specific instructions is not necessarily considered at this level—only general approaches to how things will be done.

Rule of Thumb: Explore alternatives and iterate to meet needs.

Implementation. Selecting, organizing, writing, and ordering programming and OS language instructions and verbiage to achieve a specific effect is typically referred to as coding. Intended software development toolkits are employed to develop program instructions and resources like graphic files. Use of program instructions and toolkit facilities instantiates the implementation design and the UI designs.

There are many challenges in this activity, including selection and writing of appropriate instructions and OS calls, implementation techniques and details, efficiency of resource usage, and so forth. Typical tasks include use of naming standards, programming practices, libraries of reusable components and techniques, software change control and management, and defect tracking.

Even with the use of 4GL or 5GL UI development tools, software must typically be written for:

- Screen or window opening, state setting, and closing
- Screen or window placement relative to another
- Setting focus and setting selection state
- Initializing controls
- Field validation (input and output)
- Testing content of controls
- Enabling and disabling controls
- Behavior related to keyboard and pointer events
- User feedback, error handling, and messages

   Rules of Thumb:
   - Early prototyping helps identify language and tool constraints and validate UI techniques. Start as soon as possible.
   - Explore alternatives and iterate to meet needs.

Mundane challenges of code control, software backups, use of a common development platform, efficiency, maintainability, and software documentation are addressed. Desk checking, quality reviews, and walk-throughs of the code and UI continue.

   Rule of Thumb: Be sure to use version control tools to manage UI and other code.

Problems are anticipated where possible (e.g., response time, error prone software, and reliability). Workarounds are developed when OS and programming language limitations surface.

   Rule of Thumb: Each programming language and tool has its own challenges.

Code Growth.

Actual development is conducted using an incremental and end-to-end construction approach. Just as UI design and prototypes are developed in an iterative and incremental fashion, so should actual product code be developed. Another way of saying this is to develop a little and then test, then develop a little more and test everything built to date, and repeat until done. Maintain focus on code quality, UI quality, usability, response time, reliability, and meeting other requirements. If not done up to this point, be sure to document special algorithms and techniques as the software is developed. You may need to modify the code later.

Unit Test.   A strict definition for unit test is one that requires a feature to be validated for correctness from end-to-end in an intended environment of use, such as functionality, UI, data base access, APIs, and so forth. Integration with all aspects of a software suite or system is not needed. What is needed is demonstration that a specific feature works as specified and/or intended and/or required.

Many times, it is difficult to create the actual user environment because of the state of dependent software, lack of familiarity with development tools, and access to actual production databases or networks. The time required to set up such environments can be prohibitive because of resource or knowledge constraints.

> **Rule of Thumb**: If the actual environment cannot be created during early stages of development, add time to the schedule to create the environment and perform extra testing and surprise management.

As an example, if a feature is to be accessed using a web browser, then unit test of the feature is not complete until it is tested there. Evaluation of features within an applet viewer is sufficient to test some functional features. However, the applet viewer does not demonstrate UI access technique limitations imposed by a web browser.

Many UI defects are quite devilish to resolve. Sometimes, interaction between language, system, and tool features causes problems, other times it is the sequence and timing of instructions.

> **Rule of Thumb**: Test and resolve problems as you go, especially in the intended user environment. If not immediately resolved, document the problem and return to it.

Unit Test Exit Criteria.   One measure of being done with specific software components is completion of the unit test milestone. To eliminate ambiguity, there are specific criteria for successful exit of a unit test that include:

1. Planned user features are accessible through the UI (i.e., all user accessible features can be exercised via screens, commands, links, shortcuts, etc.)

2. <u>And</u> all UI features work at the unit test level (i.e., features work correctly as best a developer and a test buddy can tell)

3. <u>And</u> help/training/EPS access is integrated and correct (i.e., help and other user information is accessible and correct)

4. <u>And</u> defect growth is minimal (perhaps zero known defects regardless of severity)

5. <u>And</u> code growth is minimal and due only to defect correction (code isn't growing by leaps and bounds weekly without apparent reason)

6. <u>And</u> usability testing with users has been performed and passes criteria (e.g., user satisfaction for an appropriate task, etc.)

7. <u>And</u> performance (response time) has been estimated or measured and is within criteria

8. <u>And</u> the developer is confidant that software is ready for system test entry (developer/buddy cannot find more defects and are ready to hand code over to the sadists doing system test)

9. <u>And</u> scheduled coding time has expired (otherwise, things keep getting enhanced/tweaked/refined without need)

Common Code Problems.   Some UI behavioral defects seem to persist across products:

- Keyboard focus is not set anywhere on a screen where a user needs it
- Tabbing causes keyboard focus to be lost on a screen (sometimes never to return)
- Response time feedback (hourglass) or progress indication is missing
- Nonstandard behavior for the Enter key or double-click of a pointing device

These items are specifically included in design and prototype information, together with an approach for how the final implementation is to handle them. Such an approach minimizes the grief of trivial UI defects and helps keep focus on function, usability, performance, and reliability.

> **Rule of Thumb**: Consider a UI Certification milestone, which demonstrates that all UI standards, guidelines, and details are implemented correctly.

A UC product team is responsible and accountable for successful completion of this milestone prior to exit of unit test.

Usability Evaluation During Code and Unit Test Activities. As usual, users are involved during code and unit test. There are always details to review with users (e.g., updated graphics and layout, field and column size adjustments, and myriad other design snippets and surprises that users may have not reviewed in detail). Participating users help with very low-level design tradeoffs and decisions by adding their view of what is important. Details are reviewed in low- or high-fidelity, depending upon the situation. Heuristic, informal, and formal evaluation methods are used as appropriate.

Rule of Thumb: Always have an executable part of the project ready to show to users and sponsors.

System and Other Tests

System, integration, and other types of testing (see Figure 19.2) validate software features within a larger environment and with other software operating and competing for resources. There are also different operating conditions, such as extreme and out-of-range input values, stress level inputs, and unusual combinations of inputs.

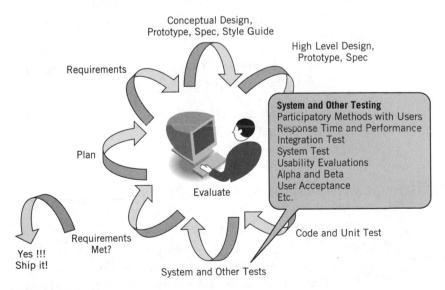

FIGURE 19.2
System and other tests.

Evaluation in the Intended Environment.   By this time, the software is definitely running within intended environments. The UI, help, training, and other artifacts of a user's experience are available. The software may not be fully functional, fully debugged, or reliable even if the unit test has completed. There are typically many residual defects to resolve. Response time issues are certainly more noticeable.

However, user participation is ongoing. Formal usability evaluations are conducted in laboratory and user environments where possible. During early phases of testing, a complete task flow may not be possible. However, complete task flows are possible in the later portions of such testing.

> **Rule of Thumb**: Be sure that the team doing system testing is trained on the platform and its basic UI style.

Long-Term Usage Evaluation.   As a system stabilizes, it is possible to have users do simulated work on the software for extended periods of time over an extended calendar timeframe. Up to this time, usability tests are relatively brief and tackle short-term learning and usage problems. However, a user who tests the software over the course of multiple weeks for multiple hours per day notices problems of a different nature—long-term learning and usage problems. In addition, all aspects of the system are tested including infrequently used paths, unimportant but essential paths, and so forth.

> **Rule of Thumb**: Involve a small set of users during system test evaluations for extended periods of time.

Users execute predefined test cases, perform ad hoc testing, and provide structured usability feedback to the UC Product Team.

Challenges, Solutions, and Lessons

Areas of Risk.   Since the implementation phase is relatively long with lots of details and complexity, some new types of risk begin to surface. Status of implementation and test is a major unknown. Response time, reliability of complex software, and training new staff are other areas of concern.

Plans.   Develop a schedule with as many milestones as the overall team needs in order to know where it is during implementation. An effective technique is to back up from the end, then go forward. Track completion of specific UI features and underlying software components.

Track progress against expectations. Statements of 80 percent complete or 90 percent complete may not be accurate if the last bit of work takes 80 percent to 90 percent more calendar time. Reality usually bites painfully, so plan using small chunks and checks to ensure balanced and accurate status and reporting of progress.

> **Rule of Thumb**: Plan, track, and report status in order to give yourself a chance to succeed.

Response Time.
Be sure to implement user feedback everywhere. Display the hourglass graphic on each command that is not likely to be instantaneous.

> **Rule of Thumb**: Just do it. It's more painful to implement user feedback later.

Staffing and Skills.
Once the gun for implementation goes off, resources are needed in place and trained to deliver what is expected. Beware of such concepts as just-in-time staffing. The entire team needs to have all required skills and knowledge from the very day that they begin. Many times, this is not realistic.

Since teams do grow as time approaches construction, use storyboards, education, walk-throughs, and libraries of documentation and presentations to train new team members.

> **Rule of Thumb**: Hyperlinks in design documentation and prototype software are useful to bind the knowledge in a meaningful manner.

Buy In.
As people are added to a development team, they must certainly be educated about the product and tools being used. Personnel must also buy in or associate with the product and development plan. Team building and other exercises are important to grow the commitment needed to meet product goals.

Separating the UI from Business Software.
There is usually a strong goal to separate UI software from business logic. This is possible, but it means extra design time and implementation cost. For example, if business rules control which fields and menu choices are enabled, a mechanism must be designed and implemented to achieve this outside of pure UI logic.

In addition, creating the software with a separation of UI and business logic has the advantage of potentially more independent development and reuse by the software engineers.

Managing Requirements and Change.   As time goes on, business needs and users change, and different design or implementation ideas become apparent. At this late stage of development, the team must resist arbitrary change to the software for business or other purposes. An arbitrary change means that it is not *really* needed for this release of the project software. It can wait until a later release.

> **Rule of Thumb**: A late change must be essential to the success of the business or project even to be considered seriously, for the risk of a delay in the project's availability to users and the sponsoring business.

Productivity.   Construction is measured using various metrics. The following are examples of metrics critical to track progress and success:

- Navigation structure between system, screens, and help implemented
- Screens and help designed and implemented using the development tool
- Help and performance support designed and implemented using the development tool
- User visible data and methods implemented
- Defect rates and severities within limits
- Percent rework

Reuse.   Plans on it, design for it, track it. Before implementing, ask Where has this been done before? Continue searching for source code examples of design and implementation techniques used on the project. Measure and reward effective reusability.

> **Rule of Thumb**: Avoid an ad hoc approach. It gets harder as team and software size increases. Remember the goal is to deliver the project.

Documenting the Code.   Since the first person to implement is not likely to be the one to implement and maintain on subsequent releases, documentation is essential to communicate what is going on for the next person. In fact, the next person is likely to be less experienced than you.

Rule of Thumb: Remember to pass your knowledge along—the business has already paid for it and shouldn't have to pay the same amount for each transition.

One could assert that unit test is not complete unless a code walk-through is conducted that verifies documentation.

Requirements Met?

The goal of testing is to demonstrate software correctness and detect defects in software functionality, UI, help, training, response time, reliability, and other important aspects of the software. Testing finds the defects, additional software engineering develops fixes that are applied to the software, and additional testing verifies that fixes are correct and nothing is defective as a result.

Hopefully, there is sufficient time in the test schedule to develop corrections, or the product could be deployed with defects, or deployment could be delayed until corrections are developed.

Functional Defects.   Typically, defects in functionality are identified, assigned a severity, and tracked until resolved or time expires. If a criterion for number of open defects of varying severity is not exceeded, then a software product is deployable. For example, a product is deployable if there are no defects of Severity 1 or 2 and less than 10 defects of Severity 3.

User Interface Defects.   Defects in UI features are handled in a manner similar to functional defects. For example, if a product implements nonstandard keyboard or pointer behavior, a Severity 2 defect should be written. Similarly, if a promised UI feature is not implemented correctly, a defect of appropriate severity should be written.

Usability Defects.   Defects related to product usability are derived from requirements developed early in the development process. For example, if a time on task requirement is not satisfied by a large margin there are probable impacts on expected business productivity. As a result, a Severity 1 defect could be written against the product. However, if the time on task is within criteria and user satisfaction criteria are slightly out of range, a low severity defect can be written.

Other Requirements.   Testing gathers sufficient information to determine whether other requirements for the software are met. Test results are compared to requirements for performance, help, training, quality, and other committed factors.

Trade-offs, Compromises, and Surprises

As in other phases of software development, there is lots of room for surprises, with the subsequent appeal to perform tradeoffs and yield compromises. Many times, acceptable design alternatives are possible that achieve requirements within constraints. Other times, alternatives are not possible and compromise reduces some desired aspect of the system. As usual, keep the users involved in the process to gain agreement on approach. At the end of the project, it's great if the deployed design is a reasonable approximation of the original design intent.

> **Rule of Thumb**: The major goal is still to deploy the best possible product that meets requirements within constraints.

Bottom Line.   When all is said and done, test results are evaluated and a judgement is made as to whether or not a product is deployable. If requirements are met, then the product deploys. If some requirements are not met, the product could be deployable with the promise of a plan to correct deficiencies and defects. If the product does not meet standards in the extreme, deployment is delayed until corrections are made or the product is canceled.

> **Rule of Thumb**: There is usually negotiation and a judgment call about whether a product is deployable. Ultimately, users, developers, and the sponsoring business must be better off with deployment of a new product.

Software development, especially that with a significant UI component, is a complex activity with many human, social, group, and organizational aspects. Clean and obvious decisions sometimes do happen. Work toward a project that makes decision making easy but be prepared for the project that is messy and requires the judgment call.

Closure of Implementation.   Prior to completion of implementation, there are the usual good things to do that are good development practices. These include:

- Code reviews

- Usability and acceptance tests
- Reviews of test cases and results
- Demonstrating that requirements are met

If change control was important during design, it is essential that change be managed very carefully during implementation. Recall that the volume of work increases dramatically during implementation. Many more people are affected.

Rule of Thumb: Late changes can kill a project.

Deployment

Some types of deployment are easier than others. Today, deploying a web-based application is potentially easier than installing a client/server application unless plug-ins and special types of workstation setup are required.

Rule of Thumb: Preparation for deployment begins during the requirements phase but certainly no later than day 2 of conceptual design.

Production Environments.   Up to this point, development and testing has taken place on development and test environments. There has probably been limited access to production environments and databases with customer and business data. The risk of compromising real business or customer data is too great for many businesses. The goal has been for development and test environments to mirror the production environment, but there are usually some minor differences. Prerequisite software, fixes to existing systems, or production database differences sometimes slip by unnoticed.

Rule of Thumb: It's a good idea to try a sample or test deployment to the production environment before the real deployment in order to smoke out serious environment problems.

All required infrastructures must be in place and user machines must be configured appropriately before the project software can be deployed to the machines for user access.

Back to the Project

As usual, the project is in a hurried state. Design is complete and it's time to drive prototyped screens to completion of build, unit test, system test, and deployment. You have about half of the overall project schedule to complete implementation design, implement through unit test, system test, integration test, and deploy to the key platforms for the web-based solution. For the sake of the project, assume that you have 60 days to work with.

Your infrastructure partner has been assigned to kick off design for the next release of the project (due within 90 days of deployment). Competitors are now aware of the project and are reacting with software proposals of their own. Speed to market with high usability and increased functionality is critical.

The project manager and you must continue to track and report status of the entire project to senior management. You will lead the project team through delivery of the initial release of the software. You will support your partner in the UI design of the next release.

Prepare an updated schedule estimate for the project. The key question is, Will the software be deployed to the key client 60 days from today? This question will be answered weekly by you and the project lead. Of course, one week is deducted from the time frame as each week goes by.

For a prototyped screen, estimate the amount of time required for achieving unit test complete for the UI software on each of the supported platforms:

- Be sure to include an estimate of unit test complete for one of the supporting dialogs, help, and training.
- Formulate a measurable implementation schedule.
- Perform the same exercise for a screen that has not been prototyped.

Then, formulate implementation design and begin construction using an implementation platform of choice. Develop all software for the UI, help, and training. Do not necessarily focus on completed functionality. Be sure to include all error handling, user feedback, response time feedback, keyboard behavior, pointer behavior, and UI mechanisms. In other words, develop the complete UI software for the screen, dialog, help and training. Be sure to test the software until it is finished and unit test criteria are satisfied. The screen and its functionality must be ready for system test, integration testing, other testing, and deployment to end users.

Be sure to track and log each work step that you perform. Compare actual development statistics to predictions. Make note of aspects of design that were not accounted for in earlier design information and prototypes. Make note of what testing remains to be done for system and other types of tests. Estimate a schedule for how long such testing takes.

The project manager has come in to tell you that one of your key UI developers has had a family crisis and is likely to be out for at least two weeks. What are the impacts to the project and what are your options for recovery? It's not likely that another person can be found on such short notice.

Continue your Web-based searches for examples, techniques, and code snippets that may be of use to the project.

Is the project on schedule for a delivery in 60 days?

Any questions?

References

Black, R., *Managing the Testing Process*, Microsoft Press: Redmond, WA, 1999.

Maguire, S., *Writing Solid Code*, Microsoft Press: Redmond, WA, 1993.

Part 4

Wrapping Up

The major steps of design and development have been explored at a high level. However, there is still a way to go. We'll look back on what should have been learned and look ahead at what may be coming in the field of UI and usability.

Chapter 20. Looking Back and Beyond

Looking Back and Beyond

What have we done and why did we do it?

Looking Back

A high level view of user-centered design and development has been provided with some focus on UI. As mentioned early on, the process is complex, nonlinear, and nonorthogonal. Furthermore, the process is somewhat opportunistic in that good ideas build upon other ideas and lead to interesting and creative solutions.

When applied with diligence and hard work, UCD provides products that meet or exceed user requirements. We've also taken a very brief and high level journey through a UCD-based software development project (as depicted in Figure 20.1).

Principles. Principles of user-centered design were discussed, namely:

351

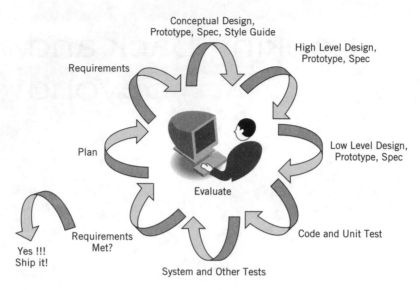

FIGURE 20.1
UCD process revisited.

- Keep users involved in the project
- Set measurable goals
- Design and prototype a total user experience
- Evaluate
- Iterate until requirements are met

Interestingly, these are industry best practices for software design and development.

UCD Tasks.   UCD tasks were discussed and applied in the context of a somewhat conventional software development process:

- A fairly conventional development organization with many business and people challenges developed the software.
- The project was complex but not uncommon or unusual for a software application that requires multiple releases over a timeframe of multiple years.
- The project time and resource constraints were fairly common.

However, even within conventional and constrained environments, UCD tasks can be performed much more often and more quickly for a 90-120 day project, or the UCD tasks can be performed very often and very quickly for a multiyear and multirelease project. If project histories serve as guidance, around half of a project's calendar time is spent in planning through design completion. The next half of a project's calendar is spent in implementation and test.

We've performed a very fast round of:

- Planning
- Understanding users, tasks, and environments
- Understanding requirements
- Design
- Design instantiation (simulation, prototype, specification)
- User evaluation and feedback
- Analysis of user feedback
- Iteration
- Implementation
- Test
- Deployment

Key facets of the overall approach are planning for UCD to incorporate user involvement, measurable criteria, evaluation, and iteration until requirements are met. Aside from implementation of key UCD principles within a project plan, more explicit awareness of the many details of UI technology was provided so as to achieve proper planning, scheduling, skills, execution, tracking of status, and risk avoidance for common problems. Each project has its own set of unique risks to address.

User-Centered Product Team.   Designing a total user experience is complex and requires many skills. A multidisciplinary team is needed to cover all the necessary bases. A user-centered product team must be staffed to achieve product goals. Key skills include engineering personnel to deal with issues related to business, UI, usability, graphics, media, information, and software. Group dynamics, organizational behavior, team building, and skill building are critical work items for a UC product team to address.

UI Style.   Three major UI styles available on current system platforms were explored during the project because of cross-platform implementation requirements. UI challenges were explored for GUI, Web, and handheld devices. In addition, the notion of an application UI style was explored. Any number of application models are applicable to any overall UI style. In a project, you would notice that:

- Many UI solutions could meet requirements for a project
- Given a choice between options, users would most likely pick one solution over the others
- No single solution is perfect
- Most solutions would likely have multiple unique and very popular features and approaches, and most of these features would be difficult to integrate into a chosen solution.

Participatory Methods.   Keeping users involved in a meaningful manner is essential to a project's success. Users provide real business and usage perspective to plans, requirements, design, prototypes, evaluation, build, test, and deployment. A UC product team begins interacting with users by observing work environments and how tasks are performed in order to gain insight into needs. Once the communication and understanding is mutual, involvement by users becomes a productive partnership. Interactions with users continue throughout a project's life cycle.

Tools.   Because of the complex nature of a software UI and UCD tasks, a UC product team needs quite a few tools to do the job. Tools include software, hardware, materials, facilities, and references. In addition, a library of examples and reusable components is needed to improve productivity and achieve consistency. A UC product team must secure the tools and be skilled in their use early in a project's life cycle.

Plan.   UCD, when applied to software UIs, is complex and full of details, and requires planning. Measurable schedules are important for proper tracking and reporting of status, especially when planning for iteration on a project. Two or three levels of scheduling may be needed (e.g., a project view, a 90-day view, and a 2-week view). Details associated with a UI can be sized for resources and scheduled so that underestimating schedule and needs is avoided.

Requirements.   Along with requirements in general, UI and usability requirements are an area to focus on. UIs have many features that require validation, planning, and sizing. Usability and other nonfeature-oriented requirements must be documented in a measurable manner. Evaluating current and competitive products is important for setting the bar for new products.

Users, Environments, and Tasks.   A UC product team analyzes the details about user characteristics, physical work environments, and social work environments. Software UIs must fit user needs within the context of physical and social needs. Various methods exist to gain the required understanding. Analysis of the information gives a UC product team sufficient understanding of intended users, environments, and tasks.

Design.   Design is a process of elaboration. Three major UI and usability design steps were discussed: conceptual, high-level, and low-level. Conceptual design sets the UI design direction and architecture. High-level design elaborates the conceptual design and provides a definition for each major feature, screen, and interaction. Low-level design provides more elaboration and completes the definition for all features and techniques. At each stage, user participation continues to shape the design.

Principles, Guidelines, and Style Guides.   The task of defining principles, guidelines, standards, and style guides for the project begins during conceptual design and continues throughout the design and implementation phases. Depending upon the requirements of a project a UC product team must create a measurable design direction that is implementable and testable. In general, consistency within and across applications is a major goal that a style guide is trying to address. A prescriptive style guide is a best practice approach to this task.

Mockups, Simulations, and Prototypes.   Design instantiation is a process of elaboration. Building a design visualization during requirements or design phases is a best practice. Numerous visualization techniques are available (e.g., mockups, simulations, and prototypes of various natures). Methods of user involvement, evaluation, and iteration are used in conjunction with visualization techniques to achieve designs that meet requirements and are liked by users. Remember that these methods may be used during the construction phase for solving problems discovered late in the development cycle.

Usability Evaluation.   Ongoing formal and informal usability evaluations are conducted to supplement information obtained from participating users. Heuristics, walk-throughs, and desk checks supplement user evaluations. As with other UCD-based tasks, careful preparation is required to ensure appropriate testing and analysis of results relative to a design and its goals. Again, this is a best practice.

Iteration.   The purpose of iteration is to improve a design that does not meet requirements or has unacceptable problems. Analysis of a design based upon usability evaluations or informal methods helps to resolve problems and find improvements. Iteration occurs during conceptual design, high-level design, and low-level design. With the right skills and environment, it is possible to perform a final iteration during implementation design and implementation that is focused on polishing, tweaking, and fine-tuning. This final iteration is as important as the others. However, great care must be exercised during implementation so as not to put delivery at risk.

Specification.   A specification is another form of design instantiation but in documented form. A minimalist specification approach provides necessary and sufficient information for a UC product team to communicate necessary and sufficient design details to others. The specification work begins during conceptual design and continues until implementation design is complete.

Code and Test.   Remember that about half of a project's calendar timeline can be spent in coding and testing. Design is transitioned to real product code, and testing verifies correct implementation. Minor iteration is possible, and final evaluations validate compliance to requirements and standards. Deployment releases the product to end users.

There Is More.   As with other engineering disciplines, there are a variety of techniques available to a user-centered product team to perform or supplement the main line tasks. A UC product team is well advised to have a toolkit of techniques and methods available to address design situations and problems.

In general, the team should address any techniques that help it involve users, staff a multidisciplinary team, formulate measurable goals, design and prototype a total user experience, evaluate, analyze results, and iterate through implementation until requirements are met and the product is deployed.

Back to the Project—A Postmortem

After any project, it is always good to step back and determine what went well and what can be improved. The project manager and senior management want to conduct a project postmortem first thing tomorrow morning.

You only have about two hours to get your story together. Management thinks you've done such a great job that you've been assigned to lead another UC product team for a new and exciting project that kicks off right after the postmortem. One of the members of the current project team will assume your responsibility for the next release.

Continue your research on the Web for any other approaches, processes, and techniques that would be helpful in future projects.

What would you do differently from a project and design point of view?

Any questions?

Looking Beyond _____

UI and usability technology is evolving—perhaps not as quickly as other technologies. However, it is moving. A UC product team must continue the search for improved methods. Existing techniques should be reviewed, internalized, and modified as appropriate to suit project and personal needs. Techniques from other disciplines such as engineering, psychology, sociology, and computer science should be explored and adapted. Techniques can be extended to suit UI, information, usability, and other needs.

In addition, a UC product team must continue to watch technology as it evolves. There are many trends relevant to UIs and UI-based application development methods. Even while focused on development of a software product, a UC product team must explore trends during a product's development and even more so in the time in between projects. An approach to study trends should consider social, human, technology, methods, and other factors likely to affect users or developers within the next five years.

> **Rule of Thumb**: Look around and note what's been going on. It does give a hint about the proximate future for the current or next project.

In General.   Progress in many areas was not as fast as expected. However, some technologies surprised many with their popularity and rapid widespread acceptance. The dominant factors influencing acceptance by users appear to be:

- Cost relative to value
- Reasonable hardware and software prerequisites
- Overall speed
- Ease of learning and use relative to the problem addressed

Rule of Thumb: A challenge with technology is being able to recognize when a revolutionary item has materialized and responding to it quickly enough.

Users. The basic tasks that a user of computer software performs have not changed much since the ever-widening expansion of computer-based technology. A user is goal oriented vis-à-vis a computer and its software. Whether the idea is creating a monthly status report or having a good time playing a game, the goal is the end and the computer and software is a tool and means of accomplishing it. Even as certain types of individual users are better understood, other users that do not fit neatly into current audience definitions are coming into the market. Within the context of a global audience, there is tremendous diversity that requires a diversity of interaction techniques.

Technology and Tools. Just look around to see the increasing power. Computers are getting smaller and more powerful. Displays are getting smaller and larger with higher resolution. Key technologies and software are being integrated in amazing ways.

Processes. More knowledge will be gained in the human and social factors of computers, software, people, and groups. Learning, reference materials and applications, and lots of practice will continue to be needed in this high skill area. For the foreseeable future, a best practice approach of iterative software development is the means of achieving great products that meet user needs.

Rule of Thumb: The overriding guideline is use of user-centered design and development that begins with users and continues with design instantiation and prototyping, evaluation, and iteration until requirements are met. Anything less than this is lip service.

Back to the Project—A Final Look

You start your new project tomorrow. However, the project manager and senior management would like your view of the future of UIs and usability and its implications to the project. They would also like a view three to five years out. They'd like for you to come to the staff meeting tomorrow with your ideas and recommended course of action for your new project.

You have two hours to do research and get your thoughts together. Your efforts may influence your next project and how senior management perceives your strategic thinking.

Any questions?

Index